CLAY AND IRON

Book 1

Dr. William R. Deagle
MD, ABFP, CCFP, CIME

Copyright © 1999 by Dr. William Deagle, M.D.
All Rights Reserved

First Printing by Gilliland Printing, 1999

Special thanks to my wife, Michelle, and my family who tolerated many long hours of research and prayer.

Cover: Image provided by Endtime Magazine, from its "Understanding the Endtime" Prophecy Home Bible Study by Irvin Baxter, Jr.

Cover Design by
Imagine Creative Services

For additional books, videos or audios, contact:

The Prophecy Club ®
P.O. Box 750234
Topeka, KS 66675

Phone: (785) 478-1112
Fax: (785) 478-1115
Internet: www.prophecyclub.com

This book is dedicated to the cell churches
of The Prophecy Club ®

FOREWARD

Called as Moses and Aaron's Staff Will be "Clay and Iron"

At the time of the encounter with the Voice of God with the commission to help the Supreme Court stop Dr. Morgentaler from setting up abortuaries, and to write "Clay and Iron" and Abortion to Armageddon" for the End Times, the Voice of the Lord said: "As Moses was you are, and as Aaron's staff was, "Clay and Iron" shall be!" This pronouncement has been many times repeated by the Lord in prayer, as when I pray I always hear the English translation. For years I ran as Jonah, hoping someone more qualified would bring this word to the Church and the world. However, by stages He was patient, and in obedience I present here today many things that are directly from the Throne Room of Heaven.

There are also many areas where I have a personal opinion, and this will be evident. Thus this text, arranged in 124 questions and answers, is a study in progression. Therefore, "Clay and Iron: Book 2" is in the works already.

As I stepped forward to speak The Prophecy Club ® and now completing the second tour, many more revelations and clarifications are forthcoming from the Holy Spirit in prayer, in vision and visitation with the angel Gabriel, and in dreams.

Many more miracles have happened, such as being translated for one half of my trip back to the airport in Minneapolis from Duluth, while praying and planning with Pastor Ricardo Baeza. Supernaturally, the Lord provided an extra 1-1/2 hours to plan a very important book that we will coauthor, with Ricardo the main author. God is good, and he has revealed much more flesh on the bones of "Clay and Iron" as I walked out in fear and trembling to do His Will. May the Grace and Peace of the Lord Jesus preserve you in that Day. Amen!!!

Daniel 2:40-43

40 And the fourth kingdom shall be strong as iron: forasmuch as iron breaketh in pieces and subdueth all [things]: and as iron that breaketh all these, shall it break in pieces and bruise.

41 And whereas thou sawest the feet and toes, part of potters' clay, and part of iron, the kingdom shall be divided; but there shall be in it of the strength of the iron, forasmuch as thou sawest the iron mixed with miry clay.

42 And [as] the toes of the feet [were] part of iron, and part of clay, [so] the kingdom shall be partly strong, and partly broken.

43 And whereas thou sawest iron mixed with miry clay, <u>they shall mingle themselves</u> **[Fallen angels!]** <u>with the seed of men</u> **[Genetically Engineered Half-Human Beings!]**: but they shall not cleave one to another, even as iron is not mixed with clay.

44 And in the days of these kings shall the God of heaven set up a kingdom, which shall never be destroyed: and the kingdom shall not be left to other people, [but] it shall break in pieces and consume all these kingdoms, and it shall stand for ever.

45 Forasmuch as thou sawest that the stone was cut out of the mountain without hands, and that it brake in pieces the iron, the brass, the clay, the silver, and the gold; the great God hath made known to the king what shall come to pass hereafter: and the dream [is] certain, and the interpretation thereof sure..

Ezekiel 33: 1-7

1 Again the word of the LORD came unto me, saying,

2 Son of man, speak to the children of thy people, and say unto them, When I bring the sword upon a land, if the people of the land take a man of their coasts, and set him for their watchman:

3 If when he seeth the sword come upon the land, he blow the trumpet, and warn the people;

4 Then whosoever heareth the sound of the trumpet, and taketh not warning; if the sword come, and take him away, his blood shall be upon his own head.

5 He heard the sound of the trumpet, and took not warning; his blood shall be upon him. But he that taketh warning shall deliver his soul.

6 But if the watchman see the sword come, and blow not the trumpet, and the people be not warned; if the sword come, and take [any] person from among them, he is taken away in his iniquity; but his blood will I require at the watchman's hand.

7 So thou, O son of man, I have set thee a watchman unto the house of Israel; therefore thou shalt hear the word at my mouth, and warn them from me.

Small Scroll of Rev 10 Revealed
A Prophecy Against America

The words of William, son of William, in the line of Aaron who was among the physicians of Colorado, which he saw concerning America in the days of Clinton, President of America, two years before Y2K.

Thus saith the Lord; Have I not called you from before the day of your birth in nineteen hundred two score, ten and second year. Did I not say to you, "At the time of the end you would know and you would tell my people!" Did you see from your eighth year from the gates of heaven and high above "my blue jewel the earth," how I will reign down judgment upon this world. Did not the prophets of old tell of such a day, but those who call themselves my people said prophesy not, but tickle our ears with comforts and ever increasing self-righteousness and power with the Holy One of Israel. Did I, Jesus, not show you these things that must happen so that all mercy, grace and justice is served, and then the end shall surely come.

Did not the fireballs rise all over my blue jewel, heat, brimstone and the red smoke of the abyss roll as a scroll across the horizon to cover in deepest darkness. Let there be two score years from the day that you, my servant, have been called until these days of the wrath of the evil one are cast upon the earth. For he knows that his time is short, and great is his wrath. When my angel casts him down into the abyss, surely he will never rise for my kingdom will be from everlasting to everlasting.

I, the Sovereign Lord of Hosts, do declare that the day of the Lord is near, even at the doors. From the going forth of this word, there will be times, times, times, times and half a times, until the great and terrible day of wrath of the Lamb. For in the fullness of the Gentile times, the prayers of the saints rise up as a fragrant incense to my nostrils and I am stirred and there will be no more time that My Spirit will strive with the spirits of men.

And this is a mystery, My wrath is to see my face and be forever forgotten from my body, the church. The wrath of the evil one is to steal, kill, and destroy until the fullness of the wrath, six trumpets, six bowls and six vials. Only when I break the seals may the wrath of the evil one be poured out upon those who bear the Mark and worship the Bearer of Light and not the Creator. I am the Holy One who died and shed the living waters of life that you would never thirst, but you would not drink. Therefore, you will receive my wrath, which is the seventh seal, the seventh trumpet, and the seventh vial in completing your iniquity and I decree a separation as an adulterous bride forever from her groom. This alone is my wrath upon a dying people and a passing world.

And he said, Thus saith the Lord; For thou, O nation, which appears as a lamb but speaks with the voice of a dragon, you who have a sea of my Word but do not drink. Thy transgressions have called out to my ears for judgment. You, America, who carry the word of my testimony to the world, have taken your heart far from Me.

Hear this word that the Lord hath spoken against you, O children of America, which I have brought up from all the lands of persecution. Your nation I have set high above all nations as a light to truth and justice, for you feared my Words. You were children of Light and not of Darkness. Therefore, I will punish you for your iniquities.

Today I blow a trumpet for my people, come out of her daughter of Babylon the Great. She has made the whole earth drunk with the wine of her outrageous profits, of every stock option, dividend and contract. You who rob the poor, crush the weak, and sell with insider information; while you convince the foolish enough to believe your lies, and buy until their wealth is dust and sand that have fallen between their fingers.

The evil one stalks a prey and I revealeth it to my servants the prophets. Those who hear these words, who heed and obey, will escape 'through' the days of trouble, as my people did to the land of Goshen, when I sent the plagues upon the land of Egypt.

Proclaim in the streets of Islam and Russia, that America knows not how to do right. I send among you Gorbachev, who seeks to tell another gospel and you write the Earth Charter as your new commandments. He bears a Green Cross and defiles the cross I bore for you my people. Because you have forsaken your first love, America, I will send you Global EcoCommunism and Islamic Terror.

Did I not tell you before it was that the city of seven hills would send one with mitre and the scepter of a shepherd to lead away all those that love not the truth, and he knows me not, but you, O wayward people, did follow the Harlot of Babylon, all you daughters of harlotry. Were not those I gave my servant Moses enough law to condemn all those upon the earth, that none are righteous, not even one? Did I not write on the flesh of your heart my commandments, to love your God with all your heart, soul and mind, and love your neighbour as yourselves? You made yourselves righteous in your own eyes.

I call upon these peoples of oil and fire for judgment upon this nation, for America knows not to do right. You, O America, who store up and prepare violence against your own people and plots to inter them in concentration camps and make covenants with the illuminated sons of Satan. I have judged you and found my cup of wrath full with anger against you.

You, O America, who conspire to spoil the bread and steal the light, to place a Mark on all your people, I have this against you. Moreover, you force the whole world to worship other gods of trees and crawling things and waters which were foreign to you, so that all may take this Mark. You croak as the voices of frogs are heard from the pits of your throats the song of a sustainable world without my Holy Name. No repentance is seen in your actions, for your hearts are far from me and my spirit will not strive long with the spirits of men. You, O America, swear by your power and might that by that false prince that comes, surely now we have "Peace and Security"! A sustainable planet will not surely die!

You, O America, who swear to destroy my people, this is what the Sovereign Lord says, I will send fire upon your coastlands and upon your cities, and I will send a hoard from Russia and Islam and all the nations with them. I will enrage them, and draw them with hooks forward into your lands for your arrogance and blasphemy against My throne and my Name. You who conspire to kill there innocents like lambs at slaughter in Iraq, and yet let there leader live to serve your purposes.

You who cry, "Leave Clinton finish his term, our portfolio is bursting with the last quarterly earnings, and peace and security are surely ours to rule the earth, and profits wash away a multitude of sins." You say, who cares if we who send His word to all the world, send gifts to our enemies of the technology and money to destroy us. For we speak as a Dragon, and who can make war with America. You call yourself a Lamb, but are like a raging lion that threatens to rain fire from heaven on all your enemies. You say in your heart, we will sell them bullets but we will bind them tightly with our computer bytes, and surely none will escape our all seeing eyes!

You, O America, who oppress the poor and sell the needy nations of the earth the seeds of famine, I will send you death. You, O America, who have set yourselves up to be the god of this world, I will bring you very low, and your murmurs for mercy will cry to Me from the dust and ashes of your nation.

You, O America, have not only shed the blood of my littlest ones but have denied care to your poor and elderly. Your have forced the heathen nations of the earth to kill there little ones and I see there blood upon your hands. It cries to Me from many lands for justice; How long, O Lord, will our sisters and brothers die in their mothers wombs at that hands of America and its multinational corporations. Have I not declared that you must not make any of your children to walk through the fire for Molech or Baal, but you did.

When your president vetoed the abomination of murder by suction at birth, where, O church, was your outrage? Where were your lawyers and physicians that call themselves by My Name? My judgment starts upon My house that sees and rebukes the demonic horde but does not speak in the houses of law and in the capitols of your cities against this outrage. Prophesy not in My name if you do not first stand in the breach for the least of your brothers and sisters, here and in many lands. I do not need your permission to rebuke the hordes of Satan. I desire only that you love and serve only Me, and not buildings and programs and warfare that sets you arrogantly at My right hand.

For I will hold you, O church, that calls yourself by my Name, and your bloodguilt, O quiet warriors. I will forever silence you unless you turn and repent for not speaking against these murders.

Henceforth, from the treaty that divides my holy city, Jerusalem, and the day upon which the house of Judah commences the sacrifice, I will anoint my people of the house of Judah who believe on my Son and on the house of Israel who believe on my Son, to prophesy to America, and all the earth for twelve hundred and three score days to this nations and all the nations who would conspire to wipe out my people and the nation of Israel.

When these days of prophesying are closed up, and on the day of my "Passing Over" my people as I did upon the firstborn of the lands of Egypt, I will send again the Death Angel upon the earth to reap a harvest into my kingdom and cast the tares into the fires of eternal torment. I have decreed for twelve hundred and threescore days wars, pestilences, death, and the greatest earthquake upon the earth until the cup of my wrath is empty and all the earth is a desolation.

Cry, you high generals and politicians of the Illuminated One, for he will not save you in the day of my wrath. Hide yourselves in NORAD and FALCON and the bowels of IRIDIUM. For in one day, at the Long Blowing, I will appear with the hosts of heaven, and those who are mine will rise to be my Bride forever. But woe to you, O daughters of Babylon, for you have set your gods of technology, medicine and genetics to create yourselves as gods. But you will not.

Therefore, eat this scroll, for its sweetness will be savored by they that hear and obey my voice, but your stomachs will turn with the sourness of destruction that will come upon the earth. Just as my voice of seven thunders has spoken, it will surely come to pass, and there will be no more delay.

The Lord God has sworn by his holiness, that, lo, the days shall come upon you, that you shall not escape from fire and brimstone and captivity. Your sons and daughters will fall in the open fields, and fall like chaff at winnowing time. I will give thee for a feast to the beasts of the field. Puzzle not at a man grasping his stomach as if in labour, though his face cries crimson in the agony as in childbirth, for I have sent fireballs of wormwood upon this people and they will surely not escape. America who for a time would rain wormwood on all those who would not take the Mark, let them drink a double portion, for a nation who called themselves My people and are not.

Escape I say, My people from this land, to the North, before the great and terrible days, for I have given you twelve hundred and three score days to prophesy to this nation of America in mercy and justice before my wrath is poured out in full.

Weep, you nations afar off, woe, woe, woe, great was the daughter of Babylon. By her sons of the Illuminated One and by their stock market, many nations and peoples have become rich. In one day has come destruction to the cities of glass and steel like mountains of light.

This is what the Sovereign Lord says, Go forth once more unto a hard and arrogant people, a righteous people full of purpose and plans, with my word on there lips but a curse in there hearts. Turn, you sheep, from the pathway that leads to destruction, and become my people again and I will turn to you and heal your land and set my tent over you and you will be my Bride. But if you do not soon turn, then in the day of my wrath I will set my face against you and you will become only a whisper in the darkness, O America.

2 Peter 1: 19-21

19 We have also a more sure word of prophecy; whereunto ye do well that ye take heed, as unto a light that shineth in a dark place, until the day dawn, and the day star arise in your hearts:

20 Knowing this first, that no prophecy of the scripture is of any private interpretation.

21 For the prophecy came not in old time by the will of man: but holy men of God spake [as they were] moved by the Holy Ghost.

MY TESTIMONY

As a child, I had a zealous love for the Lord. My heart longed for Him as I often prayed to God for answers I could not find in my church.

And so, it came as a powerful revelation when at eight years of age I had an experience that would subsequently change my life and perception of Jesus Christ. While undergoing a tonsillectomy at Colchester County Hospital, in Truro, Nova Scotia, complications lacerated the tonsillar artery and I apparently went into hemorrhagic shock. It was then that I met my Lord and Savior, Jesus Christ.

"Oh my God, he's bleeding!" The doctor implores a nurse.

"Rush! Rush! Get me a clamp and sutures!"

"Oh, no ... We're losing him..."

"You're not losing me" -- I thought to myself. "I'm right here."

But where was I? I was still me, Billy, but Billy was not on the operating table. He was floating some where near the ceiling. Doctors and nurses were rushing everywhere, panicking over the little boy on the table.

I tried to tell them I was okay but no one listened to me. As I headed toward the operating room doors, I extended by hands to push them open. To my astonishment I glided right through the double doors, like a swing through the air.

As I journeyed down the vestibule, my attention was caught by the newborn nursery. Peering through the huge glass windows that seemed to stretch so far in front of me, I marvelled at these wonderful creations all bundled up and laying on their sides. "I sure wanted to get a little closer." I leaned forward and to my amazement again, I passed through the walls and glass, as if it wasn't even there.

Two pleasantly plump attending nurses were busily chatting to each other and paid no attention to my pleas: "Why are the babies all wrapped up so tight?" "Why are some of them crying?" No one answered me and this distressed me greatly. An infant cried out and I felt helpless. Just then, everything around me started to fade until I was engulfed in absolute darkness. I was terrified, suspended in this liquid black void. In the distance appeared a pinpoint of light, and I called out as loud as I could, "God, help me!" The light became perceptibly brighter and I felt a drawing sensation all the time I was catapulting toward it. The magnetism grew stronger and in one massive squeezing, scrunching sensation I was through the pin hole and on my way through a tubular energy grid. It was then that I first became aware of the fluorescent silver cord that extended from my neck. Faster and faster my body took me through this shimmering tunnel of intersecting lines of bright light.

"Too fast, God, too fast ..." my thoughts resounded. Then, I stopped, totally bathed in a warm blanket of light, standing seemingly with pearly white clouds all around. There was brilliant light above me, below me, and on all sides.

"Where am I?" I thought. And there in front of me appeared a tall, emaciated man wearing a long shimmering white tunic. It fell to about mid-calf and was trimmed with one-half inch of solid gold "material" all along the bottom edge and around the border of his three-quarter length sleeves.

He wore a broad, golden embroidered sash around his waist, and from it dangled a double golden corded rope. On his feet were leather sandals that appeared bright like brass. Through the tremendous gleam exuded by this wonderful and overwhelmingly loving man, I could see His forehead was scarred and swollen as if recently wounded. His beard was partly plucked out. On his wrists were evidence of piercing holes that told a painful legacy of a gift given to mankind. His huge, clear eyes sat in a chiseled face wrought with compassion and love.

I knew at once, that this was Jesus. Then before me I noticed a small arch-like bridge of natural wood spanning a chasm between Him and me.

"Where am I?" I pondered to myself. "You are at the Gates of Heaven, or Paradise," He answered my thoughts. I looked down at the wooden bridge, and again, knowing my thoughts, He said in a calm, reassuring voice that the silver cord would break if I crossed the bridge and that I would not be able to return to earth.

I responded that I did not know what Heaven was like and I was only a child. I asked Jesus if He would show me what Heaven was so I could decide what to do.

Suddenly I was holding His hand and flying over the Golden City. The indescribable beauty of the city, the walls and roads of gold that seemed transparent, yet solid; the wonderous colours, creatures, and marvelous peace of Paradise was truly overwhelming.

Just as suddenly, I stood back in the place of the threshold of Heaven, and Jesus asked me to decide if I wanted to stay or go back to earth. I thought to myself that I wanted to do the right thing, and the thought came to my mind, "If I was to return, what would I do on Earth?"

Jesus held my hand and we were high above the irredescent blue jewel of planet earth. I stared down in wonderment at the beauty of the work that Jesus had created. He held forth his hand with his index and second fingers pointing to earth and said, "Behold!" with the authority of the Almighty.

As I watched, huge fireballs rose up from the earth followed by mushroom clouds. Immediately, I saw many people, beyond counting, rising to meet Jesus. I could, at that moment, feel the horrible pain and suffering of millions of people dying instantly.

I cried out in anguish to Jesus, "What is this?" With great and thunderous authority His voice penetrated the Heavens saying:

"At the time of the End, you will know and you will tell my people."

Again, standing at the gates of Heaven, I thought, "I must do the right thing," and the phrase occurred to my mind, "Let Your will be done." As I said these words, the silver cord became taut as Jesus raised His hand in authority and I felt His supernatural wave of love pass over me. It cannot be described by anything from this world. I passed down the tunnel from whence I had come, but much quicker.

"He's back." "He's coming around." "Get me some more ether." I could hear the doctors and nurses again. I began coughing and spitting up gobs of blood. The pain was excrutiating. Someone slammed an ether mask over my face in an effort to secure more stitches to stop the bleeding. I was very cold. I tried to scream to get away from the all encompassing pain. I passed out. It was many hours later that I regained conciousness.

Weeks later, I returned to private school and my favorite teacher, Sister Marie Blackie. I felt I could confide in her and she was the first person I told my experience to. Well, I was shuffled from her to Mother Superior at the Sister's Manse -- to the Monsigneur, or top priest, in charge of the school -- to Father Robertson, a junior priest in the Parish. And after many delicious brownies, cookies, and milk I was told:

"You had a special experience with Jesus."

Case closed, or so I thought. Father Robertson did stay in touch and was later to offer me paid tuition at Medical School should I become a priest. I refused the offer but was very flattered and grateful at the time. Father Robertson took an interest in me and thereby I felt he believed my experience.

In the ensuing years I had fallen away in many ways as I had no understanding of the Bible or a personal relationship with Jesus.

In 1980, I met Dr. Rawlings, a Cardiologist from Athens, Georgia, who had completed over thirty years of research into "near death" experiences of his patients. I had the opportunity to talk with Dr. Rawlings at grand rounds on "near death experiences" at the Calgary Foothills Hospital while doing a year of residency training in family medicine. He assured me that he was aware of similar reports to mine and that my experience was indeed "real". At this point in his career, Dr. Rawlings thought that the experience was "adjustable" according to his or her religious background. That bothered and confused me and I was pleased to hear that years later Dr. Rawlings became a Christian. Praise God!

Nine and one-half years ago in August 1989, after several years of returning to nominal Christianity, I borrowed a book that my wife, Michelle, was reading on the gifts of the Holy Spirit. At that time we were already "born-again" "baptized in water" - Christians for almost two years. We thought that was all there was. And truly we were happy in that and it surely was a gigantic step from our four months in Mormonism, or anything else we knew.

When I finished reading Michelle's book I received the Baptism of the Holy Spirit and spent most of the night flat on my face on the floor— praying. Praise God.

It was over the next few days that I noticed that as I read the Bible my understanding appeared magnified by an unseen counselor who gave me visions and thoughts and understanding of the words of the Bible. At the end of one week of prayer, my wife, Michelle, had two Pentecostal Pastors over to pray with us. We needed their discernment to direct us as to whether this was truly from God. The words from John were most enlightening.

1 John 4:1-6 "Beloved, believe not every spirit, but try the spirits whether they are of God: because many false prophets are gone out into the world. Hereby know ye the Spirit of God: Every spirit that confesseth that Jesus Christ is come in the flesh is of God: And every spirit that confesseth not that Jesus Christ is come in the flesh is not of God: and this is that spirit of antichrist, whereof ye

have heard that it should come; and even now already it is in the world.

Ye are of God, little children, and have overcome them: because greater is he that is in you, than he that is in the world. They are of the world: therefore speak they of the world, and the world heareth them. We are of God: he that knoweth God heareth us; he that is not of God heareth not us. Hereby know we the spirit of truth, and the spirit of error."

About one week after the Baptism of the Holy Spirit, the Lord's audible voice told me to do two things. He told me to file a complaint through the Provincial Medical Board to prevent the licensure of Dr. Henry Morgentaller, renouned secular humanist and abortion advocate. The second was that by His guidance, I would write a book called "Clay and Iron", defining the characteristics of the final empire of the world, as seen by the prophet Daniel.

As I studied the scriptures I understood that Jesus was to return and set up an eternal kingdom. My calling became clear as the illumination of the Holy Spirit brought me through each stage of repentance, not only for my sins, but for the sins of our nation, my profession and our world. The course of End Times prophecy needs a conductor to lay out an overall plan to save Gentile Christians and Believing Jews. I finally understood the reality of my calling as given to me at eight years of age.

Do not blindly receive the words of this book, but pray for the discernment as Soloman asked for from the Lord. Only the convicting Spirit of Truth can testify to the truth of this unsealing. God is a God of order, simplicity, and perfect Justice and Mercy, but most of all, He is a God of Infinite Love. Trust Jesus when He says he will return, and trust His servants with this singular message, Daniel was told to close-up and seal the words of the prophecy until the time of the end. God's Spirit is now starting to have that great outpouring. Many will join in a beautiful and perfect song of prophetic worship of the Alpha and Omega. Pray to be enslaved to the Lord by the Spirit of Truth. No matter how hard the message of these words are, I pray that you will trust only the one who is Faithful and True, Jesus Christ, our Lord and Savior.

INTRODUCTION

The process of New Testament prophecy is one of progressive unveiling. The words of this book are not only directed by the Holy Spirit. They solidly stand upon the shoulders of Old and New Testament prophets.

In prayer God said, "I am a God of order and not disorder and a God of simplicity not complexity."

To quote 2 Peter 1: 19-21 --

"We have also a more sure word of prophecy; whereunto ye do well that ye take heed, as unto a light that shineth in a dark place, until the day dawn, and the day star arise in your hearts: Knowing this first, that no prophecy of the scripture is of any private interpretation. For the prophecy came not in old time by the will of man: but holy men of God spake as they were moved by the Holy Ghost."

The Bible is like the accurate recollections of the yet future events. The prophets interpretations, from different perspectives, but of the same events when combined, give the entire picture. Just as the three separate colors combine to create a colored picture on a television screen, each from scattered and incoherent patterns of light, together they form a very clear and understandable picture. God has given me a window through which I can see this clear picture, the last seven years of this Age.

Comments in [square brackets] are mine and where they are inspired by the Spirit of God they will be qualified.

VISIONS AND DREAMS

Throughout "Clay and Iron", Dr. Deagle's visions and dreams are keyed to each question. They are placed at the end of each discussion, to confirm the synchrony with scripture and the need to have a simple and comprehensive revelation of God's will and understanding in these End Times. Pray on everything in this book. Everything must be consistent and in agreement with the Holy Scriptures, or it must be considered out of His will. May your journey help your witness and save many who will die during these perilous times. They will be gathered from the four corners of heaven and brought into the Kingdom. May the Lord Jesus be with you in the Great Harvest of the Tribulation. Amen, Come Lord Jesus!

Chapter 1

END OF THE AGE

AND

THE BLESSED HOPE

1. Why must Jesus return?

In the history of the world God has come to earth only once. Hundreds of prophecies in the Old Testament dating back thousands of years were told of the coming Messiah. The witnesses of the New Testament apostles attest to the truth of this revealed prophecy as the angel said on the night of Jesus' birth, "Peace on Earth, Good Will Toward Men."

Only when Jesus himself comes again to set up an everlasting kingdom on earth will this true peace come to earth. Jesus Christ came, as prophesied in hundreds, of separate prophecies to save godless man from self destruction. Man is technologically trying to reach forth and grasp from the Tree of Life but God will not permit fallen man a form of eternal life.

***Genesis 3:22** And the LORD God said, Behold, the man is become as one of us, to know good and evil: and now, lest he put forth his hand, and take also of the tree of life, and eat, and live for ever:*

23 Therefore the LORD God sent him forth from the garden of Eden, to till the ground from whence he was taken.

24 So he drove out the man; and he placed at the east of the garden of Eden Cherubims, and a flaming sword which turned every way, to keep the way of the tree of life.

Fetal research, abortion, new reproductive technologies and genetic engineering hold the real possibility of living extended lives in this fallen state. There were two trees in the centre of the Garden that man was not permitted to take the fruit from them. The first was man taking from the Tree of the Knowledge of Good and Evil, i.e. man doing what he thought was right aside from a prayer relationship with God and led by his spirit. That first forbidden fruit was taken at the start of man's 6,000 year downward spiral of judgment. The second tree was the Tree of Life. Man is harvesting the next generation to save the present one. Abortion and all that come from it in the new reproductive technologies, is the last acts of sin God will permit before lifting his grace and judging our world. The New Age Mother-Earth worship would no less sacrifice our children to the same dead gods of Molech that resulted in God's judgment against Israel, at the time of Amos and Hosea. Like Nineveh, may our world repent. I pray in sackcloth and ashes and advert certain Judgment.

D & V: *Thus Saith the Lord: Hands that shed innocent blood, I shall punish. You who call yourselves by my name, I demand a witness in the courts of this land. May mercy's voice will be heard before the thunder of My wrath breaks forth on an unrepentant world. Your scientists have touched the twisted coil of life within cells of my little ones and you conspired to crown yourselves co-creators. Lo, I will have no other gods before me! You will not reach forth and take from the tree of life and live forever, knowing both good and evil. The stain of your existence I will blot from the cosmos, before your stretch forth your hand and touch and defile the stars of the firmament. Repent, and I will be your father, as I am always the father to the fatherless, the aborted, the neglected and the brutalized of all ages. Your bloodguilt is equal in my eyes, you who commit these abominations and you who call yourselves by my name and yet are silent. Speak forth in mercy and take up your persecution for My name, before the Great and Terrible Day spoken of in Joel.*

2. **Why is our current time in history important to the prophetic word?**

Daniel 9:10 Neither have we obeyed the voice of the LORD our God, to walk in his laws, which he set before us by his servants the prophets.

11 Yea, all Israel have transgressed thy law, even by departing, that they might not obey thy voice; therefore the curse is poured upon us, and the oath that [is] written in the law of Moses the servant of God, because we have sinned against him.

12 And he hath confirmed his words, which he spake against us, and against our judges that judged us, by bringing upon us a great evil **[The New World Order and The Apostasy]:** *for under the whole heaven hath not been done as hath been done upon Jerusalem.*

13 As [it is] written in the law of Moses, all this evil is come upon us: yet made we not our prayer before the LORD our God, that we might turn from our iniquities, and understand thy truth.

14 Therefore hath the LORD watched upon the evil, and brought it upon us: for the LORD our God [is] righteous in all his works which he doeth: for we obeyed not his voice.

15 And now, O Lord our God, that hast brought thy people forth out of the land of Egypt with a mighty hand, and hast gotten thee renown, as at this day; we have sinned, we have done wickedly.

The Bible is the most read book in history. It was once said that a truly learned man could not consider himself educated until he was well versed in the Bible. Yet one-third of the Bible is prophecy. Most of the prophetic Word deals with the End of the Age and the Return of Jesus Christ to set up his Eternal Kingdom.

These mysteries were closed and sealed to the Prophet Daniel twenty-seven hundred years ago when he gave his prophecy to the King of Babylon, King Nebuchadnezzar. Daniel, the Jewish Prophet, first told King Nebuchadnezzar the actual dream which he had, and then gave him the interpretation from the God of Abraham, Isaac and Jacob.

Table 2 - 1

THE FAITHFULNESS OF JESUS CHRIST

Abraham -   Faith in Listening to God's Covenant
Isaac -   Faith in the Circumstances of the Impossible
Jacob -   Faith through the Eternal Promise of Life and Blessings

The first empire was represented by the head of gold indicating the Babylonian empire. The second empire represented by chest and arms of silver was of the Medo-Persian Empire. The third empire was that of Greece and of a less precious metal indicated by the stomach and thighs of copper. The last empire was of the basest of metals, iron, represented by the Roman Empire.

The Roman Empire was present at the time of the crucifixion of Jesus, and Daniel foretold that the feet and toes of this empire would be the last resurrection of the Roman Empire at the End of this Age. The feet would be made of clay and iron and would therefore not hold together. In the time of this empire, Daniel foretold, in...

> ***Daniel 2***:*31 Thou, O king, sawest, and behold a great image. This great image, whose brightness [was] excellent, stood before thee; and the form thereof [was] terrible.*
>
> *32 This image's head [was] of fine gold, his breast and his arms of silver, his belly and his thighs of brass,*
>
> *33 His legs of iron, his feet part of iron and part of clay.*
>
> *34 Thou sawest till that a stone was cut out without hands, which smote the image upon his feet [that were] of iron and clay, and brake them to pieces.*

35 Then was the iron, the clay, the brass, the silver, and the gold, broken to pieces together, and became like the chaff of the summer threshingfloors; and the wind carried them away, that no place was found for them: and the stone that smote the image became a great mountain, and filled the whole earth.

It is at the time therefore of the Empire of Clay and Iron that the events of the end of the age shall occur.

D & V: *Thus Saith the Lord: As I, the Sovereign Lord, have instructed my servant, Daniel, to close up and seal the words of the scroll I gave him, I now will unseal all at the time of the End. None of the wicked will understand, but those purified and made white in My Blood, will shine as the stars of the firmament. Knowledge has surely covered the whole earth like a sea, and I will be that compass to the Island of Truth and Wisdom. Those blasphemous ones of the unholy Grail, who call themselves my sons, will conspire to put a Mark in the right hand and in the forehead of all upon the earth. They will use the military might of America to enforce these chains, three sixes, as a personal identification. America will enforce the worship the resurrection of the unholy Roman Empire both East and Western legs., who claims sit as rightful king on my throne in Jerusalem. I alone am King of Kings and Lord of Lords, and there is no other. At the time of this last attempt to bring peace made by the hands of man when there is no peace, I will be stirred to avenge the blood of my Holy people and my Holy name. Then, all will know that I am the Holy One of Israel. My Kingdom will never perish.*

3. **Will Christians understand the times of the end of the age?**

Although prophecy has been studied for many hundreds of years, it is clear from Daniel's prophecy of:

Daniel 12:9 *And he said, Go thy way, Daniel: for the words [are] closed up and sealed till the time of the end. 10 Many shall* *be purified, and made white, and tried; but the wicked shall do wickedly: and none of the wicked shall understand; but the wise shall understand.* **[The 'Bride' or Church of Gentile Christians and Believing Jews will be made spotless by the time of Jacob's trouble. The Tribulation will make it ready for the King of Kings, Jesus Christ.]**

As knowledge increases, truly informed modern man armed with the truth of the Bible would clearly understand the signs of the end of the age. They would be able to interpret these specific prophetic messages meant to be a special comfort to believers in this time of terrible tribulation. The sequence of events is a smelting furnace of God's merciful grace on a lost and unbelieving world. We shall not shrink for fear of death for we have this blessed hope in our hearts, souls and minds. Through all these catastrophes many men, women and children on earth will be saved for eternity with God, and our hearts turned to submit to God's will through the refiner's furnace of the coming tribulation.

4. **Who will lead Christians to understanding the prophetic word in relation to current world events?**

Titus 2: 11-13

11 For the grace of God that bringeth salvation hath appeared to all men,

12 Teaching us that, denying ungodliness and worldly lusts, we should live soberly, righteously, and godly, in this present world;

13 Looking for that blessed hope, and the glorious appearing of the great God and our Saviour Jesus Christ;

As each event to the last day's events confirms the glory of God Almighty may our hearts quicken with the spirit of truth, to strengthen our resolve to hold fast until that day when Jesus returned for his own. As Joel first prophesied in Joel 2:28, to the remnant of Israel, the Jews, that turn to Jesus Christ:

Joel 2:28-29

28 And it shall come to pass afterward, [that] I will pour out my spirit upon all flesh; and your sons and your daughters shall prophesy, your old men shall dream dreams, your young men shall see visions:

29 And also upon the servants and upon the handmaids in those days will I pour out my spirit.

In these end times the Holy Spirit will guide the spirit of truth in the light of current world events as 2 Peter 1:21 for believing Christians 'Sure word of prophecy',

2 Peter 1:21

21 For the prophecy came not in old time by the will of man: but holy men of God spake [as they were] moved by the Holy Ghost.

We truly have a sure word of Prophecy if we hold fast to what the Bible teaches. We must pray to hear that still quiet voice of God speaking to our spirits to lead our minds to the truth which is Jesus Christ.

The New Testament apostles show in *Acts 2:17-18*

17 And it shall come to pass in the last days, saith God, I will pour out of my Spirit upon all flesh: and your sons and your daughters shall prophesy, and your young men shall see visions, and your old men shall dream dreams:

18 And on my servants and on my handmaidens I will pour out in those days of my Spirit; and they shall prophesy:

D & V: *Thus saith the Lord: I will send the wind of the Holy Spirit to blow like a wind of Mercy among my people. The hearts of the spiritually young will be turned for guidance and wisdom toward their spiritual elders and the hearts of the elders will turn toward their spiritual children. They will worship together, and I will be their God. Signs and wonders, visions and words from my Father, will pass among them.. A living sacrifice I demand as My worship, for My Spirit and My Word will be their spirit and their* words. *Sinew and bone will be fitted with nerve and muscle, for My Body will be glorious in That Day.*

5. **Why must modern man accept the prophetic word as the truth of God speaking to man?**

Amos* 8:11 Behold, the days come, saith the Lord GOD, that I will send a famine in the land, not a famine of bread, nor a thirst for water, but of hearing the words of the LORD:*

12 And they shall wander from sea to sea, and from the north even to the east, they shall run to and fro to seek the word of the LORD, and shall not find [it]. **[Many will claim revival but only those annointed by the Lord will speak of Mercy before Judgment!]**

13 In that day shall the fair virgins and young men faint for thirst.

2 Peter 3:*2 That ye may be mindful of the words which were spoken before by the holy prophets, and of the commandment of us the apostles of the Lord and Saviour:*

3 Knowing this first, that there shall come in the last days scoffers, walking after their own lusts, **[False prophets will prophesy Peace and Security with each evermore severe crisis or birthpangs, but there will be no peace!]**

4 And saying, Where is the promise of his coming? for since the fathers fell asleep, all things continue as [they were] from the beginning of the creation.

5 For this they willingly are ignorant of, that by the word of God the heavens were of old, and the earth standing out of the water and in the water:

6 Whereby the world that then was, being overflowed with water, perished:

7 But the heavens and the earth, which are now, by the same word are kept in store, reserved unto fire against the day of judgment and perdition of ungodly men. **[Final judgment will be with Nuclear Fire and the Fire of the Holy Spirit]**

8 But, beloved, be not ignorant of this one thing, that one day [is] with the Lord as a thousand years, and a thousand years as one day.

9 The Lord is not slack concerning his promise, as some men count slackness; but is longsuffering to us-ward, not willing that any should perish, but that all should come to repentance.

10 But the day of the Lord will come as a thief in the night; in the which the heavens shall pass away with a great noise, and the elements shall melt with fervent heat, the earth also and the works that are therein shall be burned up. **[Thermonuclear annihilation]**

11 [Seeing] then [that] all these things shall be dissolved, what manner [of persons] ought ye to be in [all] holy conversation and godliness,

12 Looking for and hasting unto the coming of the day of God, wherein the heavens being on fire shall be dissolved, and the elements shall melt with fervent heat?

13 Nevertheless we, according to his promise, look for new heavens and a new earth, wherein dwelleth righteousness.

14 Wherefore, beloved, seeing that ye look for such things, be diligent that ye may be found of him in peace, without spot, and blameless.

15 And account [that] the longsuffering of our Lord [is] salvation; even as our beloved brother Paul also according to the wisdom given unto him hath written unto you;

16 As also in all [his] epistles, speaking in them of these things; in which are some things hard to be understood, which they that are unlearned and unstable wrest, as [they do] also the other scriptures, unto their own destruction.

17 Ye therefore, beloved, seeing ye know [these things] before, beware lest ye also, being led away with the error of the wicked, fall from your own stedfastness.

18 But grow in grace, and [in] the knowledge of our Lord and Saviour Jesus Christ. To him [be] glory both now and for ever. Amen.

The crying prophet's words of impending judgment are hollow if they do not strike our hearts to seek in need to fill that spiritual emptiness. Modern man is like a man shipwrecked on a life boat in the middle of the salty ocean, thirsty for a glass of water, but he cannot drink. Just as the desalting tablets may save his physical life, only the grace of God and the conviction of his terminal helpless state allow men to receive the free gift of grace paid by the blood of God Almighty come as his son Jesus Christ. He alone paid the just penalty due for our sins. The prophets can only convict to judgment or repentance. All are given the means to escape judgment.

6. How are Christians a light to the world and point toward the only true hope?

Jonah's ministry to Nineveh stopped the judgment on that city. The action which follows must turn the hearts of the children toward their parents and the parents towards their children. This is the truth of the gospel. Grace is like a lit candle passed from those who have received the light of Jesus to those who are lost. Only by the passing of this light can the darkness of this world be banished. It has been said that when Jesus returns you will know 'them' [Christians] by the love they have for each other.

John 17: 20-26
THE PRAYER OF JESUS FOR CHRISTIAN SPIRITUAL UNITY SEEKING 'HIS' TRUTH IN PRAYER

20 Neither pray I for these alone, but for them also which shall believe on me through their word;

21 That they all may be one; as thou, Father, [art] in me, and I in thee, that they also may be one in us: that the world may believe that thou hast sent me.

22 And the glory which thou gavest me I have given them; that they may be one, even as we are one:

23 I in them, and thou in me, that they may be made perfect in one; and that the world may know that thou hast sent me, and hast loved them, as thou hast loved me.

24 Father, I will that they also, whom thou hast given me, be with me where I am; that they may behold my glory, which thou hast given me: for thou lovedst me before the foundation of the world.

25 O righteous Father, the world hath not known thee: but I have known thee, and these have known that thou hast sent me.

26 And I have declared unto them thy name, and will declare [it]: that the love wherewith thou hast loved me may be in them, and I in them.

Spirit of Elijah: Malachi 4:4-6

4 Remember ye the law of Moses my servant, which I commanded unto him in Horeb for all Israel, [with] the statutes and judgments.

5 Behold, I will send you Elijah the prophet before the coming of the great and dreadful day of the LORD:

6 And he shall turn the heart of the fathers to the children, and the heart of the children to their fathers, lest I come and smite the earth with a curse.

The spirit of the prophet Elijah must come before the blessed hope. Then Christians will turn from their denominations, seek the truth in the Bible and become informed to protect themselves physically, mentally, and spiritually as a bride preparing for her bridegroom when Jesus returns for the marriage supper and the eternal reign of Jesus begins.

***D&V:** Eight years ago I asked the Lord to give me a parable vision of salvation that I could use to explain why 'good' people can go to hell, and people who had been evil during their lives enter heaven. In a dream, Jesus took me to a hospital where he was dressed as a surgeon. In one waiting room, all the people in the room has a small piece of paper, written in Jesus blood as a permit for spiritual surgery and transplantation of the perfect body of Jesus after removal of the evil portions of their body, mind and spirit. Some looked hideous with a lifetime of horrible sins and some looked almost perfect. Suddenly, an operating room gurney would arrive to bring those waiting for surgery with Jesus. He cut off all the cursed and fallen parts and grafted in his perfect body, soul and mind. All in this first waiting room were perfect after surgery and they went home with Jesus.*

In the other waiting room, the same kinds of people both hideous and perfect were there, but none had the permission for spiritual surgery with Jesus as surgeon. When the last person was operated on by Jesus from the first waiting room, the operating room doors became bricked in and sealed and then suddenly those in the room ran out and hammered on the place where a door used to be. At that instant, the floor disappeared and they all fell in the darkness alone forever separated from Jesus. He told me to tell this story, so the people of earth would know why only through His spiritual surgery and bought by His blood, can we enter His Kingdom.

7. What is unique about Christianity?

Christianity is unique in three ways. In all other religions man reaches up to become like God. In Christianity God reaches down to give the free gift of salvation to sinful man. Secondly, Christianity has prophecy. All Old Testament prophets were one hundred percent accurate, for all false prophets were put to death if a prophecy did not occur. Thirdly, all prophecy points towards the coming, the death, the resurrection and return of Jesus Christ.

The true hope is that life does have a point, and that God's great plan is fulfilled in the resurrection of Jesus who will usher us into a personal salvation to exist with peace and joy with God forever. No other religion offers this. Any Christian religion which teaches anything less than the truth of these three prime distinctive characteristics of Christianity takes away from the truth of the 'gospel' or 'good news' to mankind.

8. How will Christians survive the fiery Tribulation?

The process of purification of the time of the end will give us the reassurance in our spirits of the thirst quenching truth of prophecy when we and our world behold judgments of the 'refiner's furnace'. The fiery judgment burns like the fires in which Nebuchadnezzar hurled Shadrach, Meshach and Abednego as shown by:

Daniel 3:25 *He answered and said, Lo, I see four men loose, walking in the midst of the fire, and they have no hurt; and the form of the fourth is like the Son of God.*

Daniel 3:28 *[Then] Nebuchadnezzar spake, and said, Blessed [be] the God of Shadrach, Meshach, and Abednego, who hath sent his angel, and delivered his servants that trusted in him, and have changed the king's word, and yielded their bodies, that they might not serve nor worship any god, except their own God.*

These same things will be echoed in the time of the end when citizens of earth are asked to worship under the power of Satan through the false prophet or messiah, accepted by Israel. The beast dictator will dictate horrible judgment against Christians and Jews in the times about to come upon the earth. Christians will have the comfort through the fiery furnace of the Tribulation, that the Son of the Living God is with them in the midst of their persecution and martyrdom.

9. What must end times Christians do with the prophetic word?

The scroll of Daniel is the same seven sealed scroll of the book Revelation. John was not told to unseal it until the time of the end when Jesus, the Lion of Judah would tell what the seven thunders spoke and breaks the seals from:

***Revelation 3:**17 Because thou sayest, I am rich, and increased with goods, and have need of nothing; and knowest not that thou art wretched, and miserable, and poor, and blind, and naked:*

18 I counsel thee to buy of me gold tried in the fire, that thou mayest be rich; and white raiment, that thou mayest be clothed, and [that] the shame of thy nakedness do not appear; and anoint thine eyes with eyesalve, that thou mayest see.

***Revelation 10:**4 And when the seven thunders had uttered their voices, I was about to write: and I heard a voice from heaven saying unto me, Seal up those things which the seven thunders uttered, and write them not.*

***Revelation 10:**9 And I went unto the angel, and said unto him, Give me the little book. And he said unto me, Take [it], and eat it up; and it shall make thy belly bitter, but it shall be in thy mouth sweet as honey.*

The scroll will be eaten, digested and become part of the end time Christians. Its sweetness is a blessed hope that Jesus will return at the end of these crisis but its bitterness is the awful judgments to come upon the earth with the ultimate judgment to many fellow men of eternal second death in the lake of fire separated from God for eternity.

10. How will the nation of Israel and Christians work together to spread the gospel?

Judah, as the remnant nation of Israel, will be a bow sent by Jesus and Christians will fill that bow and spread the gospel to an unbelieving world.

Zechariah 9:*13 When I have bent Judah for me, filled the bow with Ephraim* **[weapon to spread the gospel],** *and raised up thy sons, O Zion* **[Christian as evangelist arrows],** *against thy sons, O Greece* **[New Age Devotees],** *and made thee as the sword of a mighty man.*

Christians must verify the Abramic Covenant that the Nation of Israel must have the homeland given by God. Christians must use the preservation of the nation of Israel as verification of the character of faithfulness, justice and mercy of God. Christian nations like Canada and the U.S.A. must defend the physical nation of Israel and the spiritual nation of Israel, Christianity.

11. How will the spreading of this gospel of the kingdom set the stage for the end of the age?

Matthew 24: *14 And this gospel of the kingdom shall be preached in all the world for a witness unto all nations; and then shall the end come.* **[The Harvest of the Righteous and Jesus' Return for his Bride]**

When every person living has been exposed to the Gospel, with the wrath of Satan cast to earth let loose in the greatest time of physical and spiritual danger in all history, then Jesus will come. Only then can God's justice be served. It was because of his judgment and perfection and total intolerance to sin that God the Father sent His only Son. Through the tribulation of the end of the Age we must always remember that for the repentant believer God sits on a mercy seat, and God's mercy is stronger than justice. We will win vindication of the righteous through Jesus, rewarding of the just, and the rule of the spirit and truth.

12. **Why should another book be written about the end times prophecy?**

It is to comfort Christians and prepare them and to convince non-Christians of the truth of the gospel that Jesus, the living God, has come to earth and will return. He will save them through the horrible disasters befalling our world in the near future.

Christians must be given a clear outline of the end times, consistent with the Gospel. All of this truth will be revealed only at the end of the age, by the Holy Spirit. End times events will be understood because of the unsealing of Daniel's scroll, by called end times prophets. The testing of the truth of this unsealing will be confirmed by the prayers of the body of true Christian believers. The Holy Spirit will convict of the truth of any unsealing prophecy. Only in this manner will the Church be spared much of the physical and spiritual traps of the times about to come upon our Earth.

13. **When will the scroll of Daniel be unsealed?**

Daniel 12:4 *But thou, O Daniel, shut up the words, and seal the book, [even] to the time of the end: many shall run to and fro, and knowledge shall be increased.*

Daniel 12:9 *And he said, Go thy way, Daniel: for the words [are] closed up and sealed till the time of the end.*

10 Many shall be purified, and made white, and tried; but the wicked shall do wickedly: and none of the wicked shall understand; but the wise shall understand.

Revelation 11:1 *And there was given me a reed like unto a rod: and the angel stood, saying, Rise, and measure the temple of God, and the altar, and them that worship therein.*

2 But the court which is without the temple leave out, and measure it not; for it is given unto the Gentiles: and the holy city shall they tread under foot forty [and] two months.

3 And I will give [power] unto my two witnesses, and they shall prophesy a thousand two hundred [and] threescore days, clothed in sackcloth.

4 These are the two olive trees, and the two candlesticks standing before the God of the earth. **[Jewish and Gentile Christians]**

5 And if any man will hurt them, fire proceedeth out of their mouth, and devoureth their enemies: and if any man will hurt them, he must in this manner be killed.

6 These have power to shut heaven, that it rain not in the days of their prophecy: and have power over waters to turn them to blood, and to smite the earth with all plagues, as often as they will. **[They will prophesy for 1,260 days of the plagues to come the earth and unseal the hidden mysteries of the ancient prophecies as the last act of Mercy of a Loving God!]**

There is no necessity to set dates as the Bible so clearly states in many prophecies. At the time of the end only, will this knowledge be unsealed. Like a ship that approaches its shore, fog appears to lift as we get closer to the dock and we notice we can see the detail of the coastline and all of the other ships that are familiar to us. Such will be the clearing of the mist of time as the final events of this age are unsealed as Jesus Christ did 1900 plus years ago to the prophet John in the book of unsealing or apocalypse. A company of Jews for Jesus and Gentile Christians will prophesy starting on the first day of the Palestinian-Israeli Peace Treaty for 42 months or 1,260 days.

14. How can we take comfort from the birth pangs of the coming Tribulation?

Christians must not fear, for God is the one in control. During the disasters which will come upon the earth, he will be saving, healing, baptizing and getting his Christian house in order as a bride in preparation for her bridegroom.

***Romans 8:**22 For we know that the whole creation groaneth and travaileth in pain together until now.*

23 And not only [they], but ourselves also, which have the firstfruits of the Spirit, even we ourselves groan within ourselves, waiting for the adoption, [to wit], the redemption of our body.

The metaphor Christ gives of the birth pangs and delivery as a Tribulation to describe the second half of the seven year period is a beautiful picture of the labour pains that precedes the birth of a new child. This new child will be the earthly Kingdom of God united with heaven when Jesus comes to reign for eternity. Take comfort in Jesus's victory over the powers of darkness.

John 14:1-6

1 Let not your heart be troubled: ye believe in God, believe also in me.

2 In my Father's house are many mansions: if [it were] not [so], I would have told you. I go to prepare a place for you.

3 And if I go and prepare a place for you, I will come again, and receive you unto myself; that where I am, [there] ye may be also.

4 And whither I go ye know, and the way ye know.

5 Thomas saith unto him, Lord, we know not whither thou goest; and how can we know the way?

6 Jesus saith unto him, I am the way, the truth, and the life: no man cometh unto the Father, but by me.

15. What is the heart of the witness of this book?

The goal of the rest of this book is to show all who knock, that God listens and has the final say. We are all sinners. Those of us that accept the blood of Jesus to make us whole will walk the gleaming streets of the New Jerusalem. God loved us infinitely while we were sinners. All we must do is accept His fatherly hand, with prayer and obedience. We truly have a sure word of prophecy. As we marvel at God's omniscience, we glorify him, and make the miracle of salvation real in our lives. Only this can witness in our walk in prayer and can save others through the working of the Holy Spirit in us. The message of this book is about how Jesus would strengthen and save each and all, if we would ask.

As in the days of Noah, man's days on earth are numbered. The truth of all the prophets pointing to Jesus may soften the hardened soul and save it from an eternal state of spiritual agony, separated from all Truth and Light. May this be my witness to you, in Christ Jesus. May He give you the comfort of that Blessed Hope coming from our Saviour Lord Jesus.

As these events unfold may your daily newspaper, television and books reflect the truth of the miracle of prophecy pointing to the birth, life and resurrection of Jesus and his returning to earth soon, to judge the nations and marry his bride, the Church. His church are those sheep that listen to Jesus in prayer, fear the Lord, and walk according to His will in Spirit and Truth. At the end of this period, the Tribulation, the bride of Christ the church will truly be perfectly in white, without spot or wrinkle. Only then will she be ready for the marriage supper of Lamb with a perfect and Holy God.

Chapter 2

THE SEALS AND KEYS OF PROPHECY

16.   What is the first seal of Revelation 6?

Daniel 9:27

> *27 And he shall confirm the covenant with many for one week* **[one seven year staged Treaty]***: and in the midst of the week he shall cause the sacrifice and the oblation to cease* **[The restarted sacrifice on the Temple Mount will cease!]***, and for the overspreading of abominations he shall make [it] desolate* **[The population of East Jerusalem will be removed completely!]***, even until the consummation, and that determined shall be poured upon the desolate.*

The bible interprets itself and must be taken as one integrated whole as it is all the messages of God through his prophets. For example, comparison of Matthew 24, the Words of Jesus and Revelation 6, the prophecy given to John by Jesus, yields the interpretation of the seals of revelation,

Matthew 24:3-5

> *3 And as he sat upon the mount of Olives, the disciples came unto him privately, saying, Tell us, when shall these things be? and what [shall be] the sign of thy coming, and of the end of the world?*
>
> *4 And Jesus answered and said unto them, Take heed that no man deceive you.*
>
> *5 For many shall come in my name, saying, I am Christ; and shall deceive many.*

Matching this with Revelation 6:2

2 And I saw, and behold a white horse: and he that sat on him had a bow; and a crown was given unto him: and he went forth conquering, and to conquer.

The Antichrist will present himself as a man of Peace as he enters the city of Jerusalem to set up his throne of the Holy Roman Empire. Thus he will call himself the messiah or the christ or anointed one to bring peace to the Islamic and Jewish homeland. With the Palestinian-Israeli Peace Treaty and the securing of world peace, the Antichrist will ride forth to conquer by peace. He will claim to be the greatest enlightened politician of the Age. Christ-conciousness within will be the religious basis for this New World Order; to make a sustainable stable world without the rule of the Creator God. The empty bow is the apparent dismantled military machine i.e. no arrows. False disarmament will be that empty bow used to deceive the whole world that they need never fear a future nuclear holocaust.

The peace treaty that is the fulfillment of the Oslo Accord will allow the initiation of the sacrifice of the Oslo Accord. Such a peace will allow not only the reinitiation of the sacrifice on the Temple Mount in Jerusalem, but will allow a great symbol of the New Age to be represented to the world. That will be the false reconciliation of the Jews and Moslems everywhere.

The recent Wye Accord requires a deadline of May 4th, 99, for the partitioning of Jerusalem and transfer of the 'Occupied Territories' to the New Palestinian State. This is the most recent attempt by the United Nations lead by the United States to force a false peace on Israel, in a "Land for Peace and Security" deal. It will never work. God says in Isaiah 28, that He will annul Israel's covenant with death!

Isaiah 28:15-23

15 Because ye have said, We have made a covenant with death [the seven year peace treaty between Israel and Islamic New

Palestine], and with hell are we at agreement; when the overflowing scourge shall pass through, it shall not come unto us: for we have made lies our refuge, and under falsehood have we hid ourselves:

16 Therefore thus saith the Lord GOD, Behold, I lay in Zion for a foundation a stone, a tried stone, a precious corner [stone], a sure foundation: he that believeth shall not make haste.

17 Judgment also will I lay to the line, and righteousness to the plummet: and the hail shall sweep away the refuge of lies, and the waters shall overflow the hiding place.

18 And your covenant with death shall be disannulled, and your agreement with hell shall not stand; when the overflowing scourge shall pass through, then ye shall be trodden down by it. **[Israel will be invaded, and instead of the Treaty guaranteeing peace it will guarantee war and invasion and destruction!]**

19 From the time that it goeth forth it shall take you: for morning by morning shall it pass over, by day and by night: and it shall be a vexation only [to] understand the report.

20 For the bed is shorter than that [a man] can stretch himself [on it]: and the covering narrower than that he can wrap himself [in it]. [You Israel have reduced the land I gave you so that you do not have lands to stretch forth My People!]

21 For the LORD shall rise up as [in] mount Perazim, he shall be wroth as [in] the valley of Gibeon, that he may do his work, his strange work; and bring to pass his act, his strange act.

22 Now therefore be ye not mockers, lest your bands be made strong: for I have heard from the Lord GOD of hosts a consumption **[Judgment will come upon the whole earth for plotting to take away the lands and to destroy Israel!]**, *even determined upon the whole earth.*

23 Give ye ear, and hear my voice; hearken, and hear my speech.

The Antichrist goes forth conquering and to conquer with the first seal at the Passover on day 1,260 of the Time of Jacob's Trouble spoken of by Daniel.

Revelation 6:1-2

1 And I saw when the Lamb opened one of the seals, and I heard, as it were the noise of thunder, one of the four beasts saying, Come and see.

2 And I saw, and behold a white horse: and he that sat on him had a bow; and a crown was given unto him: and he went forth conquering, and to conquer.

Revelation 17:12

12 And the ten horns which thou sawest are ten kings, which have received no kingdom as yet; but receive power as kings one hour with the beast. **[These are the ten regional directors of the world as per the Foreign Affairs circa 1970 article on the ten global regions, e.g. North America is area 3. These global nonelected representatives will give the authority to the Russian leader to attack America and Israel and set up the headquarters for the NWO in Jerusalem. This will be a takeover by the NGO organizations and the NWO division of the world banking system with the Russian Military Machine to enforce the new order after America is crippled with a preemptive strike.]**

[They then receive their authority from the resurrected Holy Roman Empire and the Beast to rule their respective regions of the world.]

13 These have one mind, and shall give their power and strength unto the beast.

Their plan is to force the NWO on the world with this evil plan.

D & V: *In October 1998, after a busy office, I was praying and reading in Jeremiah. Suddenly, I was taken in the spirit by the angel Gabriel to the Parliament of Europe in Strassbourg, France. There he told me to observe the meeting that was happening with eighteen representatives of the European Union around a large board table. In the center, there was a silver challis, and they passed a short, appoximately 18 inch silver sword with a golden handle to all the members at the table and swore a blood oath by cutting their right thumb and marking the blood on the right ear after bleeding into the challis with blood mixed with wine. They came together in worship of Satan to setup his kingdom on earth. They also swore to destroy America.*

"By the blood of Hiram and the enlightenment of Osiris, I do pledge to the most excellent and illuminated One, to carry forth my pledge and duty to the New Order of the Ages. By my blood and with this sign, I seal my honor to do all that we have purposed here today, on pain of death by disembowelment and having my heart wrenched from my bossom. So say the Noble Knights of the Order."

I was completely overwhelmed that countries that we consider our allies would scheme to destroy our nation in order to set up the New World Order. I asked the angel when, and he again had me turn my attention to the debate as to when America would be attacked. They all came to one accord to destroy America when the EURO Dollar was completely in control of the European Economy and when all of the Illuminated Sons had removed their wealth from America and the US Stock Market into the European Banking System. Thus the sign was set and the plot hatched to destroy America when this evil plot has been brought to the fullness, and not a day earlier.

17. What is the second seal?

The spiritual war in heaven with the defeat of Satan and his armies cast down to earth coincides with the continuation of this war on the physical plane on earth.

Revelation 12:7-12

> *7 And there was war in heaven: Michael and his angels fought against the dragon; and the dragon fought and his angels,*
>
> *8 And prevailed not; neither was their place found any more in heaven.*
>
> *9 And the great dragon was cast out, that old serpent, called the Devil, and Satan, which deceiveth the whole world: he was cast out into the earth, and his angels were cast out with him.*
>
> *10 And I heard a loud voice saying in heaven, Now is come salvation, and strength, and the kingdom of our God, and the power of his Christ: for the accuser of our brethren is cast down, which accused them before our God day and night.*
>
> *11 And they overcame him by the blood of the Lamb, and by the word of their testimony; and they loved not their lives unto the death.*
>
> *12 Therefore rejoice, [ye] heavens, and ye that dwell in them. Woe to the inhabiters of the earth and of the sea! for the devil is come down unto you, having great wrath, because he knoweth that he hath but a short time.*

The army of Satan will be met with an army of overcoming Christians that will defeat Satan by (1) the Blood of the Lamb, (2) The Word of their testimony and (3) Dying in the cause of Jesus Christ in the battle. They will not be gone somewhere in a Rapture when the battle has just begun!

Revelation 12:11

> *11 And they overcame him by the blood of the Lamb, and by the word of their testimony; and they loved not their lives unto the death.*

Matthew 24:6-7

6 And ye shall hear of wars and rumours of wars: see that ye be not troubled: for all [these things] must come to pass, but the end is not yet. **[The attack on America and Israel will just be the start of the three woes. The first five seals, vials, and trumpets are all started on the Passover at day 1,260.]**

7 For nation shall rise against nation, and kingdom against kingdom: and there shall be famines, and pestilences, and earthquakes, in divers places.

In Revelation 6:3-4

3 And when he had opened the second seal, I heard the second beast say, Come and see.

4 And there went out another horse [that was] red: and [power] was given to him that sat thereon to take peace from the earth, and that they should kill one another: and there was given unto him a great sword.

The second seal is the spread of war on the world-wide basis. He would take peace from the earth. He was also given a large sword. The second seal of revelation is therefore coincident with breaking the seven year duration that opens with the first seal, or revealing of the anti-Christ (false prophet). **This war will break out at 1,260 days after the removal of the animal sacrifice initiated at the First of Tabernacles.** It will occur at the Feast of Passover. (see Fig. 23-1)

Peace will be taken from the whole world with the Jihad of Islam and the attack of Russian allies on America and Israel. This will be a pre-emptive first strike! The great sword is the nuclear superiority, and chemical and biological warfare and the will to use it. Russia, the leader and armour of the forces that invade Israel, will be the lead military power and will be the natural nation for the False Christ that had first come in peace to confirm the treaty to allow the Jews to start their sacrifice, and then come to invade and destroy their country and Israel's main ally, America.

18. What is the third seal?
Matthew 24:7-8

> 7 For nation shall rise against nation, and kingdom against kingdom: and there shall be famines, and pestilences, and earthquakes, in divers places.
>
> 8 All these [are] the beginning of sorrows.

Revelation 6:5-6

> 5 And when he had opened the third seal, I heard the third beast say, Come and see. And I beheld, and lo a black horse; and he that sat on him had a pair of balances in his hand.
>
> 6 And I heard a voice in the midst of the four beasts say, A measure of wheat for a penny, and three measures of barley for a penny; and [see] thou hurt not the oil and the wine.

Three years ago, while visiting Falcon Air Force base East of Colorado Springs, I was told the following true news that has not been available to the secular media. By the way, Falcon is now called Schriver Air Force base and is three higher levels of security than Norad, and is the central command and control center for the entire Western World.

During the Gulf War, the city of Tel Aviv had been struck by scud missiles. Prime minister Benny Begin had sixty Israeli jets in the air, and was transferring the unlocking codes for the nuclear warheads on the Israeli jets. National Security Agency intercepted this intelligence and George Bush intercepted the authorization for a nuclear attack on Damascus, Bagdad, and the plan for attack on Moscow. President Bush advised Prime Minister Begin to turn back the attack or face a long range missile lock-on by our jets in the air and Star Wars Weapons. We were for several minutes, three seconds to midnight. The time for God's judgment was yet not at the fullness. There is a time of attack by Israel when it will not turn back, and its demise is imminent from all the surrounding Islamic nations.

The occurrence of both famines and earthquakes will be triggered off by the nuclear attack of Russia and Muslim Allies in the Battle of Gog and Magog. [see reference on Dr. Gary Whiteford, Univ. of New Brunswick -- Relationship of underground testing to Richter 6 + earthquakes.] This local war on day 1,260 of the last seven years will trigger a world-wide economic collapse, and the ecological and economic effects will produce widespread famines in diverse places all over the world. Radiation will be spread around the world and the ozone layer will disappear burning sores on those that dwell on the surface of the earth, with second degree burns.

The wealthy nations will remain able to afford luxuries until the last day of the seven years. The rider of the black horse represents famines and world-wide economic depression. This depression however will not affect the entire earth. Many with wealth will be represented by those who are able to buy the oil and the wine. Many will still be able to purchase luxuries while many go hungry and require a day's wages to feed themselves for a day.

19. What is the fourth seal?

Revelation 6: 7-8

7 And when he had opened the fourth seal, I heard the voice of the fourth beast say, Come and see.

8 And I looked, and behold a pale horse: and his name that sat on him was Death, and Hell followed with him. And power was given unto them over the fourth part of the earth, to kill with sword, and with hunger, and with death, and with the beasts of the earth.

The first three events starting on day 1,260, will kill one quarter of the earth's population. The widespread Death that will occur will directly follow the nuclear attack in the Middle East, widespread earthquakes, and resulting ecological and economic collapse. The period of Peace and Security will be over and there will be no more honeymoon with the Dictator Beast. Our unprepared world will not escape the terror of these events. Destruction will come upon them without warning. Spasm after spasm of events will come upon a largely deceived world, just as birth pangs seize a pregnant woman in the active phase of labor.

1 Th 5:3 For when they shall say, Peace and safety; then sudden destruction cometh upon them, as travail upon a woman with child; and they shall not escape.

The Events of the First Five Vials and Trumpets –
Day 1,260-Passover

All of the events of the first five vials and trumpets must be understood as different perspectives of the same events, that all commence on the Passover, Day 1,260. Vial judgments reflect the perspective of the Kingdom of the First Beast - the Resurrected Holy Roman Empire and the throne of his new kingdom in Jerusalem. The trumpet judgments reflect the perspective of the world.

The plagues of Egypt are a type of the plagues that will occur at this time. The first vial judgment is skin sores that parallel the sore on the unsaved people of Egypt, while Israel was spared through this plague.

Exodus 9:8-11

8 And the LORD said unto Moses and unto Aaron, Take to you handfuls of ashes of the furnace, and let Moses sprinkle it toward the heaven in the sight of Pharaoh.

9 And it shall become small dust in all the land of Egypt, and shall be a boil breaking forth [with] blains upon man, and upon beast, throughout all the land of Egypt.

10 And they took ashes of the furnace, and stood before Pharaoh; and Moses sprinkled it up toward heaven; and it became a boil breaking forth [with] blains upon man, and upon beast.

11 And the magicians could not stand before Moses because of the boils; for the boil was upon the magicians, and upon all the Egyptians.

Those who do not have the Mark of God already on their foreheads will be affected by this plague.

In Revelation 16:1-2, the first vial judgment is parallel with the fifth trumpet of Rev 9:1-5:

Rev 16:1-2

1 And I heard a great voice out of the temple saying to the seven angels, Go your ways, and pour out the vials of the wrath of God upon the earth.

2 And the first went, and poured out his vial upon the earth; and there fell a noisome and grievous sore upon the men which had the mark of the beast, and [upon] them which worshipped his image.

Rev 9:1-11

1 And the fifth angel sounded, and I saw a star fall from heaven unto the earth: and to him was given the key of the bottomless pit. **[This is the same fall of Satan and the angelic hordes to earth spoken of in Revelation 12:7-12. He indwells the Antichrist with his power and goes forth to conquer. He was given the key to get out of the bottomless pit by God, so that the wrath of Satan which is the six seals, trumpets and vials should be complete upon a world under the curse of the law and the Old Covenant. Actual angelic encounters with demons will occur at this time. However, I prefer to call them Unidentified Fiendish Objects presenting themselves as aliens to save the world through the New World Order.]**

2 And he opened the bottomless pit; and there arose a smoke out of the pit, as the smoke of a great furnace; and the sun and the air were darkened by reason of the smoke of the pit.

3 And there came out of the smoke locusts upon the earth: and unto them was given power, as the scorpions of the earth have power. [Satan has made strategic alliances with demons at Area 51 and other military bases. America will be the base upon which the Mark of the Beast will be forced upon the whole world. In doing so America will be attacked simultaneously with Israel, and many Americans will die. This will be the start of the final civil war against the Satanic Federal Government bent on the subjugation of America to a New World Order.]

4 And it was commanded them that they should not hurt the grass of the earth, neither any green thing, neither any tree; but only those men which have not the seal of God in their foreheads.

5 And to them it was given that they should not kill them, but that they should be tormented five months: and their torment [was] as the torment of a scorpion, when he striketh a man. [This is an invasion force with the co-operation of the United States government and carried out by United Nations troops aided by the demonic hordes and the genetically hybrid MIB, just as in the days of the Nephilim before the flood of Noah. They will feel the pain of the implantation of the electronic dog tag of the Mark of the Beast consisting of a world cellular phone and database as the 6/6/6/ of Birthdate Y/M/D, Mesh Bar Code 99/99/99 sectors and subsectors for location, and the six digit genetic fingerprint.]

6 And in those days shall men seek death, and shall not find it; and shall desire to die, and death shall flee from them. [They will seek death for they are the lost and lukewarm Christians who have not prepared and now caught with the dilemma of taking the Mark or die of starvation or execution.]

7 And the shapes of the locusts [were] like unto horses prepared unto battle; and on their heads [were] as it were crowns like gold, and their faces [were] as the faces of men. [This is a "Black Operations Helicopter and Air Assault" on American civilians by United Nations forces!]

8 And they had hair as the hair of women, and their teeth were as [the teeth] of lions.

9 And they had breastplates, as it were breastplates of iron; and the sound of their wings [was] as the sound of chariots of many horses running to battle.

10 And they had tails like unto scorpions, and there were stings in their tails: and their power [was] to hurt men five months.

11 And they had a king over them, [which is] the angel of the bottomless pit, whose name in the Hebrew tongue [is] Abaddon, but in the Greek tongue hath [his] name Apollyon. **[Clearly identified is the leadership of Satan controlling and indwelling the Russian leader who will carry out the will of the NWO!]**

The first vial is breaking out of sores on those who take the Mark of the Beast within the Resurrected Holy Roman Empire. This will be a radiation burn and burns from the destruction of the ozone layer with oil well fires that will make the Gulf War fires of Saddam Hussein seem tiny by comparison.

The first trumpet of Rev 8:7, shows that this will be the destruction of the ozone layer with the particulates that can catalyze the reaction with Chlorine Monoxide that destroys the ozone layer.

Revelation 8:7

7 The first angel sounded, and there followed hail and fire mingled with blood, and they were cast upon the earth: and the third part of trees was burnt up, and all green grass was burnt up.

There is enough chlorine monoxide in the upper atmosphere to destroy the ozone layer in several days. The immediate effect will be the destruction of all the grain crops and grassy plants on the earth. This means that the attack has to be in the spring or summer to do such damage. This would coincide exactly with the feast of

Passover. As not all trees would be in bloom, only one-third would be affected by the destruction of the ozone layer.

The second vial is poured out at Revelation 16:3, and the Mediterranean sea becomes radioactive and all the sea creatures in it die. Parallel with this is the trumpet judgment with a description of a mountain burning with fire. This is the description of an ICBM and not a comet. All the events occur of the first five seals, trumpets and vials; and this is the cause of poisoning of the waters with wormwood, the Russian for Chernobyl synonymous with the meltdown and poisoning of a vast area of the Soviet Union near Kiev. This is similar to the Exodus 7:14 plague.

Revelation 8:8-9

> *8 And the second angel sounded, and as it were a great mountain burning with fire was cast into the sea: and the third part of the sea became blood;* **[ICBMs caused one-third of the oceans of the world to be poisoned with radioactivity and the primary attack areas are America and Islamic cities near Israel.]**
>
> *9 And the third part of the creatures which were in the sea, and had life, died; and the third part of the ships were destroyed.*

Revelation 16:3

> *3 And the second angel poured out his vial upon the sea; and it became as the blood of a dead [man]: and every living soul died in the sea.* **[The sea referred to here is the Mediterranean Sea, indicating an attack on coastal Israel at Haifa and Tel Aviv and other unspecified areas of the Mediterranean.]**

During the third vial, the head waters of the Tigris and Euphrates rivers are poisoned by radioactivity. This is in preparation for the invasion of the 200 million man armies of the Kings of the East, i.e. China, with the second woe. This poisoning of the waters happens on the Kingdom of the Beast, the Resurrected Holy Roman Empire, and the throne of the empire, Jerusalem. Thus European and Eastern Block, as well as Israeli and Iraqi waters, are affected. This scenario suggests that there is an Israeli nuclear retaliation for the attacks on their coastal cities and that Iraq is affected. The lack of clean fresh water and the famine from the loss of safe seafood will intensify the spread of pestilences and starvation.

Revelation 16:4-7

4 And the third angel poured out his vial upon the rivers and fountains of waters; and they became blood. **[The rivers and fountains of water are poisoned in Northern Israel and Iraq.]**

5 And I heard the angel of the waters say, Thou art righteous, O Lord, which art, and wast, and shalt be, because thou hast judged thus.

6 For they have shed the blood of saints and prophets, and thou hast given them blood to drink; for they are worthy. **[This judgment is against unbelieving Israel! Israel, according to Malachi 2:11, has done a terrible and abominable thing against the Blood of Jesus in restarting animal sacrifice on the Temple Mount. God in his anger will give them 'blood to drink'!]**

7 And I heard another out of the altar say, Even so, Lord God Almighty, true and righteous [are] thy judgments.

Revelation 8:10-11

10 And the third angel sounded, and there fell a great star from heaven, burning as it were a lamp, and it fell upon the third part of the rivers, and upon the fountains of waters;

11 And the name of the star is called Wormwood: and the third part of the waters became wormwood; and many men died of the waters, because they were made bitter. [Radioactive contamination of the oceans also now extends through the hydrological cycle to the fresh waters and one-third of the fresh water on earth must be filtered for alpha particles and radioisotopes. Many peoples die due to contamination and the effects such as thyroid failure and radiation enteritis or bowel radiation burns.] The plague of waters turned to blood is like the plagues of ...

Exodus 7:17-21

17 Thus saith the LORD, In this thou shalt know that I [am] the LORD: behold, I will smite with the rod that [is] in mine hand upon the waters which [are] in the river, and they shall be turned to blood.

18 And the fish that [is] in the river shall die, and the river shall stink; and the Egyptians shall lothe to drink of the water of the river.

19 And the LORD spake unto Moses, Say unto Aaron, Take thy rod, and stretch out thine hand upon the waters of Egypt, upon their streams, upon their rivers, and upon their ponds, and upon all their pools of water, that they may become blood; and [that] there may be blood throughout all the land of Egypt, both in [vessels of] wood, and in [vessels of] stone.

20 And Moses and Aaron did so, as the LORD commanded; and he lifted up the rod, and smote the waters that [were] in the river, in the sight of Pharaoh, and in the sight of his servants; and all the waters that [were] in the river were turned to blood.

21 And the fish that [was] in the river died; and the river stank, and the Egyptians could not drink of the water of the river; and there was blood throughout all the land of Egypt.

The fourth vial is seen in Revelation 16:8-9 with the scorching of men with heat. This may both be the thermonuclear blast and the result of particulates in the upper atmosphere that precipitate the destruction of the ozone layer releasing deadly short wave UV-A light. There will also be fierce heat from oil well fires just as in the Gulf War. Those fires were set in the Gulf War purposely by Saddam Hussein.

Revelation 8:12

12 And the fourth angel sounded, and the third part of the sun was smitten, and the third part of the moon, and the third part of the stars; so as the third part of them was darkened, and the day shone not for a third part of it, and the night likewise. **[One-third of the daylight, the moonlight, and starlight is blocked out by the particles in the high atmosphere by the thermonuclear exchange. This saves many from the total destruction of any crops and the burns to the eyes and skin of those upon the earth so that some people will survive the terrible times of the Tribulation.]**

Matthew 24:22

22 And except those days should be shortened, there should no flesh be saved: but for the elect's sake those days shall be shortened.

Mark 13:20

20 And except that the Lord had shortened those days, no flesh should be saved: but for the elect's sake, whom he hath chosen, he hath shortened the days.

The fifth vial is darkness similar to the Egyptian plague of the Exodus.

Exodus 10:21-23

21 And the LORD said unto Moses, Stretch out thine hand toward heaven, that there may be darkness over the land of Egypt, even darkness [which] may be felt.

22 And Moses stretched forth his hand toward heaven; and there was a thick darkness in all the land of Egypt three days:

23 They saw not one another, neither rose any from his place for three days: but all the children of Israel had light in their dwellings.

The darkness casts over the throne of the Beast, which is Jerusalem, for the three days after Passover, indicating an attack on Tel Aviv and Haifa. This will be for three days total in severity.

Islam will not permit a thermonuclear attack on the Holy City, Jerusalem, nor will they let their Russian allies.

Revelation 16:10-11

> 10 And the fifth angel poured out his vial upon the seat of the beast; and his kingdom was full of darkness **[Jerusalem will be covered by darkness!]**; *and they gnawed their tongues for pain,*
>
> *11 And blasphemed the God of heaven because of their pains and their sores, and repented not of their deeds.*

Revelation 9:1-2

> *1 And the fifth angel sounded, and I saw a star fall from heaven unto the earth: and to him was given the key of the bottomless pit.*
>
> *2 And he opened the bottomless pit; and there arose a smoke out of the pit, as the smoke of a great furnace; and the sun and the air were darkened by reason of the smoke of the pit.* **[This is similar to the description of the blotting out one-third of the day and the night in Revelation 16:2! This is concurrent with the five month invasion of the nations of Israel and America. This is the demonic horde and the foreign UN troops who will enforce the Mark of the Beast upon the peoples of the earth.]**

20. **What is the fifth seal?**

Then in Matthew 24:9

> *9 Then shall they deliver you up to be afflicted, and shall kill you: and ye shall be hated of all nations for my name's sake.*

Compare this to Revelation 6:9-11

> *9 And when he had opened the fifth seal, I saw under the altar the souls of them that were slain for the word of God, and for the testimony which they held:*
>
> *10 And they cried with a loud voice, saying, How long, O Lord, holy and true, dost thou not judge and avenge our blood on them that dwell on the earth?*

11 And white robes were given unto every one of them; and it was said unto them, that they should rest yet for a little season, until their fellow servants also and their brethren, that should be killed as they [were], should be fulfilled.

The fifth seal is a great persecution and martyrdom of those who follow Christ. This is signified by two companies of people. They will be Jewish and Gentile Believers in Jesus Christ. These are the two olive trees and lampstands of Revelation 11. They will have prophesied for 1,260 days and now will be killed and lie in the world for 3 and 1/2 'day years' of 360 days each, or 1,260 days, until their resurrection.

Malachi 4:4-6

4 Remember ye the law of Moses my servant, which I commanded unto him in Horeb for all Israel, [with] the statutes and judgments.

5 Behold, I will send you Elijah the prophet before the coming of the great and dreadful day of the LORD:

6 And he shall turn the heart of the fathers to the children, and the heart of the children to their fathers, lest I come and smite the earth with a curse.

They will represent the authority and ministry of Moses and Elijah. Moses led Israel out of bondage in Egypt and warned Pharaoh that plagues would descend upon his people and country if he did not let God's people go. This prophetic ministry is important to convince all people on earth to repentance and salvation or to condemnation and judgment.

Elijah represents the ministry which would turn the hearts of the fathers to their children, and of the children to their fathers. This would therefore be a caring ministry which would allow Christians to take care of each other, and for Christians and Messianic Jews to protect each other through this time of great tribulation. The caring outreach of the true church will be so important at this time.

Elijah also represents the great miracle in which Elijah raised Elisha that performed twice the miracles of Elijah that had none of the great character defects that Elijah demonstrated such as running from Jezebel. This means that there will be a great deal of teaching to the young people within our Christian congregations. It is they who will be the great evangelistic army ministering about these end time events to overtake the earth.

The ministry of Moses is just as Moses had ministered to the ancient tribes of Israel. Concrete instruction will be given to believing Jews and Christians for both physical and spiritual preparation. The prophetic word will be unsealed to reveal the truth of the plagues about to be released on earth with the wrath of Satan.

The length of time that this ministry will take place will be twelve hundred and sixty days and then a great martyrdom will occur for three and a half day years with each year being three hundred and sixty days as in the Jewish calendar. This latter period will therefore last another twelve hundred and sixty days for a total of twenty-five hundred and twenty days or the seven years of three hundred and sixty day-years.

Revelation 11:1-13

1 And there was given me a reed like unto a rod: and the angel stood, saying, Rise, and measure the temple of God, and the altar, and them that worship therein.

2 But the court which is without the temple leave out, and measure it not; for it is given unto the Gentiles: **[New World Order]** *and the holy city shall they tread under foot forty [and] two months.* **[3-1/2 Jewish Calendar Years]**

3 And I will give [power] unto my two witnesses, **[Jewish and Gentile Believers]** *and they shall prophesy a thousand two hundred [and] threescore days, clothed in sackcloth.*

4 These are the two olive trees, and the two candlesticks standing before the God of the earth.

5 And if any man will hurt them, fire proceedeth out of their mouth, and devoureth their enemies: and if any man will hurt them, he must in this manner be killed. **[The "Fire" is the fire of the Holy Spirit, and all those that curse these witnesses must die in like manner!]**

6 These have power to shut heaven, that it rain **[The Spiritual rain of the Knowledge of the Holy Spirit]** *not in the days of their prophecy: and have power over waters to turn them to blood, and to smite the earth with all plagues, as often as they will.* **[They are the witnesses that will unseal the Old and New Testament Prophecies for the End Times!]**

7 And when they shall have finished their testimony, the beast that ascendeth out of the bottomless pit shall make war against them, and shall overcome them, and kill them. **[This genocide of Jewish and Christian Believers will start with the Passover in the middle of the seven years, the exact day the Antichrist enters the Temple in Jerusalem, and the Mark of the Beast is forced by America on the whole world!]**

8 And their dead bodies [shall lie] in the street of the great city **[The massacre will start in Jerusalem with the breaking of the Treaty that partitions Jerusalem]**, *which spiritually is called Sodom and Egypt, where also our Lord was crucified.*

9 And they of the people and kindreds and tongues and nations shall see their dead bodies three days and an half, and shall not suffer their dead bodies to be put in graves. **[For 1,260 days the massacre of Jewish and Christian Believers will continue until the return of Christ for His Bride!]**

10 And they that dwell upon the earth shall rejoice over them, and make merry, and shall send gifts one to another; because these two prophets tormented them that dwelt on the earth.

11 And after three days and an half the Spirit of life from God entered into them, and they stood upon their feet; and great fear fell upon them which saw them. **[After 3-1/2 day-years or 1,260 days Jewish and Christian Believers will be resurrected.]**

Figure 20-1

		Outer Court Given to the Gentiles
2 Witnesses	**2 Witnesses**	**2 Witnesses**
Prophecy	Martyred	Martyred are resurrected
Day 1	Day 1,260	Day 2,520
Tabernacles Peace Treaty & Start of Jewish Israel, Sacrifice	Passover Iraqi and Russian Attack on Arab Neighbours & Egypt	Trumpets Rosh Hashanah

These witnesses are clothed in sack cloth and are referred to as two olive trees or lamp stands, which refer to churches or groups of people which are growing as in an olive grove with the roots being Jesus Christ. The fire that precedes from their mouth is the fire of the conviction of the prophecy of the coming times of tribulations upon the earth. The shutting up of the sky so that it will not rain is to withhold the Holy Spirit from all those who would not believe the authority of their prophesying. In the plagues with which they strike the earth are those which the Lord has prophesied in Matthew 24, and again has given the prophet John in the book of Revelation.

Malachi 2: 1-17

1 And now, O ye priests, this commandment [is] for you.

2 If ye will not hear, and if ye will not lay [it] to heart, to give glory unto my name [Accept My Son, Jesus Christ the Savior!], saith the LORD of hosts, I will even send a curse upon you, and I will curse your blessings: yea, I have cursed them already, because ye do not lay [it] to heart.

3 Behold, I will corrupt your seed **[Spiritual Seed],** *and spread dung upon your faces, [even] the dung of your solemn feasts; and [one] shall take you away with it.*

4 And ye shall know that I have sent this commandment unto you, that my covenant might be with Levi, saith the LORD of hosts.

5 My covenant was with him of life and peace; and I gave them to him [for] the fear wherewith he feared me, and was afraid before my name.

6 The law of truth was in his mouth, and iniquity was not found in his lips: he walked with me in peace and equity, and did turn many away from iniquity.

7 For the priest's lips should keep knowledge, and they should seek the law at his mouth: for he [is] the messenger of the LORD of hosts. **[The Anointed of Discernment of Clean and Unclean Falls Upon the Sons of Levi, and this is the duty of the Priests of Aaron!]**

8 But ye are departed out of the way; ye have caused many to stumble at the law; ye have corrupted the covenant of Levi, saith the LORD of hosts.

9 Therefore have I also made you contemptible and base before all the people, according as ye have not kept my ways, but have been partial in the law.

10 Have we not all one father? hath not one God created us? why do we deal treacherously every man against his brother, by profaning the covenant of our fathers?

11 Judah hath dealt treacherously, and an abomination is committed in Israel **[The Restarting of the Abomination of the Animal Sacrifice on the Temple Mount is an insult to the**

infinite sacrifice of Jesus Death on a cross, and thus this is the abomination that desolates or depopulates the city of Jerusalem and the land of Israel with the "land for peace and security" treaty of Daniel 9:27!] *and in Jerusalem; for Judah hath profaned the holiness of the LORD which he loved, and hath married the daughter of a strange god.*

12 The LORD will cut off the man that doeth this, the master and the scholar, out of the tabernacles of Jacob, and him that offereth an offering unto the LORD of hosts.

13 And this have ye done again, covering the altar of the LORD with tears, with weeping, and with crying out, insomuch that he regardeth not the offering any more, or receiveth [it] with good will at your hand.

14 Yet ye say, Wherefore? Because the LORD hath been witness between thee and the wife of thy youth, against whom thou hast dealt treacherously: yet [is] she thy companion, and the wife of thy covenant.

15 And did not he make one? Yet had he the residue of the spirit. And wherefore one? That he might seek a godly seed. Therefore take heed to your spirit, and let none deal treacherously against the wife of his youth.

16 For the LORD, the God of Israel, saith that he hateth putting away: for [one] covereth violence with his garment, saith the LORD of hosts: therefore take heed to your spirit, that ye deal not treacherously.

17 Ye have wearied the LORD with your words. Yet ye say, Wherein have we wearied [him]? When ye say, Every one that doeth evil [is] good in the sight of the LORD, and he delighteth in them; or, Where [is] the God of judgment?

Malachi 3: 1-18

1 Behold, I will send my messenger, and he shall prepare the way before me: and the Lord, whom ye seek, shall suddenly come to his temple, even the messenger of the covenant, whom ye delight in: behold, he shall come, saith the LORD of hosts.

2 But who may abide the day of his coming? and who shall stand when he appeareth? for he [is] like a refiner's fire, and like fullers' sope:

3 And he shall sit [as] a refiner and purifier of silver: and he shall purify the sons of Levi, and purge them as gold and silver, that they may offer unto the LORD an offering in righteousness.

4 Then shall the offering of Judah and Jerusalem be pleasant unto the LORD, as in the days of old, and as in former years.

5 And I will come near to you to judgment; and I will be a swift witness against the sorcerers, and against the adulterers, and against false swearers, and against those that oppress the hireling in [his] wages, the widow, and the fatherless, and that turn aside the stranger [from his right], and fear not me, saith the LORD of hosts.

6 For I [am] the LORD, I change not; therefore ye sons of Jacob are not consumed.

7 Even from the days of your fathers ye are gone away from mine ordinances, and have not kept [them]. Return unto me, and I will return unto you, saith the LORD of hosts. But ye said, Wherein shall we return?

8 Will a man rob God? Yet ye have robbed me. But ye say, Wherein have we robbed thee? In tithes and offerings.

9 Ye [are] cursed with a curse: for ye have robbed me, [even] this whole nation.

10 Bring ye all the tithes into the storehouse, that there may be meat in mine house, and prove me now herewith, saith the LORD of hosts, if I will not open you the windows of heaven, and pour you out a blessing, that [there shall] not [be room] enough [to receive it].

11 And I will rebuke the devourer for your sakes, and he shall not destroy the fruits of your ground; neither shall your vine cast her fruit before the time in the field, saith the LORD of hosts.

12 And all nations shall call you blessed: for ye shall be a delightsome land, saith the LORD of hosts.

13 Your words have been stout against me, saith the LORD. Yet ye say, What have we spoken [so much] against thee?

14 Ye have said, It [is] vain to serve God: and what profit [is it] that we have kept his ordinance, and that we have walked mournfully before the LORD of hosts?

15 And now we call the proud happy; yea, they that work wickedness are set up; yea, [they that] tempt God are even delivered.

16 Then they that feared the LORD spake often one to another: and the LORD hearkened, and heard [it], and a book of remembrance was written before him for them that feared the LORD, and that thought upon his name.

17 And they shall be mine, saith the LORD of hosts, in that day when I make up my jewels; and I will spare them, as a man spareth his own son that serveth him.

18 Then shall ye return, and discern between the righteous and the wicked, between him that serveth God and him that serveth him not.

Malachi 4: 1-6

1 For, behold, the day cometh, that shall burn as an oven; and all the proud, yea, and all that do wickedly, shall be stubble: and the day that cometh shall burn them up, saith the LORD of hosts, that it shall leave them neither root nor branch.

2 But unto you that fear my name shall the Sun of righteousness arise with healing in his wings; and ye shall go forth, and grow up as calves of the stall.

3 And ye shall tread down the wicked; for they shall be ashes under the soles of your feet in the day that I shall do [this], saith the LORD of hosts.

4 Remember ye the law of Moses my servant, which I commanded unto him in Horeb for all Israel, [with] the statutes and judgments.

5 Behold, I will send you Elijah the prophet before the coming of the great and dreadful day of the LORD:

6 And he shall turn the heart of the fathers to the children, and the heart of the children to their fathers, lest I come and smite the earth with a curse.

This will of course be the "time of Jacob's trouble" for Jews as told in the Old Testament. At the end of seven years they stand on their feet, are resurrected and are taken up to heaven while their enemies looked on. The great physical event of the tribulation of the great earthquake which moves all the mountains and islands, will occur.

We noticed also that God in the first of Revelation 11 says to measure the temple of God and the altar and count the worshippers at the end of the 1,260th day. This is like a shepherd counting his sheep before he moves them or is about to do some great work. This is the time of sealing the whole church or all the believers, Jew and Gentile from the twelve spiritual 'tribes of Israel'. This sealing will be completed on the 1,260th day after the Islamic-Israeli Palestinian Peace Treaty. The outer court is being given to the Gentiles or New World Order for 1,260 days in the last half of the Tribulation.

The first five seals, which is the number of Satan, all commence on the Passover at the 1,260th day. We shall see the first five vials and trumpets also commence on the same day. They all comprise the first woe of ...

Revelations 8:13

13 And I beheld, and heard an angel flying through the midst of heaven, saying with a loud voice, Woe, woe, woe, to the inhabiters of the earth by reason of the other voices of the trumpet of the three angels, which are yet to sound!

Revelations 9:1-11

1 And the fifth angel sounded, and I saw a star fall from heaven unto the earth: and to him was given the key of the bottomless pit.

2 And he opened the bottomless pit; and there arose a smoke out of the pit, as the smoke of a great furnace; and the sun and the air were darkened by reason of the smoke of the pit.

3 And there came out of the smoke locusts upon the earth: and unto them was given power, as the scorpions of the earth have power.

4 And it was commanded them that they should not hurt the grass of the earth, neither any green thing, neither any tree; but only those men which have not the seal of God in their foreheads.

5 And to them it was given that they should not kill them, but that they should be tormented five months: and their torment [was] as the torment of a scorpion, when he striketh a man.

6 And in those days shall men seek death, and shall not find it; and shall desire to die, and death shall flee from them.

7 And the shapes of the locusts [were] like unto horses prepared unto battle; and on their heads [were] as it were crowns like gold, and their faces [were] as the faces of men.

8 And they had hair as the hair of women, and their teeth were as [the teeth] of lions.

9 And they had breastplates, as it were breastplates of iron; and the sound of their wings [was] as the sound of chariots of many horses running to battle.

10 And they had tails like unto scorpions, and there were stings in their tails: and their power [was] to hurt men five months.

11 And they had a king over them, [which is] the angel of the bottomless pit, whose name in the Hebrew tongue [is] Abaddon, but in the Greek tongue hath [his] name Apollyon. 12 One woe is past; [and], behold, there come two woes more hereafter. **[This is the totality of the first woe: the five seals, trumpets and vials!]**

The second woe is the same as the sixth seal, vial and trumpet. It will occur at the end of the 150 days of occupation of America and Israel. It will be concurrent with the invasion of Israel with the army of 200 million men from China, and the "Kings of the East."

Revelation 9:12-21

12 One woe is past; [and], behold, there come two woes more hereafter.

13 And the sixth angel sounded, and I heard a voice from the four horns of the golden altar which is before God,

14 Saying to the sixth angel which had the trumpet, Loose the four angels which are bound in the great river Euphrates.

15 And the four angels were loosed, which were prepared for an hour, and a day, and a month, and a year, for to slay the third part of men.

16 And the number of the army of the horsemen [were] two hundred thousand thousand: and I heard the number of them. **[This is the army of 200 million men from China.]**

17 And thus I saw the horses in the vision, and them that sat on them, having breastplates of fire, and of jacinth, and brimstone: and the heads of the horses [were] as the heads of lions; and out of their mouths issued fire and smoke and brimstone.

18 By these three was the third part of men killed, by the fire, and by the smoke, and by the brimstone, which issued out of their mouths. **[One third of all remaining humanity will be killed by the conventional and nuclear war of Armageddon.]**

19 For their power is in their mouth, and in their tails: for their tails [were] like unto serpents, and had heads, and with them they do hurt.

20 And the rest of the men which were not killed by these plagues yet repented not of the works of their hands, that they should not worship devils, and idols of gold, and silver, and brass, and stone, and of wood: which neither can see, nor hear, nor walk:

21 Neither repented they of their murders, nor of their sorceries, nor of their fornication, nor of their thefts.

This is same event as Revelations 16:12-16

12 And the sixth angel poured out his vial upon the great river Euphrates; and the water thereof was dried up, that the way of the kings of the east might be prepared. **[The headwaters of the Euphrates and Tigris rivers will be dried up as a war preparation of China and America to invade Iraq and Israel. This will allow the easy transport of the massive army of 200 million from the Kyber Pass across Asia into North Israel.]**

13 And I saw three unclean spirits like frogs [come] out of the mouth of the dragon, and out of the mouth of the beast, and out of the mouth of the false prophet. **[The Sustainable Earth Doctrines of the Earth Charter 18 Commandments will still be echoed to the world as the reason for the invading forces gathering in Israel, while their real motive will be to obtain control of the oil of the Middle East.]**

14 For they are the spirits of devils, working miracles, [which] go forth unto the kings of the earth and of the whole world, to gather them to the battle of that great day of God Almighty.

15 Behold, I come as a thief. Blessed [is] he that watcheth, and keepeth his garments, lest he walk naked, and they see his shame. **[I only come as a thief to those who are not saved and walking with the Lord every day in prayer and the Spirit.]**

16 And he gathered them together into a place called in the Hebrew tongue Armageddon. **[He will gather them to the Valley of Megiddo, where the Russian navy has entered at Haifa and the troops have traversed the Valley to take control of Israel with Islam.]**

Dreams and Visions:

While praying and reading the scriptures, I received the following vision of the times spoken of by Dimitru Duduman, when the revolution would start and America would have the places like Sodom and Gomorrah attacked.

In the spirit the angel Gabriel took me to the West Coast where I saw foreign and oriental looking troops with blue hats carrying machine guns. I saw helicopters with the signs of the United Nations, and many thousands of Americans in lines waiting to receive the Mark of the Beast. He told me to watch as the Chinese navy, on the West Coast base we gave them, became a secondary staging ground for the invasion. The primary invasion was our own military bases. The angel showed me how our New World Order US government officials gave these bases to the invaders.

I was horrified as I watched. Deep below many airports and military bases, I saw those with Red badges, who were to be executed for the word of their testimony, and they did not shrink from the faith in Jesus. Others, marked by blue, worked in factories and were periodically brought to reprogramming camps and rooms where unspeakable inhumane acts were performed on them to have them repent of their belief in the Truth and the Word. Elsewhere, those with the Green Emblem smiled and went about life with peace on their well fed faces, and they feared not, for they had felt righteous in that they were saving the planet, or they knew falsely in their hearts that surely the Lord would not cast them out to outer darkness!

Surely, once saved, they thought, I have eternal security, and the Lord Jesus I once received will not reject those he has taken into his arms. Then Gabriel cringed as if in pain seeing this, for he said that their beliefs would bring them to destruction for they knew Him not!

I asked, "What is the end of these things?" He said, "Those that will hear the words of the witnesses of Jesus and the prophets of the END, would be stirred and be saved throughout the kingdom of the Beast." These would be high level masons, murderers, bankers, military men, teachers, doctors, laborers, and all the corporations of the Beast would turn over those who would receive the Mark of the Sovereign Lord on their right hand or forehead. Even those who had taken the Oath to the Evil One and those most detestable, were among their numbers! As I watched, he said, "Behold, see those who feel secure in their righteousness, are lost while these most terrible before men are now washed righteous in the Blood of the Lamb!" In the spirit I fell on my face weeping for those that call themselves by the name of the Lord, and the fate that they will face in outer darkness.

Suddenly, I was back beside the angel Gabriel, and he said, "America is Babylon and the Nation of the Annointing of Israel to bring the gospel to the world. All these things must come to pass, so that all Mercy and Justice of a Righteous God will be served." I again asked what will happen to America? He said, "Revolution will start when the Evil One is revealed in the Tabernacle, and the Holy people are trampled underfoot with the attack on America and the nations that call themselves after the name of Jesus."

21. What event will mark the beginning of the last seven years of the age?

Daniel 9: 26-27

> *26 And after threescore and two weeks shall Messiah be cut off, but not for himself: and the people of the prince that shall come shall destroy the city and the sanctuary; and the end thereof [shall be] with a flood, and unto the end of the war desolations are determined.*
>
> *27 And he shall confirm the covenant with many for one week* **[seven Jewish Calendar years of 2,520 days]:** *and in the midst of the week* **[At the 1,260th day after the Feast of Tabernacles]** *he shall cause the sacrifice and the oblation to cease, and for the overspreading of abominations* **[The Image of the New World Masonic Order will be placed in the Temple as the "god of this Age"!]** *he shall make [it] desolate* **[depopulation of Jerusalem],** *even until the consummation, and that determined shall be poured upon the desolate.* **[The Antichrist will succeed in removing all the Jewish and Christian Believers from Jerusalem, and executing them!]**

The Israelis need membership in the European Community, a water diversion treaty and domestic stability for international investment in Israel. All of those will be done on behalf of the New World Order and the returning Jews from the former Soviet Union.

We will show that this ruler is the same as Daniel 8: 9 and Daniel 8: 23. We see that the ruler will arise from the horn of the four that replaced Alexander the Greats rule. This is the new ruler of the Resurrected Holy Roman Empire.

Zechariah 14: 1-2

> *1 Behold, the day of the LORD cometh, and thy spoil shall be divided in the midst of thee.* **[The Nations of Ezekiel 38:1-6]**
>
> *2 For I will gather all nations against Jerusalem to battle; and the city shall be taken, and the houses rifled, and the women ravished; and half of the city shall go forth into captivity, and the*

residue of the people shall not be cut off from the city. **[Jewish and Christian Believers will be removed as prisoners for execution from Jerusalem!]**

We see Russia and Islam invading Jerusalem and brutalizing Christians and Jews. They will be removed from the city leaving Arab Moslem's only. Thus, the leader is Gog as Ezekiel states in Ezekiel 38:6.

The name of the Gorbachev family in Russia was Gogbachev before 1914; its nickname is "Gog"!

Only with a peace treaty with a Palestinian-Israeli peace, can the Temple sacrifice be reinstituted. Iraq is the leading foe of Israel, and its ruler is under the control of Russia who will make a peace treaty with many Arab nations, Israel and other countries, to allow the Tribulation Temple to be built and start the sacrifice. Behind Iraq and all Islamic countries is ultimately Russia, its 'amour and guard'.

We can see what will happen to this Beast Dictator who will exalt and present himself, an abomination to God, on a wing of the Temple at the Dome of the Rock.

Daniel 11: 36-45 gives his fate.

36 And the king shall do according to his will; and he shall exalt himself, and magnify himself above every god, and shall speak marvellous things against the God of gods, and shall prosper till the indignation be accomplished: for that that is determined shall be done.

37 Neither shall he regard the God of his fathers **[religion of his race, Jewish],** *nor the desire of women* **[Tammuz, the sun god, a sign of Masonism],** *nor regard any god* **[A godless atheist]:** *for he shall magnify himself above all.*

38 But in his estate shall he honour the God of forces **[Military force will be his god!]:** *and a god whom his fathers knew not shall he honour with gold, and silver, and with precious stones, and pleasant things.*

39 Thus shall he do in the most strong holds with a strange god, whom he shall acknowledge [and] increase with glory: and he shall cause them **[The New World Order]** *to rule over many, and shall divide the land for gain.* **[Control of the world oil reserves in the Middle East!]**

40 And at the time of the end shall the king of the south push at him **[Egypt will attack Russian and Islamic Allies]**: *and the king of the north* **[America]** *shall come against him like a whirlwind, with chariots, and with horsemen, and with many ships; and he shall enter into the countries, and shall overflow and pass over.*

41 He shall enter also into the glorious land, **[Israel]** *and many [countries] shall be overthrown* **[Most of the Middle East will be occupied by Russia and the allies of Ezekiel 38:6!]**: *but these shall escape out of his hand, [even] Edom, and Moab, and the chief of the children of Ammon.* [Jordan will escape from his control!]

42 He shall stretch forth his hand also upon the countries: and the land of Egypt shall not escape. **[Eventually Egypt will be defeated by the Islamic and Russian alliance!]**

43 But he shall have power over the treasures of gold and of silver [The Antichrist will effectively control oil and the world economy], *and over all the precious things of Egypt: and the Libyans and the Ethiopians [shall be] at his steps.* **[All the oil of the Middle East will be totally controlled by Russia and allies.]**

44 But tidings out of the east and out of the north shall trouble him: therefore he shall go forth with great fury to destroy, and utterly to make away many. **[Communist China and America will group to attack the Russian and Islamic alliance that now occupies the Middle East!]**

45 And he shall plant the tabernacles of his palace **[The World Headquaters of the Antichrist's Corporate Office will be on**

Temple Mount in Jerusalem!] *between the seas in the glorious holy mountain; yet he shall come to his end, and none shall help him.*

Dreams and Visions:

In 1991, while praying with my wife Michelle and Pastor Clyde Williamson of the Kereth Connection ministry, in my home in Enfield, Nova Scotia, Canada, the angel Gabriel took me in the spirit to Jerusalem. There I walked in the spirit down the Via Dolorosa, and the angel said I would meet an important Christian man named Nicola Saliba and his brother Sammy Saliba, when we went with Pastor Williamson to Israel. He was to show me special places in the church of the Holy Sepulchre and the areas of the Old City. Immediately, I was back in my kitchen, standing in a circle. I witnessed immediately as to my vision and the promise of a visit to Israel.

Three weeks later in Israel on the residence of Tom Hesse's House of Prayer on the top of the Mount of Olives, at midnight, Michelle woke me knowing we must leave now. I prayed and again the angel Gabriel took me to Tel Aviv, and said, "You must now leave without sound or notice and go and pray until I come again, when you will be brought back to Jerusalem, and the Old City. Then I will bring you to the meet Nicola Saliba, and you will see wonderous and blasphemous sights. He will know you by the glory which he will see that surrounds you two when you walk past him!"

Finally, on Friday of that week in October, while face down, the angel Gabriel came once again with a shake and firm words to arise immediately. We hurriedly left, with no preparation, and two hours later in the Old City, a Greek Orthodox stout man walked up to us and said, "I know you are Christians for I can see the Shekinah! My name is Nicola Saliba, and I am the master stone and marble mason who is renovating the church of the Holy Sepulchre. The Holy Spirit told me to walk up to you and show you the sacred and hidden places in the church. The special chambers for the Knights Templar are still taken care of by the Greek Orthodox monks. We followed and he showed us all that he was doing, including the marblestone on which the body of Jesus was prepared for burial. Then he showed a glass case on a pillar, with the silver boots and spurs of Godfrey de Bouillon, the masonic king who lead the blasphemous first crusade. All the blasphemous Kings of Europe, the Czars of Russia and the last two (at least) US Presidents (via King Edward IV) claim Davidic decent through Jesus and Mary Magdalene! He also brought us to the Great Synagogue, and the spiritual pain I felt was almost too much to bear. Michelle received a golden cross from Sammy Samiba and we met other members of the Christian Zionist Party.

22. What events must happen to allow the start of Temple sacrifice?

The Jewish sacrifice may only start when the Temple or Tabernacle of Moses is built. The Temple can only be built when the ashes of the red heifer are prepared anew. The finding of the ashes mixing a newly sacrificed and burnt heifer with the ancient ashes from the Kalal, or pottery jar, which contained the ashes of previous red heifers. This is necessary to sanctify the Sanhedrin and holy priesthood. The sacrifice must be started before it can be stopped by the Russian-Soviet and Islamic invasion.

In the Muslim's bible, the Koran, the first book is called Para, meaning of "the calf". The Muslims believe that whoever finds the ashes will rule the world. The Dead Sea Scrolls and Copper Scroll identify the specific caves. (22-1) Excavations are very close to the ashes of the red heifer.

Act 15:16-17 After this I will return **[At the second coming of the Long Blowing or Trumpets]**, *and will build again the tabernacle of David* **[Tabernacle 'Tent of Moses']**, *which is*

> *fallen down; and I will build again the ruins thereof, and I will set it up:*
>
> *17 That the residue of men might seek after the Lord* **[Many Jews will thereby be saved!]**, *and all the Gentiles* **[Many Gentiles saved who call upon Jesus!]**, *upon whom my name is called, saith the Lord, who doeth all these things.*

This shows that not only will God rebuild the temple but restore the nation of Israel after taking a Christian people for himself and then finally save all those Gentiles who would bare the name of Jesus.

23. What time periods are given by Daniel for end time events and how are they interpreted by John in Revelation?

Daniel 8: 13-14, 26

> *13 Then I heard one saint speaking, and another saint said unto that certain [saint] which spake, How long [shall be] the vision [concerning] the daily [sacrifice], and the transgression of desolation, to give both the sanctuary and the host to be trodden under foot?*
>
> *14 And he said unto me, Unto two thousand and three hundred days; then shall the sanctuary be cleansed.*
>
> *26 And the vision of the evening and the morning which was told [is] true: wherefore shut thou up the vision; for it [shall be] for many days.*

Thus from the time that the Temple Mount is taken over by Russia and Islamic allies, etc., to the reconsecration at the second coming of Jesus, it will be 1,150 days, or 2,300 evening and morning sacrifices. (See Fig. 23:1). This therefore, means that 110 days after the Antichrist enters the Temple on Mount Moriah, The War of Gog and Magog will take over the Temple Mount and the Holy City of Jerusalem. The remaining 1,150 days will bring us to the Day of the Lord on the Feast of Trumpets, or the 2,520th day after the dedication of the Tabernacle and the start of the Jewish sacrifice.

Daniel 12:6-7

6 And [one] said to the man clothed in linen, which [was] upon the waters of the river, How long [shall it be to] the end of these wonders?

7 And I heard the man clothed in linen, which [was] upon the waters of the river, when he held up his right hand and his left hand unto heaven, and sware by him that liveth for ever that [it shall be] for a time, times, and an half; and when he shall have accomplished to scatter the power of the holy people, all these [things] shall be finished. **[1 time equalling 360 days or one Jewish calendar year and 3-1/2 times equals 1,260 days]**

Daniel 12:11-12

11 And from the time [that] the daily [sacrifice] shall be taken away, and the abomination that maketh desolate set up, [there shall be] a thousand two hundred and ninety days. [Thirty days before the Passover at the 1,260th day, the sacrifice will be abolished at the Feast of Purim! See Esther 3:7 and Esther 9:18-32 for the explanation of the setting aside of this feast day to commemorate the rest of the Jews for the genocidal plans of Haman, enemy of the Jewish people!] [See Fig. 23.1].

12 Blessed [is] he that waiteth **[physical survivor],** *and cometh to the thousand three hundred and five and thirty days. . .* [Forty-five days after the Day of the Lord and world-wide nuclear holocaust!!]

We see, therefore, that from the ending of the sacrifice to the end of the seven-year period, there is twelve hundred and ninety days which places the end of the sacrifice thirty days before the middle of the seven-year period. There is also a forty-five day period after the end of the tribulation signified by the world-wide earth upheaval.

A special blessing is given to the one who waits for and reaches the end of this period of time. When asked in Daniel 12:7, how long it would be before the power of the holy people had been finally broken and all of these things completed, it was signified by a time, times, and half a time which is three and a half times, each time being one year of three hundred and sixty days. Again equal to a twelve hundred and sixty day period. (See figure 23.1).

The desolations referred to above are depopulations that will occur as a result of the abomination of the Russian King of The Unholy Roman Empire setting himself up as god. The first seal starts on day 1,260 of the seven-year period, and the fifth seal starts events which will last 1,260 days ending in persecution and martyrdom for another 1,260 days. (See Figure 23:1)

Daniel 12: 7

7 And I heard the man clothed in linen, which [was] upon the waters of the river, when he held up his right hand and his left hand unto heaven, and sware by him that liveth for ever that [it shall be] for a time, times, and an half; and when he shall have accomplished to scatter the power of the holy people, all these [things] shall be finished.

Revelation 11: 2-3

2 But the court which is without the temple leave out, and measure it not; for it is given unto the Gentiles: and the holy city shall they tread under foot forty [and] two months.

3 And I will give [power] unto my two witnesses, and they shall prophesy a thousand two hundred [and] threescore days, clothed in sackcloth.

Revelation 11: 9

9 And they of the people and kindreds and tongues and nations shall see their dead bodies three days and an half **[day-years of 360 days each]**, *and shall not suffer their dead bodies to be put in graves.*

Revelation 12: 6

6 And the woman **[Jewish and Gentile Believers]** *fled into the wilderness, where she hath a place prepared of God, that they should feed her there a thousand two hundred [and] threescore days.* **["Goshen", cities of refuge during the Tribulation!]**

Seal five, the <u>Jewish and Gentile Believing Christian</u> persecution, also starts on day 1,260 of the seven-year period. Therefore, the first to fifth seals of revelation open on day 1,260 of the seven-year period and signify the birth pangs or spasm of catastrophes which occur nearest on or before the last final great battle of Armageddon.

We see in Revelation 9, the fifth trumpet indicates the occupation type invasion. The only people affected were those people who did not have the seal of God on their foreheads. This first five months of U.N. sponsored multinational attack on Israel, will be followed immediately by surrender of the Temple Mount to Russia and her allies.

Revelation 12 paints a portrait of the nation of Israel giving birth to Jesus who had ruled the earth with an iron scepter. The 'woman' which gave birth to Him is Israel. This is the nation which would flee to a desert prepared for her by God from the Mid-point in the tribulation to be taken care of for 1,260 days by Christians and Western Jews. Those Jews who believe in the Prophetic message given by Christians, Jewish and Gentile, in the end times will be saved by fleeing to a separate place especially prepared for Messianic Jews and Christians to escape the coming of persecution and death. A Moslem holy war or Jihad which surrounds Israel and the city of Jerusalem will occur and according to:

Zechariah 14:1-6

1 Behold, the day of the LORD cometh, and thy spoil shall be divided in the midst of thee.

2 For I will gather all nations against Jerusalem to battle; and the city shall be taken, and the houses rifled, and the women ravished; and half of the city shall go forth into captivity **[Christians and Jews from the remaining Western half of Jerusalem!],** *and the residue of the people shall not be cut off from the city.* **[Moslems].**

3 Then shall the LORD go forth, and fight against those nations, as when he fought in the day of battle.

4 And his feet shall stand in that day upon the mount of Olives, which [is] before Jerusalem on the east, and the mount of Olives shall cleave in the midst thereof toward the east and toward the west, [and there shall be] a very great valley; and half of the mountain shall remove toward the north, and half of it toward the south.

5 And ye shall flee [to] the valley of the mountains; for the valley of the mountains shall reach unto Azal: yea, ye shall flee, like as ye fled from before the earthquake in the days of Uzziah king of Judah: and the LORD my God shall come, [and] all the saints with thee.

6 And it shall come to pass in that day, [that] the light shall not be clear, [nor] dark: **[Darkness in the middle of the day with the haze of nuclear attack and fires!]**

24. How is the desolation or depopulation of Jerusalem related to Jesus' return?

We can see that the city of Jerusalem will have the Jewish and Christians population removed starting at day 1,260. Then the Lord himself will return and in the day of his wrath in the valley of Meggido on day 2,520. At Jerusalem on the Mount of Olives a great earthquake will split the Mount of Olives with half moving north and half south and an east/west valley will reach between the Mediterranean Sea and the Dead Sea along the valley of Meggido. (See Map 24:1)

The description of that one day is that of one being unique without daytime or nighttime indicates the final nuclear cataclysm at the end of the seven-year period. At the time when evening comes and the end of this seven-year period the Lord himself will return and bring the light of his celestial glory.

Seal six of Revelation 6:12-17,

12 And I beheld when he had opened the sixth seal. **[The sixth seal starts at day 1,410 to 1,415 and goes to day 2,520, at the end of the 7 years.]**, *and, lo, there was a great earthquake; and the sun became black as sackcloth of hair, and the moon became as blood;* **[day 2,520]**

13 And the stars of heaven fell unto the earth, even as a fig tree casteth her untimely figs, when she is shaken of a mighty wind.

14 And the heaven departed as a scroll when it is rolled together; and every mountain and island were moved out of their places.

15 And the kings of the earth, and the great men, and the rich men, and the chief captains, and the mighty men, and every bondman, and every free man, hid themselves in the dens and in the rocks of the mountains;

16 And said to the mountains and rocks, <u>Fall on us, and hide us from the face of him that sitteth on the throne, and from the wrath of the Lamb:</u>

17 For the great day of his wrath is come; and who shall be able to stand?

The great earthquake of seals six and seven are an important signpost for end times understanding. Professor of geography and earthquake expert, Dr. Gary Whiteford, from the University of New Brunswick, Canada, has shown a direct causal relationship between underground nuclear testing and the triggering of earthquakes in diverse places on the earth.

As we read both Old and New Testament much is said of a great earthquake associated with the judgments against the world. <u>There is only one great earthquake which will move every mountain from its place, and this is that earthquake that</u>

will be set off by global movement tectonic plates triggered by a global scale nuclear war. The truth of this knowledge that only one great earthquake happens allows the various events of Old and New Testament to be laid upon one another and allow interpretation of one section of the Bible to be performed by another which brings to light the truth of what will indeed happen during these events. Much will be said of this later in tables, charts and other questions which will deal with the events of the end of the age. See Fig. 23-1. Once this key of simplicity of plan but multiple prophetic perspectives is understood, the Bible interprets itself, for it is not for private conjecture to reveal its truth.

There are numerous scriptures that describe the great final earthquake, that will move every mountain, blot out the sun and the moon and stars, and cast 100 pound hailstones to the ground. This is final thermonuclear blast that sets off the global earthquake and the blotting out of the atmosphere with dust and radioactive waste.

Revelation 6:12-14

> *12 And I beheld when he had opened the sixth seal, and, lo, there was a great earthquake; and the sun became black as sackcloth of hair, and the moon became as blood;* **[This is the time of the thermonuclear holocaust that will trigger a world-wide earthquake, at day 2,520!]**
>
> *13 And the stars of heaven fell unto the earth, even as a fig tree casteth her untimely figs, when she is shaken of a mighty wind.*
>
> *14 And the heaven departed as a scroll when it is rolled together; and every mountain and island were moved out of their places.*

Revelation 8:5

> *5 And the angel took the censer, and filled it with fire of the altar, and cast [it] into the earth: and there were voices, and thunderings, and lightnings, and an earthquake.*

Revelation 16:17-21

17 And the seventh angel poured out his vial into the air; and there came a great voice out of the temple of heaven, from the throne, saying, It is done.

18 And there were voices, and thunders, and lightnings; and there was a great earthquake, such as was not since men were upon the earth, so mighty an earthquake, [and] so great. **[The timing of the Great Earthquake is at the end of the seven-year period. There is only one Great Earthquake that will move all the mountains and the islands out of their place.]**

19 And the great city was divided into three parts, and the cities of the nations fell: and great Babylon came in remembrance before God, to give unto her the cup of the wine of the fierceness of his wrath.

20 And every island fled away, and the mountains were not found.

21 And there fell upon men a great hail out of heaven, [every stone] about the weight of a talent: and men blasphemed God because of the plague of the hail; for the plague thereof was exceeding great. **[The Great Hail will follow the firestorm of the thermonuclear holocaust of the Day of the Lord!]**

Revelation 11:13,19

13 And the same hour was there a great earthquake, and the tenth part of the city fell, and in the earthquake were slain of men seven thousand: and the remnant were affrighted, and gave glory to the God of heaven. **[This earthquake affects Jerusalem and one tenth of the city is destroyed and seven thousand people die.]**

19 And the temple of God was opened in heaven, and there was seen in his temple the ark of his testament: and there were lightnings, and voices, and thunderings, and an earthquake, and great hail.

Revelation 16:18

18 And there were voices, and thunders, and lightnings; and there was a great earthquake, such as was not since men were upon the earth, so mighty an earthquake, [and] so great.

Joel 2:10

10 The earth shall quake before them; the heavens shall tremble: the sun and the moon shall be dark, and the stars shall withdraw their shining: **[The darkness of the sun, moon and stars shall result from the dust and radioactive waste and debris that roll like a scroll across the atmosphere.]**

Joel 2:30-31

30 And I will shew wonders in the heavens and in the earth, blood, and fire, and pillars of smoke. **[The fireballs of the nuclear explosions and the pillars of smoke with the appearance of blood and fire, are exact descriptions of a nuclear war, from the times and perspective of Joel.]**

31 The sun shall be turned into darkness, and the moon into blood, before the great and the terrible day of the LORD come.

Joel 3:15

15 The sun and the moon shall be darkened, and the stars shall withdraw their shining.

Ezekiel 32:7

7 And when I shall put thee out, I will cover the heaven, and make the stars thereof dark; I will cover the sun with a cloud, and the moon shall not give her light.

Isaiah 13:10

10 For the stars of heaven and the constellations thereof shall not give their light: the sun shall be darkened in his going forth, and the moon shall not cause her light to shine.

Isaiah 14:23

23 I will also make it a possession for the bittern, and pools of water: and I will sweep it with the besom of destruction, saith the LORD of hosts.

Isaiah 29:6-8

6 Thou shalt be visited of the LORD of hosts with thunder, and with earthquake, and great noise, with storm and tempest, and the flame of devouring fire.

[The Lord will come at the time of the nuclear holocaust.]

7 And the multitude of all the nations that fight against Ariel, even all that fight against her and her munition, and that distress her, shall be as a dream of a night vision.

8 It shall even be as when an hungry [man] dreameth, and, behold, he eateth; but he awaketh, and his soul is empty: or as when a thirsty man dreameth, and, behold, he drinketh; but he awaketh, and, behold, [he is] faint, and his soul hath appetite: so shall the multitude of all the nations be, that fight against mount Zion.

Isaiah 34:4

4 And all the host of heaven shall be dissolved, and the heavens shall be rolled together as a scroll: and all their host shall fall down, as the leaf falleth off from the vine, and as a falling [fig] from the fig tree.

Isaiah 50:3

3 I clothe the heavens with blackness, and I make sackcloth their covering.

Jeremiah 4:23-26

23 I beheld the earth, and, lo, [it was] without form, and void; and the heavens, and they [had] no light. **[The earth will be in the same condition as in the times of Noah and at the time of Genesis when the earth was void.]**

24 I beheld the mountains, and, lo, they trembled, and all the hills moved lightly.

25 I beheld, and, lo, [there was] no man, and all the birds of the heavens were fled.

26 I beheld, and, lo, the fruitful place [was] a wilderness, and all the cities thereof were broken down at the presence of the LORD, [and] by his fierce anger.

Zechariah 14:1-15

1 Behold, the day of the LORD cometh, and thy spoil shall be divided in the midst of thee.

2 For I will gather all nations against Jerusalem to battle; and the city shall be taken, and the houses rifled, and the women ravished; and half of the city shall go forth into captivity, and the residue of the people shall not be cut off from the city.

[Rape of the women in Jerusalem, and incarceration of the Christians and Jews in West Jerusalem, will be the result of the Russian lead invasion of the Middle East.]

3 Then shall the LORD go forth, and fight against those nations, as when he fought in the day of battle.

4 And his feet shall stand in that day upon the mount of Olives, which [is] before Jerusalem on the east, and the mount of Olives shall cleave in the midst thereof toward the east and toward the west, [and there shall be] a very great valley; and half of the mountain shall remove toward the north, and half of it toward the south.

[The Mediterranean Sea will connect with the Dead Sea and this will be the result of the earthquake at the End of the Age.]

5 And ye shall flee [to] the valley of the mountains; for the valley of the mountains shall reach unto Azal: yea, ye shall flee, like as ye fled from before the earthquake in the days of Uzziah king of

Judah: and the LORD my God shall come, [and] all the saints with thee.

6 And it shall come to pass in that day, [that] the light shall not be clear, [nor] dark:

7 But it shall be one day which shall be known to the LORD, not day, nor night: but it shall come to pass, [that] at evening time it shall be light. **[At sundown, at the start of the Hebrew day, on the Feast of Trumpets, the Lord will return on day 2,520.]**

8 And it shall be in that day, [that] living waters shall go out from Jerusalem; half of them toward the former sea, and half of them toward the hinder sea: in summer and in winter shall it be.

9 And the LORD shall be king over all the earth: in that day shall there be one LORD, and his name one.

10 All the land shall be turned as a plain from Geba to Rimmon south of Jerusalem: and it shall be lifted up, and inhabited in her place, from Benjamin's gate unto the place of the first gate, unto the corner gate, and [from] the tower of Hananeel unto the king's winepresses.

11 And [men] shall dwell in it, and there shall be no more utter destruction; but Jerusalem shall be safely inhabited.

12 And this shall be the plague wherewith the LORD will smite all the people that have fought against Jerusalem; Their flesh shall consume away while they stand upon their feet, and their eyes shall consume away in their holes, and their tongue shall consume away in their mouth.

13 And it shall come to pass in that day, [that] a great tumult from the LORD shall be among them; and they shall lay hold every one on the hand of his neighbour, and his hand shall rise up against the hand of his neighbour.

14 And Judah also shall fight at Jerusalem; and the wealth of all the heathen round about shall be gathered together, gold, and silver, and apparel, in great abundance.

15 And so shall be the plague of the horse, of the mule, of the camel, and of the ass, and of all the beasts that shall be in these tents, as this plague.

Matthew 24:29

29 Immediately after the tribulation of those days shall the sun be darkened, and the moon shall not give her light, and the stars shall fall from heaven, and the powers of the heavens shall be shaken: **[The event of the Great Earthquake will occur at the end of the seven year period of the Time of Jacobs Trouble.]**

Matthew 27:54

54 Now when the centurion, and they that were with him, watching Jesus, saw the earthquake, and those things that were done, they feared greatly, saying, Truly this was the Son of God. **[The end of the Age will be with the greatest earthquake.]**

Luke 21:25-27

25 And there shall be signs in the sun, and in the moon, and in the stars; and upon the earth distress of nations, with perplexity; the sea and the waves roaring; **[The blotting out of the sun, moon and stars is again repeated here.]**

26 Men's hearts failing them for fear, and for looking after those things which are coming on the earth: for the powers of heaven shall be shaken.

27 And then shall they see the Son of man coming in a cloud with power and great glory.

Hebrews 12:25-27

25 See that ye refuse not him that speaketh. For if they escaped not who refused him that spake on earth, much more [shall not] we [escape], if we turn away from him that [speaketh] from heaven:

26 Whose voice then shook the earth: but now he hath promised, saying, Yet once more I shake not the earth only, but also heaven.

> 27 And this [word], Yet once more, signifieth the removing of those things that are shaken, as of things that are made, that those things which cannot be shaken may remain. **[Only the true spiritual things that give glory to Jesus and God will be unshaken, at the time of the Day of the Lord.]**

2 Peter 1:19-21

> 19 We have also a more sure word of prophecy; whereunto ye do well that ye take heed, as unto a light that shineth in a dark place, until the day dawn, and the day star arise in your hearts:
>
> 20 Knowing this first, that <u>no prophecy of the scripture is of any private interpretation</u>.
>
> 21 For the prophecy came not in old time by the will of man: but holy men of God spake [as they were] moved by the Holy Ghost.

25. What wrath are believing Christians to be spared?

We see, therefore, that the wrath from which all Christians are saved is the wrath of Jesus which is the seventh seal, trumpet and vial only, and not the destruction of all six seals, trumpets, and vials. This is the great judgment which occurs with the coming of the Lord Jesus in the third woe on Day 2,520. (See Fig. 23:1). This is equivalent to the third woe or the seventh trumpets and vials. Jesus's wrath follows the nuclear destruction of the earth during the third world war, in the battle of Armageddon, or the second woe.

Revelation 14:9-13

> 9 And the third angel followed them, saying with a loud voice, If any man worship the beast and his image, and receive [his] mark in his forehead, or in his hand, **[To fall under the wrath of God, one must serve or worship the final Beast Empire, and the image of this Empire with his or her heart, and receive the Mark of the Beast on their right hand or forehead, as world identicode.]**

10 The same shall drink of the wine of the wrath of God **[The seventh seal, trumpet, and vial judgment is the wrath of God, to be separated from the creator forever!]**, *which is poured out without mixture into the cup of his indignation; and he shall be tormented with fire and brimstone in the presence of the holy angels, and in the presence of the Lamb:*

11 And the smoke of their torment ascendeth up for ever and ever: and they have no rest day nor night, who worship the beast and his image, and whosoever receiveth the mark of his name.

12 Here is the patience of the saints: here [are] they that keep the commandments of God, and the faith of Jesus. **[The Church will be on earth to the End.]**

13 And I heard a voice from heaven saying unto me, Write, Blessed [are] the dead which die in the Lord from henceforth **[Tribulation Saints that are martyred!]**: *Yea, saith the Spirit, that they may rest from their labours; and their works do follow them.*

The third woe is a judgment to be given only to those who bear the mark of the Beast and have not repented and turned to Jesus.

26. What is the wrath of Satan?

Up to the end of the second woe or sixth seal, all of the events of the birth pains and tribulations have been the wrath of Satan. The wrath of Satan is the sixth seal, sixth trumpet and sixth vial. Trumpets and vials occur simultaneously with trumpets referred to the whole world and the vials of judgment against Mystery, Babylon, Israel its ally, in its modern, political and religious realities.

He has been let loose on earth under Gods control to turn those to Jesus or condemn those who would not listen to the gospel.

Patience and endurance are asked of the saints. (see Rev. 14:12) The faithfulness to Jesus shows that Christians will be present right up to the last moment when Jesus comes and there will still be

Christians present alive on earth, as witnesses. Jesus' Eternal reign will start at the end of the 1,335 days after bringing the sacrifice low by the abomination that desolates.

1 Thessalonians 5:9-11

9 For God hath not appointed us to wrath, **[The wrath of God is only and complete in the eternal separation from the Creator God.]** *but to obtain salvation by our Lord Jesus Christ,*

10 Who died for us, that, whether we wake or sleep, we should live together with him.

11 Wherefore comfort yourselves together, and edify one another, even as also ye do.

27. When does the first resurrection occur with the return of Jesus, King of Kings?

The first resurrection occurs with the Thermonuclear Holocaust of the Day of the Lord!!

1 Thessalonians 4:13-18

13 But I would not have you to be ignorant, brethren, concerning them which are asleep, that ye sorrow not, even as others which have no hope.

14 For if we believe that Jesus died and rose again, even so them also which sleep in Jesus will God bring with him.

15 For this we say unto you by the word of the Lord, that we which are alive [and] remain unto the coming of the Lord **[who survive until the end of the seven years]** *shall not prevent them which are asleep.*

16 For the Lord himself shall descend from heaven with a shout, with the voice of the archangel, and with the trump of God **[the last trumpet at the end of the tribulation heralding the Coming of Jesus]**: *and the dead in Christ shall rise first:*

17 Then we which are alive [and] remain shall be caught up together with them in the clouds, to meet the Lord in the air: and so shall we ever be with the Lord.

18 Wherefore comfort one another with these words.

The Lord will return <u>at the last trumpet</u> of Revelation 11:15,

15 And the seventh angel sounded; and there were great voices in heaven, saying, THE KINGDOMS OF THIS WORLD ARE BECOME [THE KINGDOMS] OF OUR LORD, AND OF HIS CHRIST; AND HE SHALL REIGN FOR EVER AND EVER.

From Matthew 24:29-31 we know that after the sky is darkened by the great war that Jesus will return after the sign of the Son of Man in the sky. Jesus words tell us that the sequence is: Falling away, Man of Sin revealed, Tribulation of Seven Years and Jesus singular Second Coming. His elect are gathered from the four winds just as described in 1 Thessalonians 4:13-18.

Matthew 24:29-31

29 Immediately after the tribulation of those days shall the sun be darkened, and the moon shall not give her light, and the stars shall fall from heaven, and the powers of the heavens shall be shaken:

30 And then shall appear the sign of the Son of man in heaven: and then shall all the tribes of the earth mourn, and they shall see the Son of man coming in the clouds of heaven with power and great glory.

31 And he shall send his angels with a great sound of a trumpet, and they shall gather together his elect from the four winds, from one end of heaven to the other.

Paul's description of the same event occurs in **1 Corinthians 15:50-52**

50 Now this I say, brethren, that flesh and blood cannot inherit the kingdom of God; neither doth corruption inherit incorruption.

51 Behold, I shew you a mystery; We shall not all sleep, but we shall all be changed,

52 In a moment, in the twinkling of an eye **[thermonuclear flash],** *at the last trump* **[seventh trumpet at day 2,520]:** *for the trumpet shall sound, and the dead shall be raised incorruptible* **[resurrection],** *and we shall be changed.*

We see that this event occurs at the last trumpet according to verse 52.

Revelation 11:15-19

15 And the seventh angel sounded; and there were great voices in heaven, saying, THE KINGDOMS OF THIS WORLD ARE BECOME [THE KINGDOMS] OF OUR LORD, AND OF HIS CHRIST; AND HE SHALL REIGN FOR EVER AND EVER.

16 And the four and twenty elders, which sat before God on their seats, fell upon their faces, and worshipped God,

17 Saying, We give thee thanks, O Lord God Almighty, which art, and wast, and art to come; because thou hast taken to thee thy great power, and hast reigned.

18 And the nations were angry, and thy wrath is come **[The Wrath of Jesus],** *and* **[Three purposes: 1]** *the time of the dead, that they should be judged, and that* **[2]** *thou shouldest give reward unto thy servants the prophets, and to the saints, and them that fear thy name, small and great; and* **[3]** *shouldest destroy them which destroy the earth.* **[White Throne Judgment and the Second Death of Eternal Torment]**

19 And the temple of God was opened in heaven, and there was seen in his temple the ark of his testament: and there were lightnings, and voices, and thunderings, and an earthquake, and great hail.

In verse 18 that the reward was give to the bond servants, to prophets, and to the saints and those that fear the name of Jesus. As Jesus says that his reward is with him in ***Revelation 22:12***

12 And, behold, I come quickly; and my reward [Resurrection into the Kingdom] *[is] with me, to give every man according as his work shall be.*

The reward that Christ brings with him is the resurrection to eternal life. We, therefore, see that the rapture [thermonuclear disintegration] occurs at the sounding of the seventh trumpet. Later we shall see an analysis that shows that the trumpets and vials are parallel. Refer to Fig. 23-1 for an outline of the sequence of events throughout the tribulation.

We can see that the parallel of the tribulation is similar to the plagues sent on Pharoah and Egypt in Exodus 1, and that many of the plagues were for the people to convince them to enter the Land of Goshen. Many would not have moved to the area of safety until several, or almost all, of the plagues had befallen on Egypt. This is, therefore, a refining furnace to save all that would be saved during the times of the tribulation.

28. What are the three objectives of the wrath of God?
Revelation 11:18

18 And the nations were angry, and thy wrath is come **[Now we have God's wrath],** *and* **[1]** *the time of the dead, that they should be judged, and that* **[2]** *thou shouldest give reward unto thy servants the prophets, and to the saints, and them that fear thy name, small and great; and* **[3]** *shouldest destroy them which destroy the earth.*

Three purposes for the tribulation being number one, judging of the dead, resurrecting the saints and prophets, and those which are followers of Jesus, and thirdly, to destroy those that destroy the earth. In God's sovereignty the wrath of Satan which is included in all of the six seal, six vial and trumpet, and in the physical destruction of earth in a human conventional and finally nuclear holocaust. We see, therefore, that 777 or the wrath of God is a spiritual wrath, judging the dead, resurrecting the believers, and spiritual destruction for those that are the enemies of God. Just prior to this, 666 includes the physical destruction by Satan upon the earth. This clearly sets out the specific things that are included within the third woe or the wrath of God and shows that only at this point at the seventh trumpet has a wrath of God been poured out after the resurrection of those who follow Jesus. (See Fig. 23-1).

The Beast Dictator

29. What issues will be the platform of the beast?

Daniel 9 and from Revelation 13: 11 speaks of the ruler of the resurrected Roman Empire, of a New World Order Government, who will present himself at the end time as a man of peace. . . This term was reported on September 11, 1990, in a speech by President George Bush.

Crises of the environment, Mideast peace, population explosions, and social problems such as the war on drugs have unified the New World Order agenda. The Orwellian Socialist left has propelled all Western nations toward less democratic freedoms and more anti-Christian pluralistic socialism. This comes at a time when the Soviet Union has made apparent attempts at increasingly democratic reforms.

We see August 3, 1991 false coup of Mikhail Gorbachev's Government and the subsequent breakup of the Soviet Union into the Confederation of Independent States. Russian alliances have been made with Europe, and militarily with the Moslem republics north of Iran, Iraq and Turkey. The sale of Russian nuclear technology and the transfer of Russian scientific knowledge and expertise, with the collapse of the Soviet economy, has armed the Moslem fundamentalist states. On the surface the beast empire will have signed a peace treaty with Israel. With the unification of Germany and the apparent breakup of the Soviet empire, a perfect candidate leader of the powerful European community, which would include the Soviet Union former states would be Mikhail S. Gorbachev.

Gorbachev proposed a Green Cross, according to McIlvany, to be a symbol of the world-wide environmental crusade. He is now the President of the Green Cross, the largest single environmental organization in the world. The environment and worship of the creation rather than the creator will be the issue to unify the world under a counterfeit sense of peace and security. **These unifying global environmental crisis are:**

        (1)   **The Greenhouse Effect**
        (2)   **The Ozone Hole**
        (3)   **Toxic Pollution**

These are being proposed by the media and political left that can only be tackled by a New World Order. Such a government can overrule national governments in the delusion that this will be the only way to save Mother Earth.

1 Thessalonians 5: 1-5

1 But of the times and the seasons, brethren, ye have no need that I write unto you. **[You know the circumstances but unsealing will happen at the time of the end]**

2 For yourselves know perfectly that the day of the Lord so cometh as a thief in the night. **[to them, the unwise nonbelievers]**

3 For when they shall say, Peace and safety; then sudden destruction cometh upon them, as travail upon a woman with child; and they shall not escape.

4 But ye, brethren, are not in darkness, that that day should overtake you as a thief.

5 Ye are all the children of light, and the children of the day: we are not of the night, nor of darkness. **[You can read God's Word and know that the wrath of Satan is coming and then Jesus salvation.]**

The Beast Dictator will, therefore, be a man of peace, environmental concern and revival of freedom to allow religious freedom as well within the former republics of the Soviet Union. Behind the scenes, however, he will be militarily dominant within this new Clay and Iron Empire of great economic wealth and military power linked together. Political and economic compromises as well as military alliances with Moslem fundamentalist states will bring this empire into direct conflict with the presence of the state of Israel; and, ultimately threaten its very existence. He will subdue areas of the ten region C.F.R. #2, #5, #7 to reform the Unholy Roman Empire, ie., three ribs in his month of the bear.

Please read the Earth Charter and the tenants that follow. The "Ten or Fifteen Commandments" as referred to by Gorbachev in Rio+5 to July 97 Summit, set the Ecological Laws upon which to basis a Godless Eco-Communist New World Order!!

The Earth Charter:
An Overview by Steven Rockefeller

It is the objective of the Earth Charter to set forth an inspiring vision of the fundamental principles of a global partnership for sustainable development and environmental conservation. The Earth Charter initiative reflects the conviction that a radical change in humanity's attitudes and values is essential to achieve social, economic, and ecological well-being in the twenty-first century. The Earth Charter project is part of an international movement to clarify humanity's shared values and to develop a new global ethics, ensuring effective human cooperation in an interdependent world. There have been numerous Earth Charter consultations and efforts to draft a Charter over the past ten years. An Earth Charter Commission has recently been formed by the Earth Council and Green Cross International. The Commission has prepared a Benchmark Draft Earth Charter, and it plans to circulate a final version of the Charter as a people's treaty beginning in mid-1998. The Charter will be submitted to the United Nations General Assembly in the year 2000.

31. Historical Background, 1945-1992

The role and significance of the Earth Charter are best understood in the context of the United Nations' ongoing efforts to identify the fundamental principles essential to world security. When the UN was established in 1945, its agenda for world security emphasized peace, human rights, and equitable socioeconomic development. No mention was made of the environment as a common concern, and little attention was given to ecological well-being in the UN's early years.

However, since the Stockholm Conference on the Human Environment in 1972, ecological security has emerged as a fourth major concern of the United Nations. Starting with the Stockholm Declaration, the nations of the world have adopted a number of declarations, charters, and treaties that seek to build a global alliance that effectively integrates and balances development and conservation.

In addition, a variety of nongovernmental organizations have drafted and circulated their own declarations and people's treaties. These documents reflect a growing awareness that humanity's social, economic, and environmental problems and goals are interconnected and require integrated solutions. The Earth Charter initiative builds on these efforts. The World Charter for Nature, which was adopted by the UN General Assembly in 1982, was a progressive declaration of ecological and ethical principles for its time. It remains a stronger document than any that have followed from the point of view of environmental ethics.

However, in its 1987 report, *Our Common Future,* the UN World Commission on Environment and Development (WCED) issued a call for "a new charter" that would "consolidate and extend relevant legal principles," creating "new norms needed to maintain livelihoods and life on our shared planet" and "to guide state behavior in the transition to sustainable development." The WCED also recommended that the new charter "be subsequently expanded into a Convention, setting out the sovereign rights and reciprocal responsibilities of all states on environmental protection and sustainable development." The WCED recommendations, together with deepening environmental and ethical concerns, spurred efforts in the late 1980s to create an Earth Charter.

However, before any UN action was initiated on the Earth Charter, the Commission on Environmental Law of the World Conservation Union (IUCN) drafted the convention proposed in *Our Common Future*. The IUCN Draft International Covenant on Environment and Development presents an integrated legal framework for existing and future international and national environmental and sustainable development law and policy. Even though the IUCN Draft Covenant was presented at the United Nations in 1995, official negotiations have not yet begun on this treaty which many environmentalists believe is urgently needed to clarify, synthesize, and further develop international sustainable development law. The United Nations Conference on Environment and Development (UNCED), the Earth Summit held in Rio de Janeiro in 1992, did take up the challenge of drafting the Earth Charter. A number of governments prepared recommendations. Many nongovernmental organizations, including groups representing the major faiths, became actively involved.

While the resulting Rio Declaration on Environment and Development is a valuable document, it falls short of the aspirations that many groups have had for the Earth Charter. It does not reaffirm commitment to the World Charter for Nature, and its anthropocentric emphasis is a step back from the more balanced approach of the World Charter for Nature. The Rio Declaration does call for the protection and restoration of ecosystems, but it does not affirm the intrinsic value of all life forms and articulate clearly a principle of respect for nature. Unless human beings adopt an attitude of respect for Earth and come to appreciate the intrinsic value of all life, it is unlikely that they will make the radical changes in behavior required to achieve protection of the environment and a sustainable civilization.

II. The Earth Charter Project, 1994-2000

A new Earth Charter initiative began in 1994 under the leadership of Maurice Strong, the former Secretary General of UNCED and chairman of the newly formed Earth Council, and Mikhail Gorbachev, acting in his capacity as Chairman of Green Cross International.

The Earth Council was created to pursue the unfinished business of UNCED and to promote implementation of Agenda 21, the Earth Summit's action plan. Jim MacNeill, former Secretary General of the WCED, and Prime Minister Ruud Lubbers of The Netherlands were instrumental in facilitating the organization of the new Earth Charter project. Ambassador Mohamed Sahnoun of Algeria served as the executive director of the project during its initial phase, and its first international workshop was held at the Peace Palace in The Hague in May 1995. Representatives from thirty countries and more than seventy different organizations participated in the workshop.

Following this event, the secretariat for the Earth Charter project was established at the Earth Council in San José, Costa Rica. A world-wide Earth Charter consultation process was organized by the Earth Council in connection with its independent Rio+5 review in 1996 and 1997. The Rio+5 review was organized to complement and contribute to the official 5-year review of UNCED that culminated with Earth Summit II, involving a UN General Assembly Special Session in June 1997. The objective of the independent and official reviews was to assess progress toward sustainable development since the Rio Earth Summit and to develop new partnerships and plans for implementation of Agenda 21.

The Earth Charter consultation process engaged men and women from all sectors of society and all cultures in contributing to the Earth Charter's development. A special program was created to contact and involve the world's religions, interfaith organizations, and leading religious and ethical thinkers. An indigenous peoples network was also organized by the Earth Council.

Early in 1997, an Earth Charter Commission was formed to oversee the project. The twenty-three members were chosen on the basis of their commitment to the cause and their ability to advance the project. They represent the major regions of the world and different sectors of society. The co-chairs include Kamla Chowdhry of the Centre for Science and the Environment, New Delhi (Asia); Mikhail Gorbachev of the International Foundation for Socio-Economic and Political Studies, Moscow (Europe); Mercedes Sosa, a performing artist from Buenos Aires (Latin America); Maurice Strong (North America); and General Amadou Toumani Touré, former president of Mali (Africa).

The Commission issued a Benchmark Draft Earth Charter in March 1997 at the conclusion of the Rio+5 Forum in Rio de Janeiro. The Forum was organized by the Earth Council as part of its independent Rio+5 review, and it brought together more than 500 representatives from civil society and national councils of sustainable development. The Benchmark Draft reflects the many and diverse contributions received through the consultation process and from the Rio+5 Forum. The Commission extended the Earth Charter consultation until early 1998, and the Benchmark Draft is being circulated widely as a document in progress.

It is hoped that many organizations will conduct their own workshops on the Benchmark Draft and report their findings and recommendations to the Earth Council. A number of workshops and conferences in different regions of the world have taken place and many more are being planned. At the end of the consultation period, a final version of the Earth Charter will be prepared.

The Commission is scheduled to announce the final version after its June 1998 meeting. There will then follow a period of advocacy on behalf of the Earth Charter with the goal of enlisting wide support for the document and its principles in civil society, religious communities, and national councils of sustainable development. Special efforts will be made to promote the adoption of Earth Charter values in all sectors of society and to integrate Earth Charter values into educational programs. With a demonstration of wide popular support, it is hoped that the Earth Charter will be endorsed by the United Nations General Assembly in the year 2000.

III. The Earth Charter Concept

A consensus has developed that the Earth Charter should be: a statement of fundamental principles of enduring significance that are widely shared by people of all races, cultures, and religions; a relatively brief and concise document composed in a language that is inspiring, clear, and meaningful in all tongues; the articulation of a spiritual vision that reflects universal spiritual values, including but not limited to ethical values; a call to action that adds significant new dimensions of value to what has been expressed in earlier relevant documents; a people's charter that serves as a universal code of conduct for ordinary citizens, educators, business executives, scientists, religious leaders, nongovernmental organizations, and national councils of sustainable development; and a declaration of principles that can serve as a "soft law" document if endorsement by the UN General Assembly can be secured.

It is hoped that the Earth Charter will inspire regional, national, local, religious, and other groups to develop their own charters that give expression to the universal values of the Earth Charter within a framework and in a language appropriate to their distinctive traditions. The Earth Council will actively promote this process. The Earth Charter concentrates on fundamental principles. It does not seek to set forth the many practical and legal implications of these principles. It leaves to the IUCN Draft Covenant on Environment and Development and other hard law treaties to lay out in full the legal principles that should guide state behavior and interstate relations.

The Earth Charter endeavors to complement and support the IUCN Draft Covenant by making clear the fundamental principles that are the ethical foundation for the Covenant. In addition, when the Earth Charter is finalized it will be accompanied by supporting materials that discuss the goals and actions that will lead to implementation of Charter principles.

The Earth Charter Commission does not plan to turn the drafting of the Earth Charter over to a formal intergovernmental process. It attaches special importance to the role of the Charter as a people's treaty, and it is concerned to ensure a very strong document that reflects the emerging new global ethics. UN endorsement of the Earth Charter is an important objective.

However, quite apart from the UN, the Earth Charter can serve as a powerful influence for change. The Earth Charter project draws upon a variety of resources, including ecology and other contemporary sciences, the world's religious and philosophical traditions, the growing literature on global ethics and the ethics of environment and development, the practical experience of people living sustainably, as well as relevant intergovernmental and nongovernmental declarations and treaties.

At the heart of the emerging new global ethics and the Earth Charter is an expanded sense of community and moral responsibility that embraces all people, future generations, and the larger community of life on Earth. Among the values affirmed by the Benchmark Draft are: respect for Earth and all life; protection and restoration of the diversity, integrity, and beauty of Earth's ecosystems; sustainable production, consumption, and reproduction; respect for human rights, including the right to an environment adequate for human dignity and well-being; eradication of poverty; nonviolent problem solving and peace; the equitable sharing of Earth's resources; democratic participation in decision making; gender equality; accountability and transparency in administration; the advancement and application of knowledge and technologies that facilitate care for Earth; universal education for sustainable living; and a sense of shared responsibility for the well-being of the Earth community and future generations.

The Earth Charter Commission

A.T. Ariyaratne Sri Lanka; **Mother Tessa Bielicki** USA; **Kamla Chowdhry** *Co-Chair* India; **Mikhail Gorbachev** [President of the Green Cross and the Gorbachev Foundation, Princeton Full Professor, Future Anti-Christ] *Co-Chair* Russian Federation; **John A. Hoyt** USA; **HRH Princess Basma Bint Talal** Jordan **Pierre Calame** France; **Paulo Freire** (d. 6-97) Brazil; **Wakako Hironaka** Japan; **Yolanda Kakabadse** Ecuador; **Ruud F.M. Lubbers** The Netherlands; **Elizabeth May** Canada; **Enrique Peñalosa** Colombia; **Henriette Rasmussen** Greenland; **Maurice F. Strong** [Originator of the Biodiversity World Conferences] *Co-chair* Canada; **Wangari Maathai** Kenya; **Federico Mayor** Spain; **Shridat Ramphal** Guyana; **Mohamed Sahnoun** Algeria; **Mercedes Sosa** *Co-Chair* Argentina; **Severn Cullis Suzuki** Canada; **Amadou Toumani Touré** *Co-Chair* Mali; **Pauline Tangiora** New Zealand

For additional information on the Earth Charter, contact: The Earth Council, P.O. Box 2323-1002, San José, Costa Rica. Website: http://www.ecouncil.ac.cr.

Comments and recommendations regarding the Benchmark Draft may be forwarded directly to Steven Rockefeller, Professor of Religion at Middlebury College, who is coordinating the drafting process for the Earth Charter Commission, at: P.O. Box 648, Middlebury, VT 05753 (fax: 802-388-1951; e-mail: rockefel@panther.middlebury.edu)

Click here to return to "Women's Views on the Earth Charter" Table of Contents
Click here to return to "Buddhist Perspectives on the Earth Charter" Table of Contents

THE EARTH CHARTER BENCHMARK DRAFT
Reviewed and Presented during the Rio+5 Forum - March 18, 1997
(Text also available in **Spanish, French, Portuguese, Chinese**)
*IAU has signed a **Memorandum of understanding** with the Earth Council. Apart from the overall interest for the EC Web site, this also explains the special link of the Earth Council's Web site to the IAU Web site on Sustainable Human Development.*

Background

The objective of the Earth Charter is to set forth an inspiring vision of the fundamental principles of a global partnership for sustainable development and environmental conservation.

The Earth Charter initiative reflects the conviction that a radical change in humanity's attitudes and values is essential to achieve social, economic, and ecological well-being in the twenty-first century.

The Earth Charter project is part of an international movement to clarify humanity's shared values and to develop a new global ethics, ensuring effective human cooperation in an interdependent world.

There have been numerous Earth Charter consultations and efforts to draft a Charter over the past ten years. An Earth Charter Commission has recently been formed by the Earth Council and Green Cross International and the Earth Charter Management Committee.

A Benchmark Draft was prepared as a result of this initial consultation process and is being circulated widely as a document in progress.

The consultation process is extended until late 1998, and it is hoped that many organizations will conduct their own workshops on the Benchmark Draft and report their findings and recommendations to the Earth Council.

It is hoped that the Earth Charter will be endorsed by the United Nations around the year 2000, and mainly that this process of values internalization generates public awareness and the necessary change towards a better future.

The Earth Council welcomes your contributions to this process. The Earth Council welcomes your creative contributions to this process and comments on the Benchmark Draft such as:

1. Which principles expressed in the Benchmark Draft are applicable to your carrier/profession? And how can these be translated into practice?
2. Are all the requirements and interests of your group represented in the 18 principles of this Draft?
3. In which way could your professional Association implement it in daily life?
4. Which principles expressed in this draft are contrary to your culture or to the behavior of your group and why?
5. Do you wish to suggest new principles? (please include short philosophical reference or reasons).

Earth is our home and home to all living beings. Earth itself is alive. We are part of an evolving universe. Human beings are members of an interdependent community of life with a magnificent diversity of life forms and cultures. We are humbled before the beauty of Earth and share a reverence for life and the sources of our being. We give thanks for the heritage that we have received from past generations and embrace our responsibilities to present and future generations.

The Earth Community stands at a defining moment. The biosphere is governed by laws that we ignore at our own peril. Human beings have acquired the ability to radically alter the environment and evolutionary processes. Lack of foresight and misuse of knowledge and power threaten the fabric of life and the foundations of local and global security. There is great violence, poverty, and suffering in our world. A fundamental change of course is needed.

The choice is before us: to care for Earth or to participate in the destruction of ourselves and the diversity of life. We must reinvent industrial-technological civilization, finding new ways to balance self and community, having and being, diversity and unity, short-term and long-term, using and nurturing.

In the midst of all our diversity, we are one humanity and one Earth family with a shared destiny. The challenges before us require an inclusive ethical vision. Partnerships must be forged and cooperation fostered at local, bio-regional, national and international levels. In solidarity with one another and the community of life, we the peoples of the world commit ourselves to action guided by the following interrelated principles:

18 Commandments of the NWOrder Sustainable Earth

1. Respect Earth and <u>all life</u>. Earth, each life form, and all living beings possess intrinsic value and warrant respect independently of their utilitarian value to humanity. **[value of Human life = animal and plant life forms]**
2. Care for Earth, protecting and <u>restoring the diversity</u>, integrity, and beauty of the planet's ecosystems. Where there is risk of irreversible or serious damage to the environment, <u>precautionary action</u> must be taken to prevent harm. **[Nature preserves = All Parks to be controlled by the Eco-Police]**
3. Live sustainably, promoting and adopting modes of consumption, production and <u>reproduction</u> that respect and safeguard human rights and the <u>regenerative capacities of Earth</u>. **[Regional limits on fossil fuel use and consumption of raw materials. Total population control and regulated reproduction will be under the bureaucratic control of**

the New World Order Officials, in balance with the Ecosystem!]

4. Establish justice, and defend without discrimination the right of all people to life, liberty, and security of person within an environment adequate for human health and spiritual well-being. People have a right to potable water, clean air, uncontaminated soil, and food security. **[Positive Tolerance = There are no religious heirarchies and all people must give equal honor to the Buddhist or the Homosexual. All pathways lead to God, and none is better than the other in this theology!]**

5. Share equitably the benefits of natural resource use and a healthy environment among the nations, between rich and poor, between males and females, between present and future generations, and internalize all environmental, social and economic costs. **[The Rich Nations will be taxed with a world EcoTax to redistribute the wealth and developmental resources of the planet.]**

6. Promote social development and financial systems that create and maintain sustainable livelihoods, eradicate poverty, and strengthen local communities. **[Communism, communism, communism!!! And the New World Disorder]**

7. Practice non-violence, recognizing that peace is the wholeness created by harmonious and balance relationships with oneself, other persons, other life forms, and Earth. **[All guns will be eliminated from all citizens of all national and militia groups, as the New Eco-Communist Disorder will not tolerate opposition! Forget it NRA!!]**

8. Strengthen processes that empower people to participate effectively in decision-making and ensure transparency and accountability in governance and administration in all sectors of society. **[Global Beauracracies will make ALL the IMPORTANT DECISIONS!!]**

9. Reaffirm that <u>Indigenous and Tribal Peoples</u> have a vital role in the care and protection of Mother Earth. They have the right to retain their spirituality, knowledge, <u>lands</u>, territories and resources. **[Huge tracts of <u>lands will be given back to the Native peoples</u> under the guise that they will be the guardians of Mother Earth, but be the minions of the NMO Communists!]**

10. Affirm that gender equality is a prerequisite for <u>sustainable development</u>. **[<u>Affirmative action</u> will extend despite abilities to all minorities, and white males will be on the endangered list, as they will be last to given an EQUAL opportunity!!]**

11. Secure the right to <u>sexual and reproductive health</u>, with special concern for <u>women and girls</u>. **[Abortion on demand of the state with no interference from parents, as the <u>UN Charter on the Rights of the Child</u> will be inforced with the rule of World Law!!]**

12. Promote the participation of <u>youth as accountable agents of change</u> for local, bio-regional and <u>global sustainability</u>. **[A N.W.O. version of the Hitler Youth Movement to turn the hearts of the children against the parents and rewrite history!!]**

13. Advance and put to use scientific and other types of knowledge and technologies that promote <u>sustainable living and protect the environment</u>. **[A return to a non-energy intensive lifestyle with the <u>world population dramatically and forcefully reduced by extermination, internment slave labour camps</u> and indoctrination of the remainder in the Utilitarian Death when the life-value quotient is below N.W.O. thresholds.]**

14. Ensure that <u>people throughout their lives</u> have opportunities to acquire the knowledge, values, and practical skills needed to <u>build sustainable communities</u>. **[Continuing education

and indoctrination throughout your life with N.W.O. mandated educational seminars on the creation of a sustainable world!!!]

15. Treat all creatures with compassion and protect them from cruelty and wanton destruction. [**No more animals will be consumed by humans and the hunting of game in the wild will be a capital offence!!!**]

16. Do not do to the environment of others what you do not want done to your environment. [**Of the Ten Regions of the Earth - the High Court of the Earth Council will rule against nations that do not adhere to the export of environmental pollution of air, water or industrial waste, and huge fines will be leveed against offending Western Industrialized Nations!!!**]

17. Protect and restore places of outstanding ecological, cultural, aesthetic, spiritual, and scientific significance. [**We, the Earth Council, take all special Parks and Religious Places under our control and our Global Sovereignty!!!**]

18. Cultivate and act with a sense of shared responsibility for the well-being of the Earth Community. Every person, institutions and government has a duty to advance the indivisible goals of justice for all, sustainability, world peace, and respect and care for the larger community of life. [**We will eliminate war and take care of all qualified adult humans with a varifiable quality life, eliminate crime and nuclear war and promise to do this for the remaining population of the earth that in our view allows the Earth to sustain a human population under stable and absolute population control!!!**]

Embracing the values in this Charter, we can grow into a family of cultures that allows the potential of all persons to unfold in harmony with the Earth Community. We must preserve a strong faith in the possibilities of the human spirit and a deep sense of belonging to the universe. Our best actions will embody the integration of knowledge with compassion.

* *

In order to develop and implement the principles in this Charter, the nations of the world should adopt as a first step an <u>international convention</u> that provides an <u>integrated legal framework</u> for existing and future environmental and sustainable development law and policy. **[The <u>United Nations Will Adopt the Earth Charter</u> and all the nations of the Earth, <u>Lead by the United States</u> that will enforce it on the whole world!!!]**

Newsletter #9 - Fall 1997

Spring Consultation Suggests Charter Changes "We call upon the earth, our planet home, with its beautiful depths and soaring heights, its vitality and abundance of life, and together we ask that the earth teach us and show us the way." This invocation from the Chinook Indian tradition opened the Earth Charter consultation session held June 14th at the BRC. On a near-perfect spring day in Cambridge, over sixty scholars, activists, students, religious leaders, and other concerned citizens of our planet met to review, discuss, and critique the current Benchmark Draft of the Earth Charter. "What we have today is a draft," remarked Eileen Gannon, who together with Carol Zinn facilitated the day-long consultation on behalf of Global Education Associates. "It is still evolving. It's still trying to state clearly the underlying values and ethics that people hold in their hearts." The Earth Charter Project, which has its roots in the 1992 Rio Earth Summit, aims to set forth an ethical framework for humanity's relationship with the planet; to provide a moral standard in the form of a global covenant, similar to the United Nations Declaration of Human Rights, to which governments, corporations, and peoples will be held accountable. It is, in the words of Gannon: "a moral contract with the earth." Fundamental to achieving this framework is the development of a global consensus on ethical principles among such disparate groups as the economically developed and developing societies, men and women, young and old, environmental activists and multinational corporations, and indigenous peoples and modern urbanites. "Obviously, we all have a stake in the environment," noted Gannon. "But if we only sit and talk to people who think like us, then we don't arrive at a "common ground" language. We need to bring together around a table people from every different thinking field, from every different professional background. You don't get an agreement going if the only people you talk to are people who think the way you think. We need to bring the wisdom of older people together with the enthusiasm of younger people."

Eileen Gannon (standing) and Carol Zinn (right) facilitate the June 14th Earth Charter consultation This process of bringing together people of differing viewpoints, and learning how to hear those viewpoints, was the purpose of the day's meeting. And while it was clear that not all of the earth's constituencies were represented in the consultation, it provided a good starting point. This became evident in the notable atmosphere of respect and genuine listening that imbued the discussions in the numerous small groups. Convened between the opening and closing plenaries, these groups reviewed the details of the Charter; and then decided what they agreed with, what they questioned, and what they disagreed about. Specifically, there was general agreement with the sentiments set forth in the document's preamble, but numerous suggestions for improving the language. On the other hand, discussion of the Charter's eighteen specific principles led to a number of substantive questions and recommendations, which were reported during the afternoon's closing plenary session. Among the issues raised were:

1. Shouldn't a prohibition against the unwarranted destruction of another species be included?
2. Do social-justice issues like gender equality and reproductive health–issues addressed in other documents like the UN

Declaration of Human Rights and the Beijing Platform for Action–belong in this Charter?
3. Can shelter be added to clean water and air as a basic human right?
4. Shouldn't the Charter recognize the differences in power and/or vulnerability of different peoples and different social groups, and thus delineate responsibility accordingly?

These along with the many other comments, suggestions, and objections expressed at the gathering have been collated, reviewed, summarized, and reported to Steven Rockefeller, Professor of Religion at Middlebury College, who has been enlisted by the Earth Charter Commission to gather input on the document in the final year of consultation, slated to end in March 1998. "But the value of today is not necessarily in the words you changed," Gannon noted in her closing remarks. "The value of today is that you looked seriously at a document and saw how it could be used." Indeed, for the many leaders and activists who attended, the Earth Charter session provided a useful and practical model that they in turn could employ with their respective community, environmental, and religious groups. And on departing the BRC, and rejoining that nearly perfect spring day in Cambridge, one could envision the ripples of dialogue, debate, and discussion that would spread from this point, contributing in time to a genuine covenant between humanity and the earth. -- **Bill Aiken**

Mikhail Gorbachev
Earth Charter Speech at the Rio+5 Forum
March 18th, 1997

Good afternoon, ladies and gentlemen, dear colleagues on our mutual quest for improving the ecological situation on the Earth.

I greet all of you again here in Rio de Janeiro, as this is a great event in itself, and there are quite a few reasons to consider this meeting to be both very important and necessary. Having made a lot of contacts and being engaged in discussions for the last two days, I am fully aware of the fact that we all have been brought here by the same concern about the present and future, both of our planet and humankind.

Those who act mainly within the framework of non-governmental organizations might feel the difficulty to keep track of that new paradigm which could substitute the old one, within the limits of which we have lived and developed for the last three hundred years. And I think you will agree with me, that it is enormously difficult to change the situation for the better. **We all have confronted the choice of either being swept away by time and nature, or of facing the realities, assessing the present situation in our world, in nature, to our relationships with our fellow human beings, their situations and their needs. All of this forces us to accept the fact that this civilization has already outlived itself, and we all have to think about the difficult transition based on consensus on the main values which could help us to build our future.**

The Rio+5 motto which we all can see above this table, appeals to me greatly, and I think you would have voted for my suggestion to give an award to the author. **We all feel now that Agenda 21's ecology goals must move into what we call sustainable development; it is high time to progress to real action.**

Moreover, I am convinced that we are shamefully behind schedule! Life severely punishes us for this lack of speed, courage and insight. Having found myself as a guest at the final session held by the Earth Council, I have felt the deep concern of the members of this commission.

Speaking from Rio de Janeiro, this beautiful city, we, representatives from many countries, people who have access to a wider range of ecological knowledge and information than others, we have to tell to all the people of the world, all the governments, businesspeople, that our hopes for Rio 92 have yet not come true.

I do not know whether all of you will support me, but I would only like to express this conclusion as my own assessment as well that of the Green Cross (a global organization which operates in 20 countries, with more waiting to join).

This assessment is a cause for great concern. Both the time and the present ecological situation make us to undertake resolute actions.

In spite of the fact that the Rio 92 Declaration was a unique and momentous event (and I want here to pay tribute to my friend, Maurice Strong and his colleagues who made the 1992 meeting possible), this Declaration has expressed only what it could at that period. It was not enough from the conceptual point of view, as it remained on anthropocentric position. This is its main and serious drawback.

We cannot afford to overlook ecological problems, to try to pretend that nothing really is going on, that everything could somehow settle by itself.

We all witness those tremendous pressures to which the global ecosystem is subjected! Within this global ecosystem, limited by its own parameters (as has already been proved by scientists), there has developed a new societal subsystem, whose impact has grown by factors of tens, even hundreds times and is still growing.

Total world GNP by the beginning of this century came up to only US$60bln, while modern economy creates a daily GNP of exactly the same volume!

Here are the rates of growth of this new societal subsystem, which also means the growth of wastes, consumption of natural resources, of new stresses on the ecosystem. The population of the Earth has grown by five times since the beginning of the 20th century. Consumption of clear water has grown from 360 cubic kilometers to 4,000 cubic kilometers, more than by ten times.

It has become widely accepted that if our humankind continues to develop by the old patterns, the consequences may include such things as uncontrollable growth of population, dramatic ecological changes and even irreversible changes in our biosphere, up to the total extermination of a human being as a species.

This was the verdict of 1,500 scientists (101 Nobel Prize winners among them) who gathered in 1992 in Washington: if everything goes on according to old patterns using the same technologies and not changing our present lifestyles, irreversible changes will occur in a biosphere in 30-40 years. Just imagine, it seems like yesterday, but five years have already passed since this verdict was pronounced. Time flies very fast!

If we once had 30 years at our disposal, now we have only 25 years, the span of one generation. Still, I do not think that this situation is fatal. We must not just kneel and close our eyes in hope that everything will be resolved somehow.

A change from the well-trod roads of civilization is necessary and inevitable. Human beings have already exceeded all Nature's credit limits. In one word, we, the humankind, have to live according the demands of objective laws of our biosphere. Our choice is quite limited, and we also have not much time left: we either float along the currents of fate or, having drawn

right conclusions, undertake necessary actions, make first steps.

I think, that when we speak about living within the limits set by biosphere, it in no way means that the evolution of the humankind must stop at this point. Evolution of civilization, development of a human spirit, culture, do not have any other limits but those set by biosphere.

It is extremely important to understand and accept our situation. Such understanding and acceptance should be the starting point for all our further steps and decisions, both political and practical. We have to make transition from the idea that a man is a king of nature, to the understanding that a man is a part of the biosphere. This change of civilizational orientations is by no means easy; this has been proved by discussions which we held while preparing of the Earth Charter by the initiative of Prime Minister Lubbers and in contact with the Earth Council. It is always very difficult to get to the vista of a free thought which could enlighten our future and also give guidelines for our everyday life.

It has already become a commonplace to speak about the difficulties of such transition. I would only stress the fact that we have at last achieved the consensus on urgent necessity of changes. This is only the first step, which allow us to think about a long road ahead. **We have to set directions and act on planetary, national and individual levels. The main goal of the Earth Charter, the draft of which we adopted yesterday, is formation of a new outlook; a new set of values.**

The discussion on these issues was extremely difficult. We have even debated the desirability of addressing this semi-finished document to the world public, governments, business.

Yes, I admit that this document is far from being ideal. It is far from those 10 or 15 Commandments which we all know about and which have played their role for 2,000 years. But

here is the document which can be considered as an important step toward those famous testaments. Yesterday we came to the conclusion that we need this intermediate version, a preliminary draft which should be taken from the shuttered world of conferences and round tables to the turbulent world of the world public. All of you can obtain this draft Earth Charter today. I am sure that everyone will find something important for oneself.

For the last two days we have come to an agreement that all considerations regarding the Earth Charter are in their nature thoughts about humankind. Our planet Earth existed billions of years. There was long periods of transitions from one form of life to others, without a human. If we do not change our behavior it might happen again, and this depends on us. In its essence the Earth Charter shifts the focus to people on the Earth, their responsibilities, their morals and spirituality, their way of consumption. I liked the formula, expressed yesterday, which I would like to repeat now: to save humankind and all future generations, we must save the Earth. By saving the Earth, humankind saves himself; it is that easy to understand! Our Charter gives an answer to the question: what does humankind need to do to provide an answer the global ecological challenge?

One more thing to add here: we address our Charter to civil society. We all see that bureaucratic procedures within the UN labyrinths. Governments and other institutions strangle all ecological initiatives. Both the Earth Council, Maurice Strong and we in the Green Cross feel the difficulties which we encounter, trying to implement ideas of radical changes in our everyday life, thus answering the challenge of the biosphere.

That is why our addressee is a world-wide civil society. I firmly believe that if the civil society doesn't become the master of its own destiny in the nearest future, all the projects, including the one which has been subjected to the UN for consideration, will be doomed. The legal document which is buried somewhere in the UN corridors is very important for harmonization and standardization of all the national environmental legislation acts. In spite of the fact that all the governments represented in the UN had received this document, none of them has offered any proposals to include it into the agenda at least at the Committees' level, to start discussions. Here is to the fate of these initiatives!

That is why the Earth Charter is so important for us: with its help we can address all the people who feel an urgent need to adopt it and who will follow it. That is the reason for our issuing the Charter without giving it the final polish. We want to expose it to the world-wide discussions and criticisms, thus waking up people, provoking action. This Charter is the most important factor in realization of the ideas discussed by you at the final stage of Rio+5 Forum.

We looked at the world with open eyes, we fully acknowledge existence of countries which have left the rest of the world far behind in their socio-economic development. We believe that without solidarity on a planetary level we can't answer the challenge of ecology; we simply can't make it if there still is poverty in the world, and this painful issue must be considered by us as one of the top global problems.

We look at the world and see that we cannot ignore lessons of the past and we cannot make the same mistakes of imposing upon peoples various utopias and concepts. We all have recently witnessed the crash of one of the largest experiments of our time-the communist model of bringing happiness to humankind.

As soon as we have managed to set ourselves free and open the way to the freedom of choice and democratic institutions for realization of those choices, there appeared new prophets declaring that the only way out for now is "westernization of the world." I do not think that it is a wise decision. It is just a new attempt to dictate some artificial scheme which many countries would not accept. And what is to be expected in the world if someone tries again to impose their way of development using one's economic, technological and military domination? That is why we declare in our Charter: the world is integrated unity, but it is also the integration of diversity; all of us are equal on the Earth, in the face of Nature, in the face of each other, one nation in the face of the others. We specifically emphasize the unique input made not only by the great nations but also indigenous peoples, which could be referred to as great peoples due to their knowledge of a caring and friendly relationship with nature.

This is exactly what our Charter declares and offers as a milestone for the future. We have already expressed our meaning that it is impossible to move toward future development based on only one option. Here we have the spectacular Brazilian experience: local scientists have come to a conclusion that Brazil could adopt mechanically neither the experience of developed countries, nor the experience of the new industrial Asian countries. They have prudently considered that their development strategy should be focused on inner potentials of society, as well as on its ability to make an input into the world's experience of development. I wholeheartedly greet this approach.

Unfortunately in Russia the situation is reverse; the IMF has dictated its concept of development there. Based on this foreign concept, these reforms have inevitably collided with the Russian national mentality, culture, experience, and finally, the Russian people rejected them. Moreover, the country has found itself in a most severe crisis.

There we have the results of imposing alien ideas, having no respect to the other peoples. That is why we see the future as a cooperation of peoples, which implies a dialog of cultures, religions, traditions. We are trying to use this model as a cornerstone for our Charter, in hope that we will create the document addressed to the Planet Earth.

Our document begins with the words: "We declare our respect for the Earth," we treat her as a living being, and we are grateful to Mother Earth for her gift of life for the numbers of generations of humankind in spite of mistreatment with which these generations paid back to her.

I want to state here, that we are terribly separated now, and everything which is taking place now in Rio serves the purpose of consolidation of all public, cultural and ecological movements for the benefit of our mutual future. Isn't it a great achievement that we, representatives from all countries, can openly meet here and share our thoughts, offer our considerations? Yesterday, working on my speech, I said to my Russian colleagues that some 10-15 years ago the question: "What kind of future we must build?"- would be answered quite easily. The socialist world would have answered that communism is our future, the opposite side would have declared that our future is freedom, market and capitalism. Everything is "crystal clear", and everything would have been very simple and very frightening.

Now we have got the chance to get together as people concerned about our mutual future, as people who accept the Earth in all her diversity and also as an entity, united by a mutual destiny. Now we have a perfect chance to use our intellectual, moral and spiritual experience to answer the challenges of the next millennium.

I believe that all those involved both at the governmental and civil society levels, as well as the Earth Council and non-governmental ecological institutions as, for instance, the International Green Cross have to help people get rid of their fear of the future. People are demoralized nowadays. They are demoralized by worsening of the general situation in the countries which were stable and secure only recently. People are concerned about their workplaces, about their own future and the future of their children, health, and poverty problems. Many of them try to escape from those problems by hiding from harsh realities of our world. This is very dangerous because such a person disconnects oneself from real life, thinking that he may be safer there.

Actually, a person may try to save oneself by cutting off all the connections with this world, by getting lost as a tiny wave in the ocean. But it is extremely dangerous from the point of view of global challenges, which we have to answer on the threshold of the 21st century.

I believe that our Charter gives ethical and moral orientations that will help to strengthen the human spirit. Only a person who has self-confidence, open to friendship and solidarity, can answer the challenges of our time.

I want to conclude my speech by stating that the Earth Charter is not a draft which seeks to dictate for the future civilization, future humankind. I think we are wise enough not to repeat our past illusions. Nobody can foresee what kind of future is in a store for us, but we can use experience of the founding fathers of the United States' Constitution. They decided to create such documents which would have become a picture of a perfect motherland for all the future generations of the US citizens. But then the founding fathers of the US Constitution decided to elaborate a set of rules for the functioning of institutions and human relationship which could be used by future generations with inevitable corrections imposed by future historic realities. And so appeared the set of rules.

The idea of creating a set of rules seems to me quite appealing for our mutual work on our Charter. The Earth Charter is a set of rules of its own kind, but in this case I am afraid that the word "rules" somehow diminishes the real meaning of this idea. It is rather a set of moral and practical orientations, ethical imperatives, that provide us with a possibility to create our future in full awareness of modern global environment, possibilities to move forward to rearranging our life on this planet for the better, to dramatic changes in our consciousness, in politics, business life, in public life of all humankind.

This idea was used as a basis for our work on the Earth Charter, this was the reason for our presenting you with this draft, as it is. I just wanted to share with you our considerations, our concerns, our plans, so that you could understand our ultimate motives.

I believe that the Earth Charter opens a new phase not only in ecological movement, but also in the world's public life. We must do everything we can so that this Charter is accepted exactly as it was designed: a set of vitally important rules.

I must tell you that I have met quite a few cynics in my life, and their number will still multiply. Somehow we have all got used to the fact that everything is in the hands of politicians, that our main goal is to please the UN, so that they would treat our Charter benevolently, and that business is not too aggressive to our ecological demands.

It is not that our Charter is the basis for the total war against everyone, not at all! All we want to achieve by working on this document is to show to all peoples of the world, politicians and business circles, that we have only one option, that is to live within the demands of nature. We must do everything we can to be worthy of our time, to prove that we are a mature society, able to assess our situation and act wisely and responsibly in the interests of the present and future generations.

Standing ovation

The Earth Charter Campaign, International Secretariat
The Earth Council | Apdo. 2323-1002 | San José, Costa Rica
Tel: +506-256-1611 | Fax: +506-255-2197 | e-mail: echarter@terra.ecouncil.ac.cr

Dreams and Visions:

Thus Saith the Lord: As I, the Sovereign Lord, have instructed my servant Daniel to close up and seal the words of the scroll I gave him, I now will unseal all at the time of the End. None of the wicked will understand, but those purified and made white in My Blood, will shine as the stars of the firmament. Knowledge has surely covered the whole earth like a sea, and I will be that compass to the Island of Truth and Wisdom. Those blasphemous ones of the unholy Grail, who call themselves my sons, will conspire to put a Mark in the right hand or in the forehead of all upon the earth. They will use the military might of America to enforce these chains, three sixes, as a personal identification. America will enforce the worship the resurrection of the unholy Roman Empire both East and Western legs, who claims sit as rightful king on my throne in Jerusalem. I alone am King of Kings and Lord of Lords, and there is no other. At the time of this last attempt to bring peace made by the hands of man when there is no peace, I will be stirred to avenge the blood of my Holy people and my Holy name. Then, all will know that I am the Holy One of Israel. My Kingdom will never perish.

30. What was the purpose of the Iraq-Kuwait war?

As Dave Hunt states in "One World: Bible Prophecy and the New World Order": "The war in the Gulf was not about the price of oil at the pump — it was about the New World Order." The United States acted as the world cop as displayed on the front cover of Time magazine shortly after the Gulf War opened. In its function it acted as the military enforcer of the edicts passed by the United Nations' Security Council. The oil price was secondary to the issue of enforcing political edicts of a world government, by its forerunner, the United Nations.

31. Why will this New World Order arise?

This humanistic New World order offers unity of purpose without God and the arrogant blasphemy that man can create utopia without divine revelations and interventions. These are the foundations upon which the last terrible empire will rise, the Kingdom of the Antichrist made of CLAY AND IRON. The clay and the iron will not hold together, but will self destruct and usher in the Eternal Reign of Jesus, King of Kings.

This New World Order will come about because people will worship the creation. There is no real peace without the Prince of Peace. As Jeremiah 6:14 and 8:11 says how people will cry out for peace but there will be none.

Jeremiah 6:14 and Jeremiah 8:11

Jeremiah 6:14 They have healed also the hurt [of the daughter] of my people slightly, saying, Peace, peace; when [there is] no peace.

1 Thessalonians 5:3-5

3 For when they shall say, Peace and safety; then sudden destruction cometh upon them, as travail upon a woman with child; and they shall not escape.

4 But ye, brethren, are not in darkness, that that day should overtake you as a thief.

5 Ye are all the children of light, and the children of the day: we are not of the night, nor of darkness.

6 Therefore let us not sleep,

Man has not yet grasped the truth of the judgment passed on man by his initial sin, choosing to know good and evil as the serpent or Satan lied to them in the garden. ***Genesis 3:1-5,***

'THE LIE'

1 Now the serpent was more subtle than any beast of the field which the LORD God had made. And he said unto the woman, Yea, hath God said, Ye shall not eat of every tree of the garden?

2 And the woman said unto the serpent, We may eat of the fruit of the trees of the garden:

3 But of the fruit of the tree which [is] in the midst of the garden, God hath said, Ye shall not eat of it, neither shall ye touch it, lest ye die.

4 And the serpent said unto the woman, Ye shall not surely die:

5 For God doth know that in the day ye eat thereof, then your eyes shall be opened, and ye shall be as gods, knowing good and evil.

[STOP PRAYER AND DIRECTION FROM GOD'S HOLY SRIRIT]

The initial lie is that surely you will not die if you choose to decide what is good or what is evil. The result of our society making these choices by ourselves away from God's Spirit without prayer over six thousand years has brought us to the brink of disasters that secular humanists are very aware of. This is the global crisis which has caused to come to the fore the concern over the environment, and mother earth. Rather than forsake their worship of man's wisdom and creative ability to solve these problems, they have continued to believe the lie and, therefore, will accept the New World Order rather than return to God and be saved. This is the 'strong delusion' that God will allow to be sent to deceive those that would believe a lie, for they do not love the truth. God's perfect Justice will be served.

32. What is God's purpose of allowing the New World Order?
2 Thessalonians 2: 9-12

9 [Even him], whose coming is after the working of Satan with all power and signs and lying wonders,

10 And with all deceivableness of unrighteousness in them that perish; because they received not the love of the truth, that they might be saved.

11 And for this cause God shall send them strong delusion, that they should believe a lie:

12 That they all might be damned who believed not the truth, but had pleasure in unrighteousness.

The lie is that great lie of Satan's that caused mankind's downfall.

Genesis 3:4

4 And the serpent said unto the woman, Ye shall not surely die:

5 For God doth know that in the day ye eat thereof, then your eyes shall be opened, and ye shall be as gods, knowing good and evil.

This was an invitation by Satan to realize that she had 'goodness' within her and she could decide good from evil. When she accepted this lie she worshiped her own wisdom and not the Lordship of her Creator-God. This is the lie of the New Age Movement.

Matthew 24:5

5 For many shall come in my name, saying, I am Christ; and shall deceive many.

Matthew 24: 23-28

23 Then if any man shall say unto you, Lo, here [is] Christ, or there; believe [it] not.

24 For there shall arise false Christs, and false prophets, and shall shew great signs and wonders; insomuch that, if [it were] possible, they shall deceive the very elect.

25 Behold, I have told you before.

26 Wherefore if they shall say unto you, Behold, he is in the desert; go not forth: behold, [he is] in the secret chambers; believe [it] not.

27 For as the lightning cometh out of the east, and shineth even unto the west; so shall also the coming of the Son of man be.

28 For wheresoever the carcase is, there will the eagles be gathered together.

The Christ of the New Age Movement is Christ consciousness. They refer to this as though everyone must only realize they are anointed with divinity. It is for this reason that the False Prophet to the Jews will be a New Age Leader, 5th Buddha to the Buddhists and possess the charisma to convince other religious groups that he is their messiah. This man is the false prophet and is accepted by the higher levels of the New Age Movement world-wide as the New Age messiah.

Thus the New World Order enforced militarily by the United Nations is allowed by God. His purpose is to condemn those who do not love the truth, but would believe a lie. Man with modern science is a scientific behemoth but a moral microbe. Earth worship through ancient goddess names such as Diana or Gaia will not save us. Behind a green environmentalist cross, there is only the same lie in the garden of Eden. Only the cross of Jesus can save us, our planet, and all humanity from total destruction.

The coming American President will be such a leader, first in the political realm, and then he will be accepted by diverse religious groups as the teacher of the N.W.O. gospel. He will force the worship of the resurrected UnHoly Roman Empire lead by the Russian leader, and the Islamic vassal, who will represent the Imam Mahdi to Islam. Their deception will be universal and completed on a religious level after the economic, political and military realities are evident.

33. How does Royal Arch Masonism differ from the New Age in what they expect as Messiah?

In Royal Arch Masonism this ruler will claim to be a blood line descendent of Jesus, and therefore, a Davidic king acceptable to the Jews. The history of the Masonic tradition gives the answer to this question.

The 17th level of the Scottish Rite gives the name of the angel they must call upon at death to bring them to their reward. His name is

Abaddon. Revelation 9:11 calls the angel of the Abyss, Abaddon in Hebrew. This is none other than Satan worship.

Masonism controls international banking, global and national politics, higher education and the professions, military and security systems world-wide. It considers itself a more all encompassing religion and thus a 'superreligion'. Masons either control or have infiltrated the power structures of every religion on earth. Only some Spirit filled born-again Christian congregations are free of their Satanic control. The Mormons, commonly known as the Church of Jesus Christ of Latter-Day Saints are all Masons but have been instructed at their temple ordinances that they have the correct endowment. It is identical to Masonism's elevation of Satan to the Godhead and it preaches of another Jesus and another gospel. They are one of the most dangerous and wealthiest of the sham-Christian cults on Earth.

To be acceptable as Messiah to the Masons, the Messiah must be of the bloodline of David of the tribe of Judah. The Books, "The Holy Blood and the Holy Grail" and "The Messianic Legacy" state that great Masonic blasphemy that the Royalty of Europe are all bloodline descendents of Jesus. They claim that Jesus was never crucified but was taken with Mary Magdalene, Jesus' supposed wife, to Marseilles, France, thereby propagating the bloodline.

All the current efforts to unify Europe are based not on the economic advantages of union but on the Masonic hope of ruling the world from the resurrected Holy Roman Empire. Masonic authors such as the eminent pastor, Thomas Poole, wrote of the fact of the British and Celts being the lost tribes of Israel after the Babylonian invasion. He even shows their evidence that the Druids of Europe and Great Britain were Baal worshipers combined with Judaism. The last two presidents, through King Edward IV, Clinton and Bush are "blood line" decendants of this Merovignian blasphemous blood line!!

The stone of David was taken to Scotland and later to Ireland, then to reside to the present in the Royal Throne Room of the Queen or

King of England. The King or Queen of England is the titulary head of world Royal Arch Masonism, headquartered in London, England. These mason's believe the Royal bloodline will rule the world. Doesn't this sound like a Davidic bloodline counterfeit to the rightful ruler of our world, Jesus Christ, King of Kings and Lord of Lords?

The woman who rides the beast is the harlot or religious prostitute that has many daughter prostitute religions, and is epitomized by the nation founded by Royal Arch Masonary, America!!

Masons worship Jah-Bal-On, a triune god composed of Jahweh, the Creator God, Baal the fertility god and Osiris, the god of the underworld. They therefore worship the sources of all good and all evil. This is the basis for all eastern mysticism including Buddhism, Hinduism and is embodied in the ancient Chinese principle of Ying and Yang. The Arab term for it is Ramaat, Ra being the sun god, and maat, being the destroyer, embodied by the sunset and death of the sun at the end of the day. Mastery of these forces is their aim, so by accumulating good works, they can qualify for the Grand Lodge in the heavenlies.

In opposition to the Masonism, within the New Age and Islam (Shiite), the False Prophet or Messiah will be a positive Christianity type leader in the New Age tradition, of God within, acceptable to the religions of the earth. He will make everyone worship the economic system based on a resurrected Germany. The E.C.U., or European Currency Unit, will be based on the engine of the Fourth Reich of Germany and this will be the central currency standard of the world and not the U.S. dollar.

Revelation 13:14-18

14 And deceiveth them that dwell on the earth by [the means of] those miracles which he had power to do in the sight of the beast; saying to them that dwell on the earth, that they should make an image to the beast, which had the wound by a sword, and did live.

15 And he had power to give life unto the image of the beast, that the image of the beast should both speak, and cause that as many as would not worship the image of the beast should be killed.

16 And he causeth all, both small and great, rich and poor, free and bond, to receive a mark in their right hand, or in their foreheads:

17 And that no man might buy or sell, save he that had the mark, or the name of the beast, or the number of his name.

18 Here is wisdom. Let him that hath understanding count the number of the beast: for it is the number of a man; and his number [is] Six hundred threescore [and] six.
[UNIVERSAL 666 IRIDIUM ELECTRONIC TRACKABLE IMPLANTABLE IDENTICODE]

34. What is the basis for the New World Order economy?
America's Iridium = M.O.B. Earth!
"Al Capone is dead but there will be MOB rule!"

Revelation 13:16-17

16 And he causeth all, both small and great, rich and poor, free and bond, to receive a mark in their right hand, or in their foreheads:

17 And that no man might buy or sell, save he that had the mark **[#1 - implantable 6/6/6 trackable iridium biochip],** *or the name of the beast* **[#2 - access account to the beast internet/iridium global communications],** *or the number of his name.* **[#3 - 3 global citizen 6/6/6 number - This can be a simple RFID number as those that are implanted in animals now!]**

Rev 13:11-18

11 And I beheld another beast coming up out of the earth **[America-Daughter of Babylon the Great!];** *and he had two horns like a lamb, and he spake as a dragon.*

12 And he exerciseth all the power of the first beast before him, and causeth the earth and them which dwell therein to worship the first beast, whose deadly wound was healed.

13 And he doeth great wonders, so that he maketh fire come down from heaven on the earth in the sight of men,

14 And deceiveth them that dwell on the earth by [the means of] those miracles which he had power to do in the sight of the beast; saying to them that dwell on the earth, that they should make an image to the beast, which had the wound by a sword, and did live.

15 And he had power to give life unto the image of the beast, that the image of the beast should both speak, and cause that as many as would not worship the image of the beast should be killed.

16 And he causeth all, both small and great, rich and poor, free and bond, to receive a mark in their right hand, or in their foreheads:

17 And that no man might buy or sell, save he that had the mark, or the name of the beast, or the number of his name.

18 Here is wisdom. Let him that hath understanding count the number of the beast: for it is the number of a man; and his number [is] Six hundred threescore [and] six.

Key Components of the M.A.R.C!

Multiply Addressable Readable Chip

Ascent of Information Technology

American-Russian Global Communications Network

1] Iridium: Global "Citizen" Cellular Communications

Iridium Satellite Global Communications

66 L.E.O. Satellite

World "Cellular Phone Number" = Mark of the Beast !!!

Number and Master File

Hot Button Issues

1] Nationalized Health Care / Social Services Card

2] Terrorism Prevention

3] Illegal Immigration

4] Gun Control

5] Taxation at Transaction (Value Added Tax, V.A.T.)

The Implantable M.A.R.C.

1st Number: Birthdate Y/M/D

2nd Locator Code: 6 digits Sector##/Subsector##/Local Sector##

3rd DNA Fingerprint: 6 digits

Iridium Satellite - Chandler, Arizona

2] Biometrics Located in the Chip Implant to Provide absolute authorized access - Fingerprint, Retinal Scan, and Genetic Fingerprints e.g. current electronic dog tags used in the US Military!

3] Satellite Trackable - Intelligent Neural Network Trackable Locator Patent from Intellabs in Denver with Multiple Models Intelligent Neural Network Tracking Technology!

4] All Global Citizenship and Health, Military, and Criminal Records with Financial and Banking Accounts!

Atmel Corporation RFID Chip # 8T24RF08 (2.0 mm by 3.5 mm) with encapsulation with Cross Technologies, WI and Sokymat Corporation, Switzerland

Medical Smart Card Technologies 4MB of memory password protected and addressably controlled!

5] Worship of the Sustainable Planet as a living being and the need for abortion and euthanasia and eugenics on demand!

(This identifies any global economic system as the "MARK"!)

The Iridium Project
Y2K and the Mark of the Beast

The **Y2K** nightmare, is less than 500 days away. The dawn of the third millenium is closing quickly. During the past four years working and living in Colorado, I have been exposed to numerous sources of information about the new system that will replace the current electronic financial system. The *Iridium System*, is the replacement. The atomic number of Iridium is 77, and this is a precious element for military and electronic devices. This title was selected by a think tank in the early 80's in Dallas, sponsored by Motorola. The plan was to develop the next generation Internet. A full sixty-six satellites in geocentric orbit were later found necessary to cover the globe. The name was not changed to reflect the new atomic number, and the Iridium Project was birthed.

Like a "who's who" the list of corporations involved in this consortium includes: Martin-Lockheed, MCI, Hewlett Packard Digital Satellite Division, Symbios Logic, Rockwell, Atmel Corporation, Storage Tek, Lucent Technologies, Sun

Microsystems, etc. Most of this system is centered in Denver and Colorado Springs with some main players in California and Texas, and numerous subcontractors across the country. Clinton-Gore signed the bill authorizing the Digital Superhighway two weeks after winning the first term elections. "Full steam ahead" has been the slogan of this powerfully backed organization of companies.

This SuperInternet will be very fast–100 hundred thousand megabytes per second data transfer across the backbone of the network. More importantly, it will be immune to the Y2K bug that threatens to initiate civil breakdown of all our institutions. The IRS, the Justice Department, and Social Services have all had computer simulations of their mainframe systems with the clock advanced to January 1st, 2000. This recently took place at the Denver, "Silver Palace" facility of Martin-Lockheed.

Martin-Lockheed's WAN or wide area network satellite interlink research complex, located just west on Denver, was the place of "The Tests!". All crashed miserably with the dawn of "00" on their operating systems.

One Senator recently was reported as stating that the Y2K is so serious that the drafting of *new laws regarding identification and martial law* will be necessary, as all the government agencies and businesses here in the US and in all other countries are going to receive an "F grade" for preparedness in the face of **Y2K**.

My source at Martin-Lockheed identified that within 60 days a public offering to government and businesses in America would be made to completely shift their current communications and financial systems to Iridium. By November 1998, businesses will be given an "offer they can't refuse", convert or face financial chaos!

Each individual in the Western world will be given special identification to access this database and all the benefits. This system entails the assignment of three unique identifiers to each person. The first is the six digits of year/month/day of birth. The second identifier is based on the GPS or Global Positioning System, that the US military use for targeting artillery. It is called the Mesh Bar Code. Conceptually, the world is divided into 99 global sectors, with 99 subsectors inside each of these. Finally, within each of these subsectors, they are subdivided into 99 subsubsectors. This allows for long-range targeting to an accuracy of less than 250 radial yards anywhere on the planet. An individual residence is targetable. How Iridium works relies on the position of the signal source and the identity of the source signal. Having the Mesh Bar Code of the source individual allows for more accurate and efficient signal routing. However, it has the unpleasant side effect of absolute control of the digital airwaves. The identity of the individual and locations of any signal whether phone, computer, radio, etc., and will allow no one access to this SuperNet, who is not authorized. Each allowed database zone will be protected by a virtually impenetrable "firewalls" with security protections against unauthorized access.

This database now exists but for the third identifier. "Genetic fingerprinting" was central to the legal cases of O.J. Simpson and more recently President Clinton. In the case of O.J. Simpson, they used the unique identification of the patterns on five bars of DNA. It took weeks. Newer systems will cut this to less than one hour with high speed PCR or polymerase chain reaction analyzers.

The new reports of the last month have come out the government has recommended the DNA fingerprinting of all US citizens. When this is available, it will be linked to all manner of biometric database information, such as fingerprints, laser retinal scans, etc., depending on security clearance and access past specific SuperNet "firewalls".

Everyone will be issued a universal identifier number with access to military, medical, criminal, tax, and security/travel records. John spoke of it in Revelation. Although the devil might sit on this system for a century, being an overachiever, he will act quickly to force a Treaty on Israel. The coming financial collapse and the resurrection of the economic "Peace and Security" of the SuperNet, will catch offguard the lost and those brothers that do not see the gathering storm. Know that the God of Abraham, Isaac and Jacob, is the same yesterday, today, and forever. Israel was saved through the Egyptian plagues. Watchmen hear the Voice of God and discern the times and seasons of His coming!

All Wealth to Eurodollars

The German economy is the powerhouse of Europe. The Deutchmarke will soon be phased out, starting January 1st, 1993. Its replacement will be the European Currency Unit, or E.C.U., an electronic currency.

States of the former Soviet Union are about to be swallowed up in this expanding economic alliance with Germany. On the agenda is Russian membership in the G7 Nations Economic Alliance and the soon tieing of the ruble to the E.C.U. In a Trilateral World, Germany would be the center of a Euro-Asian Empire from the Atlantic to the Pacific, with three times the population of the United States and the potential of five times the manufacturing capacity. Germany will thus become the economic centre of the trilateral world and the E.C.U. will thus be the base currency standard.

Control of world wealth through the G7 or Group of Seven Nations will move quickly toward a global electronic economic control. Referring to the documents published by the Club of Rome, reviewed by Gary Kah, this world economy would be controlled by the first three nations of the ten economic-political regions of the world. They are North America, Europe, and Japan and the Eastern Rim Countries. Germany will be the cornerstone in the New World Order as the powerhouse of a newly expanded Euro-Asian Empire. Now we are seeing the first glimmers of the rise of the Fourth Reich.

European Unification took its first shape with the Treaty of Rome. In 1967, European Community Nations were to have expanded. It was to be a new first stage of the United States of Europe, with their watchword, "Many Languages, One Voice". Monetary exchange rate controls took the form of the S.N.A.K.E., a currency control board that prevented the buffeting of currencies by no more than 2% from the internal standard, primarily set by Germany. This put further pressure on capital to cause greater growth in the European heartland of Germany. An even greater flood of capital surged into the German economy with the Unification of East and West Germany and the July 1990 free flow of capital between all European countries.

Nazi Germany, destroyed in the second world war, followed closely the destruction of the first world war. We are witnessing the rise of the "Beast" of Revelation 13:1-10. This nation, is spoken of in Rev13:3, which receives a deadly wound but is miraculously resurrected.

Rev. 13:3 "And I saw one of his heads as it were wounded to death; and his deadly wound was healed: and all the world wondered after the beast."

Maastricht, the plan for economic unification of Europe, sets forth the grand timetable of the grand architects of this plan. Total integration is to be completed by 1999. January 1st of 1993 starts this process in earnest with the effective pegging of the E.C.U. with the German Deutschmarke. The twin challenge of Denmark and Ireland rejecting the Treaty, and the grudging French "oui", has had a serious cooling effect on the momentum for total economic integration. This is in direct opposition to the New World Order, which forsees the crowning jewel of its next step to World Government as the Unification of Europe. Even the "Economic Terrorism" of the international exchange controls was unable to force a strong "yes" from the French. During the latest tremor, the week prior to the French Maastricth, both Britain and Italy, left the S.N.A.K.E., the currency exchange control board for Europe. Sweden, a non-European Community Country, was unable to keep its currency afloat with 500 percent interest rates during the days after the currency rally. The events of the week of 13, September '92, will go down in world history as the economic straw that broke the camel's back and sped the demise of the Deutchmarke and the ascendancy of the E.C.U..

The **E.C.U.** which can buy little more than a fast food meal in Brussels will be the electronic gold of the 90s. Once this is accomplished, the E.C.U. will made exchangeable with the ruble, Russia's currency. The Russian people are the best savers in the world, due to the lack of consumables and the absence of public financial institutions. A fully convertible **ruble** would make the Market Communism of Gorbachev a real possibility, while all the while supporting the greatest war machine in world history. In the last two years the International Monetary Fund (I.M.F.) and the World Bank have pledged 24 billion dollars to stabilize the ruble's international exchange rate.

Germany publicly fears a right wing coup of the kind attempted with the Aug 3rd, 1991 ouster of Mikhail Gorbachev. They feel it is their best interests to finance investment in an economy which will foster a more docile Russian bear on their Northern border.

This entire process will culminate with the formation of a world government with ten economic-political kingdoms, according to the Bible and confirmed by Club of Rome documents. Daniel's vision of the statue in Nebuchadnezzar's dream, foresaw a statue with feet of **Clay and Iron**. Clay will be represented by the building blocks of a New World Order, nations with great resources such as oil. Military force, the Electronic Monitoring and Currency Controls will be the Iron of Daniel's statue. Only at this time in history, and with our current technology, could this Empire encompass the whole earth. A period of world-wide economic fascism is about to plunge the world into a fanatically environmental, spiritually perverse socialist Utopian nightmare.

[Documents Reproduced In Public Domain of the Internet]

GLOBAL FINANCIAL DATA

THE EURODOLLAR: THE CURRENCY FOR THE TWENTY-FIRST CENTURY

Currently, about $1.5 trillion in currency is traded on a daily basis. This works out to $300 per day for every human being on the planet, or $100,000 per year for every person alive. The cost of carrying out these foreign exchange transactions is enormous, and hardly constitutes an efficient use of resources. We have a proposal for resolving this problem.

In January 1999, members of the European Union will introduce a single currency, the Euro. In 2002, the Euro will replace national currencies, and each country's currency will cease to exist. It is our belief that within the next ten years the Euro should be merged with the Dollar to create a Eurodollar, which would act as a single currency for both the United States and in Europe, and eventually for other countries.

The Eurodollar summarizes our views on how and why the world should move toward a single currency. This article explores how the world has moved toward single currencies in the past, what the economic costs and benefits of a single currency would be, the political impact of introducing a single currency, the impact on financial markets of a single currency, and it provides a timetable for moving to a single currency in the next decade.

If you enjoy this article, you might also want to read the five more detailed articles that explore the impact of the transition to a single international currency.

A History of Universal Currencies spans monetary history from ancient Mesopotamia to modern times to analyze currency unions of the past. This article shows that whenever it has been politically and economically feasible, governments have introduced a single currency over a wide economic area in order to facilitate economic trade. The article looks at universal currencies in ancient Rome and ancient China, in medieval times, and in modern times. The article looks at the Latin Union in the 1800s, the gold standard, Bretton Woods, the CFA Franc, and the upcoming introduction of the Euro.

The Economic Benefits and Economic Costs of a Eurodollar analyzes the economic impact of introducing a single currency for the United States and Europe. The article discusses optimum currency area theory and sees whether it applies to the United States and Europe. The article analyzes the economic benefits and the economic costs of introducing a single currency for the United States and Europe, and it discusses the economic impact of the single currency.

The Political Economy of a Eurodollar looks at the political impact of introducing a single currency for the United States and Europe. Politics influences the existence of currencies just as much as economics does. First, the article looks at the role political plays in the introduction of a single currency. Second, the article discusses the political and economic aspects of creating a Global Reserve Bank that would oversee the single currency. Third, the article looks at the influence of interest groups on the introduction of a currency union. Fourth, the article analyzes the impact of a Eurodollar on the rest of the world. Finally, the article focuses on the political benefits of introducing a Eurodollar.

The Eurodollar and Financial Markets looks at the impact of the introduction of a single currency on financial markets. The first section looks at the impact on currency markets. The second section looks at the Global Reserve Bank, which would act as the central bank for the currency union between the United States and Europe. The third section analyzes the impact on stock markets and futures markets. The fourth section studies the impact on interest rates and on inflation rates. The final section looks at the financial impact on corporations.

A Timetable for the Introduction of a Eurodollar details how the world can gradually move to a single currency for the entire world. The article discusses why the world economy is ripe for the move to a single currency. Next, the article provides a timetable for the introduction of the Euro in Europe. Then, the article provides a timetable for linking the Dollar and the Euro into a single currency over the next ten years. Finally, the article discusses how countries outside of North America and Europe could join the Eurodollar bloc.

After reading these articles, we hope that you will conclude with us that if the rallying cry of the twentieth century was to be "Workers of the world, unite!" then the rallying call of the twenty-first century could be "Currencies of the world, unite!"

Our goal is to help investors to conduct their own research, not to offer investment advice. The information and data in this report were obtained from sources considered reliable. Their accuracy or completeness is not guaranteed.

The Eurodollar

October 1998

Bryan Taylor II, Ph.D., President
Global Financial Data

Introduction

Currencies have been at the focus of the international economy in the past year. On the one hand, there have been currency collapses in many East Asian countries and in Russia, with the fear that these currency collapses could lead to a world-wide economic recession. On the other hand, in January 1999, members of the European Union will introduce the Euro, which will replace national currencies in 2002.

It is our belief that there is a simple solution to the problems which currencies are causing the international economy. Within the next ten years the Euro should be merged with the Dollar to create a Eurodollar, which would act as a single currency for both the United States and Europe, and eventually for the rest of the world.

We believe that history, economics and politics all point toward the benefit of moving toward a single international currency. To prove our point, we first provide a brief economic history of money and currencies, showing that whenever it has been politically and economically feasible, the world has moved toward a single currency. Next, we look at the economic and political impact of a single currency, and we see how a single currency would affect financial markets. Finally, we provide show how the United States and Europe can introduce a single currency for them, and eventually, for the rest of the world.

A History of Single Currencies

Whenever economic and political stability have enabled international trade to expand, attempts have been made to introduce a universal currency that meets the demands of trade. Because of the political benefits of introducing a universal currency, a single monetary standard has usually followed the expansion of political power. The Roman Empire, the Chinese Empire, and the British Empire all established a single currency standard for the regions over which they ruled. Although there are economic reasons for having a universal currency, history suggests that politics, and not economics, has been the chief determinant of currency areas in the past and today.

The first attempts to create an international currency for Europe occurred in 1800. The German Zollverein was introduced in 1834 and the German currencies were consolidated into the mark in 1873. The Latin Monetary Union was established in 1865, and lasted until 1914, with France, Belgium, Switzerland and Italy as charter members. Each country agreed to mint coins to a single standard that would be accepted as legal tender by government offices in any of the member countries.

The relative success of the Latin Monetary Union led to the International Monetary Conference of 1867, which tried to create a single monetary standard for Europe and the United States by minting a common coin equal to 25 French Francs, 5 U.S. dollars and 1 British pound; however, the idea fell through. Without a single European government or international currency agreement, the gold standard was the closest the world could get to a universal currency. Currencies were fixed to gold, and gold fixed currencies to each other. The result was the virtual elimination of currency fluctuations among the world's major currencies between the 1870s and 1914 when World War I forced countries to suspend their currency conversion.

Despite numerous attempts to stabilize the international financial system after World War I, any success was only temporary. The Bretton Woods established a dollar standard to replace the gold standard. The value of the dollar was fixed to gold at $35 to the ounce, and the world's currencies were fixed to the dollar. Exchange rates were fixed in the short run, but flexible in the long run. By the early 1970s, however, the world had changed dramatically from 1944, and in 1973, Bretton Woods collapsed. Flexible exchange rates replaced system of the fixed exchange rates.

The current push for monetary union in Europe began with the Delors report of 1988, which advocated a gradual move toward a single currency. This was the basis for the Maastricht Treaty, signed in 1992, which set the timetable for the move to a single currency by January 1, 1999.

There have been other attempts to form currency unions since World War II, and the record shows that currency unions have succeeded in two cases. The first has been when a small country tied its currency to a larger country's currency, and second when several countries gave up control over their monetary policy to a supranational central bank. Belgium and Luxembourg have been in a currency union since World War II. Similarly, Swaziland, Lesotho and Namibia have all tied their currencies to the South African Rand.

Only two multinational currency unions have worked since World War II. The smaller success story has occurred among the islands of the East Caribbean, which has continued since the British Caribbean Currency Board was established in 1950. The most successful currency union has been the Communaute Financiere Africaine (CFA) which has continued a successful currency union among its members since the former French colonies gained their independence in the early 1960s. Fourteen countries in west and in central Africa share the CFA Franc.

In countries that do not share a single currency, economic necessity and technological change have pushed the world toward a single monetary standard. US dollars are accepted almost everywhere. It has been estimated that about half the United States' outstanding currency, and the majority of its $100 bills, are held outside of the United States.

Technology has unified the world's currencies in a way that is fundamentally different from either the era of the gold standard or from Bretton Woods. Over 1.5 trillion dollars in currency is traded every day or about $300 for every person on the planet every single day. Currency crises can lead to, and can produce, recessions and political change. Given this, it is not difficult to imagine the massive savings that could occur by the introduction of a universal currency.

In short, history shows a continuous desire to move toward a single currency when such a change is economically and politically feasible. The reason is simple, the benefits of having a common currency exceed the costs. Though political trends have been moved toward greater plurality in the world, finance, technology and economics have moved toward greater integration. Yet, there is no reason to believe that monetary integration in the form of a single currency could not coexist with political plurality.

The Economics of a Single Currency

The introduction to a single currency for the United States and Europe will produce both economic benefits and economic costs. On average, the net economic benefits for society should exceed the costs.

The theory of optimum currency areas was first elaborated by Robert Mundell back in the 1960s. The benefit of having different exchange rates between countries is that they help countries adjust to asymmetric economic shocks. A single currency eliminates the ability to adjust prices between different economic regions through changes in the exchange rate. Consequently, economic adjustments must be made in one of three ways.

First, labor must be mobile so workers can move from an area suffering from recession to one that is enjoying an economic boom. Second, wages and prices must be flexible in order that the economy can respond to changes in supply and demand. Third, there must be some way of transferring resources to the country or region which is in dire economic straits in order to help it recover from its recession. Given these three criteria, it is unlikely that the United States and Europe would fit Mundell's definition of an optimum currency area. However, it is also unlikely that many countries that have a single currency, such as the former Soviet Union, China, India or Italy are optimum currency areas. No government in modern times has allowed different currencies to circulate within its borders, regardless of any economic benefits that would occur.

The real question, however, is whether having a single currency for the United States and Europe would be more efficient than having a multitude of currencies. Whether the United States and Europe move on to a single currency will be determined by the net political and economic benefits that come from introducing a Eurodollar.

Money is a public good. If the government provides the coin of the realm, then society does not have to incur the costs of agreeing on a standard for carrying out economic activity. Having a single currency for the United States makes economic transactions easier than having a different currency in every state of the union. There are several reasons why a single currency increases economic efficiency.

First, a single currency increases the transparency of prices. Whether you buy or sell goods in New Hampshire or in California, consumers can compare price in the United States in a single currency. If you are in Europe, and you are trying to find the best price, you will have to compare prices in fourteen different currencies.

Second, a single currency reduces the transaction costs of buying and selling goods because you don't have to convert money from one currency to another. Multinational corporations, which operate in ten or twenty different currencies, would see a large decrease the cost of managing revenues and costs would be reduced dramatically.

Third, a single currency would eliminate exchange rate risk among the countries that shared the currency. Foreign exchange risks and the cost of hedging these risks are a major cost of multinational corporations' operations. Having a single currency eliminates foreign exchange risk as companies that operate exclusively in the United States already know.

Fourth, when a currency union exists, countries can no longer use devaluations as part of their economic policy to gain an advantage over other countries. Fifth, because the Central Bank which oversees the currency union is not controlled by a single government, it will be easier for the Central Bank to focus on its primary objective-to control prices and fight inflation.

Although there are many economic benefits from a single currency, there are also costs. The primary benefits of a single currency are microeconomic. The single currency enables individuals and businesses to carry out economic transactions more efficiently. There are also macroeconomic benefits from having a single currency. A single currency encourages international trade, and reduces the disruptions that result from currency fluctuations. Nevertheless, most of the costs of having a single currency are macroeconomic and political, and there are several important costs that nation sharing a common currency incur.

First, a single currency forces a country to forgo an independent monetary policy. After the currency union begins, the country's monetary policy is determined by the supranational central bank and not by the domestic central bank. This is why the theory of optimal currency areas emphasizes the importance of flexible prices, labor mobility and fiscal transfers. Because flexible prices and labor mobility become more important when a currency union exists, governments have an incentive to make markets work more efficiently.

A second effect of the currency union is less regional economic differentiation. The Federal Reserve in the United States cannot lower interest rates in one part of the United States which is in a recession while simultaneously raising interest rates in another part of the country which is booming. Interest rates and prices become similar throughout most of the currency area.

Third, there are also political costs to a currency area. If the government loses control over monetary policy to the supranational central bank, politicians are limited to using fiscal policy to influence the macroeconomy.

The primary question we want to address here is whether a single currency for the United States and Europe would be more efficient than multiple currencies. Some would argue that the main difference between a currency union for the United States and a currency union for the United States and Europe would be the inability to use fiscal transfers to offset asynchronous regional economic cycles between the United States and Europe. However, special funds could be set up to address this problem.

Another benefit of introducing a single currency would be that individuals and corporations would have greater economic choice. The single currency would encourage trade which could in turn place pressure on governments to reduce the barriers to trade that currently exist between countries, and force governments to reduce structural barriers to trade. The market reforms that will inevitably follow from the introduction of a single currency should be included in the list of benefits that a Eurodollar would provide.

The Political Economy of the Eurodollar

Were the introduction of a single currency for Europe and the United States a purely economic concern, a Eurodollar and a supranational Global Reserve Bank probably would have been introduced long ago, because the economic benefits of a single currency exceed the costs.

Even if economics and history provide convincing arguments for the introduction of a single currency for the United States and Europe, or for the rest of the world, political factors have been and will continue to be the primary barrier to the introduction of a single currency. This section will focus on the political problems of establishing a currency union, and of establishing a supranational Global Reserve Bank to oversee the currency union. Many people already believe that central banks, which are independent but accountable to their governments, have too much power already, and ceding power to a supranational central bank would increase the central bank's power even more. In order for governments to be willing to cede this power, they must believe that the benefits of a single currency will exceed the costs.

The process of introducing a single currency has been difficult enough in Europe, which has carried out multinational cooperation for decades. Getting the United States and Europe to agree on a single currency will be even more difficult. The United States was one of the last developed countries to have a central bank, and only in the past few years has the United States allowed nationwide banking, something which has been taken for granted in every other country in the world for most of this century. The United States' willingness to participate in international economic organizations is evidenced by its membership in the WTO, the IMF, the World Bank and NAFTA.

The primary political reason for opposing a supranational Central Bank would be the loss of economic sovereignty that would occur. However, it is important to differentiate between independence, accountability, and political control. Even though it would be a supranational agency, the Global Reserve Bank would never have complete independence from domestic political control. It would be accountable to the countries that would give the GRB its power. If the Global Reserve Bank forsook its accountability and acted against the interests of the United States, the US could leave the currency union just as some French African countries have left the CFA Franc currency union. The threat of exit would force the GRB to remain accountable.

The basis of democracy is a system of checks and balances, which limits the powers of each branch of government. Although members of the Federal Reserve have a large degree of freedom from political influence, Congress must approve Federal Reserve appointees, and the appointees are subject to impeachment. Similar control over appointees to the Global Reserve Bank would be necessary for the U.S. Congress to approve US membership. The Global Reserve Bank can be both independent and accountable. The two are not mutually exclusive.

In some ways, it would be easier to establish an independent, supranational Central Bank than to establish other supranational agencies. First, by definition, the Federal Reserve is supposed to be independent of political influence on a day-to-day basis. Second, because the Federal Reserve makes a profit from the reserves that are deposited with it by banks, it does not require any Federal funding. Third, the Federal Reserve has coordinated its actions with other central banks in the past. The Global Reserve Bank would institutionalize this cooperation. Fourth, by their very nature, financial markets are international, and the dollar is an international currency with about half of U.S. currency currently outside of the United States. A Global Reserve Bank would probably make policy coordination between the world's central banks easier than it is today.

A final economic cost of the currency union would be that the United States would no longer be able to issue bonds in its own currency. Given the credit history of the United States, there would be few worries about default through non-payment, and the introduction of a Eurodollar could reduce the risk to bond holders because the government could no longer default through inflation.

One way of understanding the future debate over the Eurodollar will be to look at which interest groups will come out in favor of a currency union and which will oppose the currency union. In the case of a Eurodollar currency union, direct losers would be few. Although there might be ideological opposition, economic opposition would come mainly from firms that would fear that the currency union would favor large multinationals at their expense.

The introduction of a Eurodollar would also have political repercussion outside of the United. Many European countries found it difficult to convince their citizens to give up their own domestic currency for one controlled by the European Central Bank. Convincing Europeans to give up their currency for one jointly controlled by Europeans and Americans might be even more difficult. Outside of Europe, the introduction of the single currency would produce a group of insiders who were part of the world's leading currency, and outsiders who were not. The world could become divided between Eurodollar countries and everyone else. For this reason, arrangements would have to be made for countries outside of Europe and North America to join the Eurodollar bloc.

Once the transition to a single currency for Europe and the United States was made, the transition to a single currency for the entire world could come with a speed that might surprise many. The world might easily moving from having almost 200 currencies today to having one within a decade, and twenty-five years from now, historians would wonder why it took so long to eliminate the Babel of currencies which existed in the twentieth century.

The fear that economic integration inevitably leads to greater political integration is unfounded. In fact, the opposite is probably true. Economic unity can coexist with and support political diversity. Countries which have been part of the Deutsche Mark bloc (Denmark, Netherlands, Belgium, Luxembourg, France, Switzerland, Austria) have seen no reduction in political freedom as a result of linking their currency to the Mark. In some ways, having a currency union could enhance political sovereignty since it would reduce the role of monetary policy in politics.

One benefit of a currency union between the United States and Europe would be that it could strengthen the Euro. Many Europeans fear that the Euro could fail, but if the Euro were seen as an intermediate step on the path to a currency union between the United States and Europe, many reservations about the Euro could be removed.

Greater financial and economic integration within the world could also reduce the likelihood of conflict between countries. With a single currency being used throughout the world, and multinational corporations operating in dozens or even a hundred different countries, the potential for war due to economic reasons would be reduced substantially. This fact has been a driving force behind the economic integration of Europe since World War II.

The Impact of the Eurodollar on Financial Markets and on Banking

The greatest direct impact of the introduction of a Eurodollar would fall on financial markets, and particularly on foreign exchange. Currency markets transact over $1 trillion in foreign exchange operations every day. The introduction of a Eurodollar would dramatically reduce international currency transactions in the spot market, the futures market, swap market and forward markets. The need for currency hedging between the United States and Europe would be eliminated overnight. Moreover, once a Eurodollar was introduced, it would become the principal, perhaps the only, reserve currency in the world.

One consequence of introducing a Eurodollar would be the need to create a central bank, perhaps to be called the Global Reserve Bank (GRB), which would oversee the currency union. The Global Reserve Bank would probably be modeled on the Federal Reserve Bank. The Global Reserve Bank would build on the foundations of existing central banks to link the banks of all member countries together.

At the Fed, policy is centered in the Federal Open Market Committee with the Federal Reserve Bank of New York carrying out the policy actions of the FOMC. The Global Reserve Bank's version of the FOMC could include twelve members. Six members would come from the GRB (one of whom would be the Chairman), three from United States district banks (one of whom would be from New York), and three from European central banks. Europeans could rotate their positions among different countries as they do now.

In addition to running monetary policy, the Federal Reserve in the United States plays an important role in regulating the banking system. The Comptroller of the Currency charters national banks, the FDIC provides deposit insurance that is backed by the full faith and credit of the United States government, and the Fed supervises banks. Countries would have to meet common standards for bank supervision and deposit insurance, which would be similar to the standards that currently exist in the United States. Banking regulations would have to be rewritten in both the United States and in Europe to harmonize them with each other. International accounting and transparency standards for countries that would be part of the Eurodollar bloc would have to be applied in all member countries.

These rules would be applied to other countries that wanted to join the Eurodollar. Although countries would be free to link their currency to the Eurodollar as Argentina has to the Dollar, joining the Eurodollar bloc would entail agreeing to the same regulatory standards as occur within the United States and European countries.

The globalization of financial markets, which would occur in banking, would extend to stock and futures markets. World stock markets would become more integrated because the single currency would make it easier to trade stocks on multiple exchanges. Firms that did an initial public offering or a secondary offering could offer shares in both the United States and Europe giving them a larger capital base to draw upon.

The savings to corporations and to individuals of introducing a single currency would be enormous, both in terms of the costs of carrying out international economic activities, and in the reduction in foreign exchange risk that would occur. Corporations would see a virtual elimination of transaction risk, economic risk and translation risk overnight.

It should be obvious that foreign currency markets are expensive. Governments force corporations to spend billions of dollars each year dealing with the consequences of operating in almost 200 currencies world-wide. Introducing a single currency for the

United States and Europe would go a long way toward reducing these costs for corporations and for individuals.

A Timetable for the Introduction of a Eurodollar

Though the economic benefits of a single currency have long been obvious from a purely theoretical point of view, no currency for the entire world has been introduced until now because the political and economic costs of making this change have been too great. The real problem is, how do you go from having almost 200 currencies to having only one?

If there were a single world government, there would also be a single world currency, but a single world government is neither likely to occur, nor desirable. The current global financial crisis has made a single currency more feasible, because some people are beginning to question the efficiency of the current exchange rate system.

What is unique about the current world economic and financial situation is that for several reasons, it is now possible to convert to a single currency for the United States and Europe, and the rest of the world at a minimal economic cost.

First, financial markets throughout the world have become increasingly integrated. Financial firms span the globe and international transactions increase annually. In a world that is brought closer together everyday through airplanes, telecommunications and the Internet, having almost 200 different currencies seems an absurd, inefficient anachronism. In our opinion, the economic cost of maintaining almost 200 national currencies exceeds the cost of converting to a single currency.

The introduction of the Euro enables the world to make the first step toward a single currency for the United States and Europe. The Dollar and the Euro could be linked together to form a single currency at a 1:1 parity with each other. Linking the Dollar and the

Euro would be a relatively simple step compared with creating the Euro out of the eleven currencies that preceded it.

The Euro will be introduced on January 1, 1999 in accordance with the Maastricht treaty. Participating countries will fix their domestic currencies to the Euro, and after that, their currencies will not be allowed to fluctuate against the Euro or against each other. The European Central Bank will begin running the monetary policy of the countries which are members of the Euro. On July 1, 2002, the German Mark, French Franc, Italian Lira and other currencies will cease to exist.

The introduction of the Euro simplifies the transition to a Eurodollar in a number of ways. First, once the Euro has been introduced, it reduces the cost of joining Europe's currencies to the U.S. dollar because these currencies have already made the transition to a single currency. Second, it introduces the technology that is necessary to make the transition.

Third, the rough similarity in the value of the Euro and the Dollar means that the two currencies could be set at par to one another. Since one dollar is worth less than a Euro, this will put the United States at a disadvantage because it would automatically raise the prices of U.S. goods relative to European goods. However, finding a conversion rate other than par would probably make linking the currencies almost impossible. After the link is established, prices of goods will gradually adjust to insure that goods in the United States and Europe are priced similarly.

The earliest date which the Euro and the Dollar could be linked together at a 1:1 ratio would be January 1, 2003. The initial goal would be to establish the Eurodollar as a single currency, rather than to eliminate the Euro and the dollar altogether. Time would be needed to establish confidence in the new currency.

The other change that would occur on January 1, 2003 would be that the Federal Reserve Bank and the European Central Bank would begin cooperating with one another and would lay the foundations for the Global Reserve Bank, which would replace them. Similar ties would be established between other government agencies in the United States and Europe, which oversee financial markets and would be affected by the introduction of the single currency. Corporations would also begin preparing for operating their financial accounts in a single currency.

The Eurodollar could be established as the legal tender of all member countries two years later on January 1, 2005. The GRB would take control of monetary policy for member countries on this date, and the regional Federal Reserves in the United States and European central banks would henceforward carry out the policies of the Global Reserve Bank.

The third step would begin after the Eurodollar and the Global Reserve Bank had been firmly established. In this phase, other countries would be allowed to join the Eurodollar bloc and use the Eurodollar as their legal tender currency. Every country that wanted to join the Eurodollar bloc would have to go through a two-year probationary period.

During this time period, the country would have to set up a currency board and fully back its currency with Eurodollars, as Hong Kong and Argentina do today with the US Dollar. During this probationary period, the country would have to link its currency to the dollar and maintain that link. Second, each country would have to allow the GRB and other agencies which oversaw the financial system in the United States and Europe to establish regulatory control over the financial institutions within its own country. Third, each country would have to agree to strict limitations on government deficits and other aspects of fiscal policy that could jeopardize participation in the Eurodollar bloc. If the country had managed to maintain a stable link to the Eurodollar for two years, and if it had met all the regulatory requirements of the Global Reserve Bank and its sister agencies, the country would be allowed to introduce the Eurodollar as its legal tender currency.

Non-members could be allowed to link their currency to the Eurodollar beginning on January 1, 2005 when the Eurodollar would become legal tender in Europe and the United States. Countries would not be allowed to introduce the Eurodollar as their currency until January 1, 2007.

Conclusion

For the first time since the world moved to a system of flexible exchange rates back in 1973, it is possible to establish a single currency for Europe, the United States, and possibly for the rest of the world. The Eurodollar would move beyond Bretton Woods and the Gold Standard by establishing a single currency rather than a system of fixed exchange rates as had existed before.

Conditions are ripe for this transition. The introduction of the Euro has created the momentum to move to change to a single currency. The technology for making this change has been introduced in Europe, and because of the rough parity between the Euro and the Dollar, the transition to a single currency for Europe and the United States could be made at a minimal cost.

The only condition that is lacking is the political will to make this change. As with the Euro in Europe, making the transition will require strong leadership in both the United States and in Europe to see through the transition to a single currency. At some point in the near future, people will see that the benefits of having a single currency far outweigh the costs, and people will begin to ask if we can afford not to have a single currency. At that point, the single currency will become a political and economic fait accompli, and a world that has almost 200 currencies will be seen as an inefficient anachronism.

If the rallying cry of the twentieth century was to be "Workers of the world, unite!" then the rallying call of the twenty-first century could be "Currencies of the world, unite!"

Timetable for the Introduction of a Eurodollar

October 1998

Bryan Taylor II, Ph.D., President
Global Financial Data

Timetable for the Introduction of a Eurodollar

In January 1999, members of the European Union will introduce a single currency, the Euro. In 2002, the Euro will replace national currencies, and each country's currency will cease to exist. It is our belief that within the next ten years the Euro should be merged with the Dollar to create a Eurodollar, which would act as a single currency for both the United States and in Europe, and eventually for other countries. These articles explore the impact of this transition to a single international currency.

Though the economic benefits of a single currency have long been obvious from a purely theoretical point of view, no currency for the entire world has been introduced until now because the political and economic costs of making this change have been too great.

In the past, the expansion of a currency area occurred under one of two circumstances. First, an expansion of political power enabled the government to impose its currency on the countries that it conquered. The Roman and Chinese Empires introduced a single currency to the lands which they ruled over, and the Pound Sterling was used throughout the colonies which it had settled.

The second reason for the introduction of a new currency area or currency arrangement was that an economic or financial crisis had left international financial markets so unstable and unsettled that a new set of exchange rates and foreign currency ties was deemed preferable to the chaos which existed. Bretton Woods provides a perfect example of this. The global need for financial stability superceded parochial economic interests that preferred the status quo.

During World War II, President Roosevelt suspended foreign exchange transactions, and the pre-war exchange rates lost all economic meaning. Introducing a new foreign exchange system based on the dollar was preferred by the Allies to the inter-war chaos that had existed in international financial markets between 1918 and 1939. Prior to World War I, the world had avoided the need for a single currency by linking their currencies to gold, fixing the exchange rate between countries on the gold standard. Since currencies are no longer tied to any commodity, the gold standard would not be an alternative today.

Under peacetime and stable economic conditions, it is difficult to get countries to agree to substantial changes in their currencies. If there were a single world government, there would also be a single world currency, but a single world government is neither likely to occur, nor desirable. A global economic crisis might push the world toward changing the foreign exchange system, but this would be an awfully high price to pay for pushing the world toward currency unification.

What is unique about the current world economic and financial situation is that it is now possible to convert to a single currency for the United States and Europe, and the rest of the world. Several factors have caused both the political and economic costs of making the transition low enough that the introduction of a single currency is now a viable solution.

Several changes in recent years have made this possible. First, financial markets throughout the world have become increasingly integrated. Financial firms span the globe and international transactions increase annually. Over $1 trillion in foreign currency is traded on a daily basis. In a world that is brought closer together everyday through airplanes, telecommunications and the Internet, having almost 200 different currencies seems an absurd, inefficient anachronism.

In the United States, most legislation of the 1920s and 1930s, such as the Glass-Steagall Act or the McFadden Act, which were designed to keep financial firms limited in both their geographic and operational scope, have been repealed. Deposit banking is no longer completely separated from investment banking. Banks can offer deposits, insurance, security and real estate services in any state in the union. Nationwide universal banking will soon be possible in the United States.

Multinational corporations operate in numerous countries and the cost of monitoring operations in different countries, converting currencies, hedging currencies, and so forth has become substantial. Technology has made it possible for corporations to operate in every country in the world. Today, the economic cost of maintaining almost 200 national currencies exceeds the cost of converting to a single currency.

But the biggest problem in any major institutional change is how do you get from the old system (multiple currencies) to the new system (one currency) with a minimum of economic cost and disruption? The current system may not work, but how do you fix it?

The introduction of the Euro enables the world to make the first step toward a single currency for the United States and Europe. The Dollar and the Euro could be linked together to form a single currency at a 1:1 parity with each other. Linking the Dollar and the Euro would be a relatively simple step compared with creating the Euro out of the ten currencies that preceded it.

Now that we know how the world could move toward a single currency, we can look at the steps that would be taken to create a single currency for the United States, Europe and the rest of the world.

The Timetable for the Euro

The Euro will be introduced on January 1, 1999 in accordance with the Maastricht treaty. Participating countries will fix their domestic currencies to the Euro, and after that, their currencies will not be allowed to fluctuate against the Euro or against each other. Government financial transactions, such as issuing bonds, will take place in Euros, and most corporations will convert their accounts into Euros. The European Central Bank will begin running the monetary policy of the countries which are members of the Euro. Domestic central banks will give up their control over monetary policy. Initially, prices of goods will be quoted in both Euros and in the local currency. Only when local currencies are eliminated will all goods and services be priced in terms of the Euro.

The Euro, as a currency, will not be introduced until January 1, 2002. Individuals will have until July 1, 2002 to convert their domestic currency into Euros when domestic currencies will cease to have legal tender status. On July 1, 2002, the German Mark, French Franc, Italian Lira and other currencies will cease to exist.

Implicit in this transition is the cost to governments, corporations, financial markets and individuals of converting into a single currency. Already, governments and corporations are setting up the infrastructure for making the transition to a single currency successful. A financial change of this magnitude has never occurred before, and there is a learning curve to making the adjustment. This is why there is a three-year period between the introduction of the Euro and the elimination of domestic currencies.

Without the introduction of the Euro, the introduction of a Eurodollar would have been extremely difficult to achieve, if not impossible. The introduction of the Euro simplifies the transition to a Eurodollar in a number of ways. First, once the Euro has been introduced, it reduces the cost of joining Europe's currencies to the U.S. dollar because these currencies have already made the transition to a single currency. Second, it introduces the technology that is necessary to make the transition. This will lower the overall cost of converting into a single currency for a second time.

Third, the rough similarity in the value of the Euro and the Dollar means that the two currencies could be set at par to one another when the two currencies are linked together. One Euro will equal one U.S. dollar. Since one dollar is worth less than a Euro, this would put the United States at a disadvantage because it would automatically raise the prices of U.S. goods relative to European goods. Although this is an imperfect solution, it is probably the best one. The prices of most goods are changed several times over the course of a year. After the link is established, prices of goods will gradually adjust to insure that goods in the United States and Europe are priced similarly.

Finding a conversion rate other than 1:1 would probably produce so many costs, both in terms of converting prices to the new currency, and in terms of agreeing to a single exchange rate, that any other solution would be prevent a Eurodollar from ever being introduced. Even if the technology were available to make a non-par conversion, finding an exchange rate everyone could agree on could undermine the whole process. It is easier to require prices in Europe and the United States to gradually adjust to smooth out differences between American and European prices than to fix the currency at any rate other than par.

One potential barrier to the introduction of a Eurodollar would be the failure of the single currency in Europe; however, if the introduction of the Euro were seen as an intermediate step on the way to a single currency for both the United States and Europe, this fact would strengthen the Euro and help to guarantee its success.

The reason for making the change to a single currency now is that there is momentum to move to a single currency, the technology of doing so is readily available, and the transition to a single currency can be made at a small cost once Europe has a single currency.

A Timetable for a Eurodollar

While Europe is going through the process of introducing the single currency between 1999 and 2002, preparations can be made for the next step in this process, introducing a single currency for the United States and Europe.

There will be a number of differences between the transition to a single currency for Europe and for a Eurodollar. The Maastricht treaty established convergence criteria which countries had to meet in order to join the Euro. The convergence criteria were introduced both to harmonize economic policies before the Euro was born, and to keep inflationary countries out of the Euro. Participation was limited to countries whose inflation rates and government bond interest rates were close to the average for the rest of Europe, which had a government deficit which did not exceed 3% of GDP, and which had a government debt/GDP ratio below 60% or moving toward 60. The first criterion was not a problem, countries adjusted their expenditures and taxes to meet the 3% rule on time, and the 60% rule was basically ignored since only Luxembourg met this requirement of the eleven countries which will form the Euro.

In the case of a Eurodollar, the monetary policies of the Federal Reserve and the European Central Bank would make the convergence criteria unnecessary. Instead, the focus would be on forming the institutions and means to introduce the single currency. All countries that are currently members of the Euro will be grandfathered into the Eurodollar. Britain, Sweden and Denmark, which opted out of the Euro, would probably join the Eurodollar. The only other countries that might be among the founding members would be Canada and Switzerland. A conversion of 1.5 Canadian Dollars or Swiss Francs to the Eurodollar could be used.

Provision would also have to be made for countries outside of the Eurodollar bloc to make the Eurodollar their legal tender currency. Several countries, such as Argentina and the Bahamas, tie their currency to the dollar at par, and the CFA Franc bloc ties their currency to the French Franc at a 100:1 ratio. These countries would probably want to join a Eurodollar bloc, rather than simply remain linked to the Eurodollar. The process for adding new members to the Eurodollar will be discussed below.

Timetable for Transition to a Eurodollar

Since Europe will not introduce its single currency for everyday transactions until 2002, it would be impossible to introduce the Eurodollar before that time. Moreover, time would be required to lay the foundations for the institutions that would administer the monetary policy of the Eurodollar. The Eurodollar could only be introduced once the Euro had replaced domestic currencies. Once this was done, the transition to a single currency for Europe and the United States would follow in three steps.

The earliest date which the Euro and the Dollar could be linked together at a 1:1 ratio would be January 1, 2003, and linking the two may not even take place then, but it is certainly a feasible goal. Although the Euro and dollar would be linked to one another at this point, the initial goal would be to establish the Eurodollar as a single currency, rather than to eliminate the Euro and the dollar altogether. Time would be needed to gain confidence in the new currency, and establish the single currency as a credible replacement for the Euro and the dollar. The Dollar and the Euro could be made legal tender on both sides of the Atlantic.

The other change which would occur on January 1, 2003 would be that the Federal Reserve Bank and the European Central Bank would begin cooperating with one another and would lay the foundations for the Global Reserve Bank which would replace them. The Fed and the ECB, however, would continue to run monetary policy among their member countries.

Similar ties would be established between other government agencies in the United States and Europe, which oversee financial markets and would be affected by the introduction of the single currency. The SEC, which oversees security markets, the FDIC, which provides deposit insurance, and the Comptroller of the Currency, which supervises national banks, would link up with their sister agencies in Europe to make the transition to a single currency.

Corporations could begin preparing for operating their financial accounts in a single currency. Their job would be relatively easy. Having made the transition from eleven European currencies into one, making the transition from two currencies into one would seem relatively simple.

The Eurodollar could be established as the legal tender of all member countries two years later on January 1, 2005. The GRB would take control of monetary policy for member countries on this date, and the regional Federal Reserves in the United States and European central banks would henceforward carry out the policies of the Global Reserve Bank.

At this point, the new Eurodollar currency could be introduced which would replace the Dollar and the Euro. A new currency would not be necessary. Just as Scottish pounds are accepted in Britain, and vice versa, the United States and Europe could either introduce a new currency, or continue with their own versions of the Eurodollar.

The third step would begin after the Eurodollar and the Global Reserve Bank had been firmly established. In this phase, other countries would be allowed to join the Eurodollar bloc and use the Eurodollar as their legal tender currency. Every country that wanted to join the Eurodollar bloc would have to go through a two-year probationary period.

During this time period, the country would have to set up a currency board and fully back its currency with Eurodollars, as Hong Kong and Argentina do today. During this probationary period, the country would have to link its currency to the dollar and maintain that link. Second, it would have to allow the GRB and other agencies which oversaw the financial system in the United States and Europe to establish regulatory control over the financial institutions within its own country. Third, the country would have to agree to strict limitations on government deficits and other aspects of fiscal policy that could jeopardize participation in the Eurodollar bloc. If the country had managed to maintain a stable link to the Eurodollar for two years, and if it had met all the regulatory requirements of the Global Reserve Bank and its sister agencies, the country would be allowed to introduce the Eurodollar as its legal tender currency.

Non-members could be allowed to link their currency to the Eurodollar beginning on January 1, 2005 when the Eurodollar becomes legal tender in Europe and the United States. Countries would not be allowed to introduce the Eurodollar as their currency until January 1, 2007.

Inevitably, the benefits of a quick or a gradual transition to a single world currency will become a topic of debate, just as it was debated whether the former Communist countries of Eastern Europe should make a speedy or a gradual adjustment to capitalism after Communism fell. We believe that a speedy adjustment is the best choice. The reason for this is that once it is seen that the transition to a single currency is possible, momentum will build to move in that direction. If financial markets believe that a single currency for both the United States and Europe will work, the value of the Dollar and Euro will quickly move to parity even before the Eurodollar is introduced. Because the benefits of the Eurodollar are so large, once the Eurodollar has gained credibility, it could establish itself de facto even before it has established itself de jure.

Conclusion

For the first time since the world moved to a system of flexible exchange rates back in 1973, it is possible for financial markets to not only move back to a system of fixed exchange rates, but to a single currency for Europe, the United States, and possibly for the rest of the world. The Eurodollar would move beyond Bretton Woods and the Gold Standard by establishing a single currency rather than a system of fixed exchange rates as had existed before.

Conditions are ripe for this transition. The momentum to move toward a single currency exists, the technology for making this change has been introduced in Europe, American law now allows banks to operate across state lines and offer an array of financial services, and because of the rough parity between the Euro and the Dollar, the transition to a single currency for Europe and the United States could be made at a minimal cost.

The only condition that is lacking is the political will to make this change. As with the Euro in Europe, making the transition will require strong leadership in both the United States and in Europe to see through the transition to a single currency. At some point in the near future, people will see that the benefits of having a single currency far outweigh the costs, and people will begin to ask if we can afford not to have a single currency. At that point, the single currency will become a political and economic fait accompli, and a world that has almost 200 currencies will be seen as an inefficient anachronism.

If the rallying cry of the twentieth century was to be "Workers of the world, unite!" then the rallying call of the twenty-first century could be "Currencies of the world, unite!"

The Economic Benefits and Economic Costs of a Eurodollar

October 1998

Bryan Taylor II, Ph.D., President
Global Financial Data

The Economic Benefits and Economic Costs of a Eurodollar

In January 1999, members of the European Union will introduce a single currency, the Euro. In 2002, the Euro will replace national currencies, and each country's currency will cease to exist. It is our belief that within the next ten years the Euro should be merged with the Dollar to create a Eurodollar, which would act as a single currency for both the United States and in Europe, and eventually for other countries. These articles explore the impact of this transition to a single international currency.

The introduction to a single currency for the United States and Europe will produce both benefits and economic costs. This is true of any economic change. Any movement toward free trade between nations entails benefits to consumers who can now purchase foreign goods at lower prices and costs to producers who can no longer compete, or workers who lose their jobs when the company they work for can no longer compete. On average, however, the net economic benefits for society are positive. The same is true of a single currency. Although there are costs and benefits, the benefits will exceed the costs. The purpose of this article is to examine exactly what the costs and benefits of a single currency for the United States and Europe would be.

The first part of this article will look at optimum currency area theory that provides the economic justification for currency areas. It then analyzes whether the United States and Europe is an optimum currency area. The second part of the article looks the economic benefits, then the economic costs, of introducing a Eurodollar. Finally, the article analyzes the economic impact of introducing a single currency to the United States and Europe.

Optimum Currency Areas

The theory of having a single currency is known as optimum currency area theory, which was first elaborated by Robert Mundell back in the 1960s. Mundell analyzed the costs and benefits of having a single currency to determine under what circumstances a single currency between economic regions would be beneficial or harmful. Historically, the introduction of a single currency has had more to do with politics than with economics, and optimum currency area theory has attempted to put economics at the center of this issue. To solve this problem, Mundell asked what economic factors, rather than what political factors, make a single currency succeed. In short, why do countries have different currencies?

The benefit of different exchange rates is that they help a country adjust to asymmetric economic shocks. A sudden collapse in exports, inflation or other economic shocks can lead to a recession. One way out of the recession is to lower prices, which will increase demand for goods, but prices of labor and goods can increase more easily than they can fall. A decline in the value of the currency in effect lowers the price of all goods within the country enabling the country to become more competitive because it is easier to lower prices through the exchange rate than by getting everyone to agree to accept lower wages.

A single currency eliminates the ability of currencies to adjust prices between different economic regions. Consequently, adjustments must be made in some other way. Optimum currency area theory focuses on three adjustment mechanisms, which can act in lieu of currency devaluation to resolve economic problems.

First, labor must be mobile so workers can move from an area suffering from recession to one that is enjoying an economic boom. If labor cannot, or will not move, economic adjustment becomes more difficult. Even where there are no legal barriers to labor mobility, cultural and linguistic barriers may inhibit the movement of labor.

Second, wages and prices must be flexible in order that the economy can respond to changes in supply and demand. Third, there must be some way of transferring resources to the country or region which is in dire economic straits in order to help it recover from its recession The less often major economic shocks occur, the more successful the currency area will be.

As our review of the history of currencies shows, once a universal currency is introduced, it usually continued until severe economic or political pressures forced the elimination of the universal currency. Tsarist Russia had a single currency for all of Russia, but when Russia fell apart after World War I, each local government introduced its own currency until it was conquered by the Soviets. Once Russia was reunited under Soviet leadership, a single currency replaced the dozens of currencies that had existed between 1918 and 1923. When the Soviet Union broke up in 1991, each country within the CIS reintroduced their own currencies.

Economic and political regions are not necessarily the same. If there are large economic disparities within a country, it could theoretically benefit from having more than one currency. Italy is often used as an example. There are strong economic differences between southern and northern Italy and some economists have suggested that different currencies for the north and the south would be beneficial. If northern Italy were to secede from the south, they would immediately introduce their own currency, just as the constituent parts of Yugoslavia and the Soviet Union did once they gained their own political independence.

This example shows that politics has been just as important a factor as economics in determining currency areas. No government in modern times has willingly allowed different currencies to circulate within its borders. Governments may allow several entities with its borders to issue currency. Several Scottish banks are allowed to issue currency that is accepted as legal tender in England, but the Scottish pound complements the pound sterling rather than compete with it. Governments do not allow currency disunions within their borders, but they can pursue currency unions as has happened in Europe, and this is where the theory of optimum currency areas becomes useful. Now let's apply the optimum currency area theory to the United States and Europe.

Would the United States and Europe Be an Optimum Currency Area?

To answer this question, we will need to review each of the criteria for an optimum currency area.

With respect to labor mobility, the likelihood that labor would freely flow between the United States and Europe after a currency union is low. Many people have pointed to labor mobility as one reason why the United States has succeeded as an optimum currency area. In Europe, however, labor mobility within European countries, much less between European countries, is often very low.

Labor can move quickly from one region to another in the United States, though without perfect flexibility. In fact, labor mobility between Mexico and the United States is probably as great as it is between some European countries. This occurs despite the obvious legal, linguistic and cultural barriers to labor mobility between the United States and Mexico.

These facts alone do not condemn the United States and Europe as an optimum currency area. There are two ways in which the labor mobility problem can be solved. First, multinational corporations, which operate in several countries that share a single currency, can switch their operations to low cost regions, just as corporations have switched production from the northern states to the southern states in the U.S. Businesses can adjust rather than labor.

Second, the introduction of a single currency encourages labor mobility to a degree that might not exist prior to the introduction of a currency union. A single currency makes it easier for individuals and corporations to find jobs outside of their own region, and it increases their willingness to move from one region or country to another.

Wage and price flexibility is not one of the strong points of Europe's economies. How crucial this factor is remains debatable. The lack of wage and price flexibility has never prevented a country from having a single currency within its borders, nor should this factor, in and of itself, prevent a single currency for the United States and Europe. It would be difficult to show that the lack of wage and price flexibility has kept currency unions between French African countries, or between Belgium and Luxembourg, from succeeding.

If labor mobility and wage and price flexibility are lacking, these problems can be alleviated through fiscal transfers between different regions of the country or currency area. Even though a country may be unified politically, that does not mean that it is unified economically. Oklahoma may depend on oil, Kansas on agriculture, California on the Pacific Rim, Florida on Latin America and New York on Europe. The Federal government plays an important role within the United States because it can transfer resources between booming regions and those that are in a recession.

This is one of the concerns economists have expressed about the Euro. There is no mechanism in Europe similar to Federal government transfers in the United States to alleviate regional recessions. This fact would be equally true were Europe and the United States to have a single currency.

Whether the lack of fiscal transfers is sufficient to justify forgoing a single currency between the United States and Europe is debatable. Even if no fiscal mechanism for expenditures were set up, a loan facility, similar to the loan facility of the International Monetary Fund, could be set up to offset asymmetric shocks which would affect the United States or one of the European countries. The Fund could loan the country money on a temporary basis to help offset the economic shocks it is suffering.

Based upon these criteria, the United States and Europe probably do not qualify as an optimal currency area, according to Mundell's criteria. However, it is questionable whether Europe and French Africa, or even a country, such as Italy or India, meets these qualifications. Does this mean a single currency for the United States and Europe would not be beneficial?

The answer is the fact that the United States and Europe do not fully qualify as an optimum currency area, a Eurodollar could still work. Many countries that have a single currency within its borders would probably not qualify as optimum currency areas. No attempt has been made to break countries up into optimum currency areas because politics, rather than economics, is the primary driving force behind the determination of currency areas.

Whether the United States and Europe move on to a single currency will be determined by the net political and economic benefits that come from introducing a Eurodollar. To see whether a Eurodollar would succeed, we must analyze the costs and benefits of the new currency in more detail.

The Economic Benefits of a Eurodollar

Economics sees money as a public good. A public good is one from which everyone benefits without incurring any costs. Money acts as a medium of exchange, a store of value and a unit of account. If the government provides the coin of the realm, then society does not have to incur the costs of agreeing on a standard for carrying out economic activity. The greater the reach of the government's currency, the lower the cost of carrying out economic transactions.

Having a single currency for the United States makes economic transactions easier than having a different currency in every state of the union. This obvious fact has propelled Europe to introduce a single currency for the European Economic Community. By comparing the impact of a single currency for the United States and multiple currencies for Europe, we can see why a Eurodollar would be beneficial to the United States and Europe.

First, a single currency increases the transparency of prices. If you are in Europe, and you are trying to find the best price, you will have to compare prices in fourteen different currencies. Even when you find the lowest price, changes in the exchange rate, or the cost of converting to the other currency, could eliminate your cost advantage. These facts discourage people from using comparative shopping across international borders. Although individuals may not travel to different countries to compare prices, the Internet and mail order can be used to compare prices.

The inability to compare prices directly hurts corporations as well as individuals because multiple currencies limit the corporations' ability to sell goods in other countries. Corporations know that consumers may not want to compare prices in a dozen different currencies to find out which is the lowest, so they reduce their marketing efforts.

Compare this situation with the United States where the currency is the same whether goods are ordered from New Hampshire or from California. Prices can easily be compared, and corporations have an incentive to pursue customers across the country. Corporations would also benefit from a Eurodollar because it would make it easier for corporations to compare their own costs in different countries to determine which countries or which suppliers have the lowest production costs.

Second, a single currency reduces the transaction costs of buying and selling goods. Even if you find a better price for a good in another country, you still have to convert to that currency, and this will entail a cost. Anyone who has traveled through Europe can immediately recognize the benefit of having a single currency. Changing small amounts of currency can cost anywhere from 5-10% of the face value of the amount that is converted, and this cost is incurred every time a border is crossed. The Economist magazine once estimated that if you converted $1.00 into each of Europe's twelve currencies you would end up with about 50 cents once all the transaction costs were paid. With foreign exchange transactions totaling over $1 trillion every day, the introduction of a single currency would substantially reduce currency conversion costs, saving corporations billions of dollars.

These costs would be reduced in another way as well. Today, multinational corporations represent a substantial portion of the world's output. A major corporation might operate in ten, twenty, or even more countries. Managing revenues and costs in these different currencies, and consolidating these revenues in costs requires a substantial dedication of resources. With a single currency, the cost of managing revenues and costs would be reduced dramatically.

Third, a single currency would eliminate exchange rate risk among the countries that shared the currency. Foreign exchange risks are a major cost of multinational corporations, but they are willing to bear these costs because expanding the firm's operations internationally opens up new markets and enables the firm to diversify its operations. However, currency fluctuations can and have generated substantial losses and profits, for firms operating in different countries.

The solution to the problem of foreign exchange risk is to hedge this risk by using futures contracts, forward contracts, money market hedges, options, swaps and other hedging techniques. In practice, these techniques cannot fully hedge all foreign exchange risks, and hedging those risks can be expensive.

Sudden changes in exchange rates affect both individuals and corporations. When the Asian currencies collapsed in 1997, many students in America were forced to return home because they could no longer afford to live in the United States. Similarly, corporations can see sudden changes in their costs of producing goods, or in their competitors' costs which will suddenly make their goods uncompetitive through no efforts of their own. Years of efforts to reduce costs and remain competitive can be wiped out in a few months because of currency depreciation or appreciation. Having a single currency eliminates this foreign exchange risk as companies that operate exclusively in the United States already know.

The problem of facing a sudden change in the value of the currency is especially severe in countries where the government tries to control the exchange rate rather than leave its value to the supply and demand of the market. Governments prefer exchange rate stability because a depreciating currency is often seen as a sign of poor economic management, and because it can produce inflation or recession within the country. Large fluctuations in the value of the currency create uncertainty, which can reduce the amount of international trade and investment that occurs.

Smaller countries address this problem by pegging their currency to another currency, such as the U.S. dollar, French franc, German mark or other major currency. This only gives the country stability relative to the currency the country is linked to. If the dollar appreciates, or depreciates, so will a currency such as the Hong Kong Dollar relative to the rest of the world.

If the country has different inflation rates or monetary policy than the country they are pegged to, the real economy will be affected. Governments must use their currency reserves, their control over interest rates, or controls over international trade and capital flows to maintain the pegged exchange rate if the currency link comes under attack. Governments will postpone a currency devaluation until they no longer have a choice, usually denying that any devaluation will occur until hours before it actually takes place. If the peg cannot be maintained, there will be a sudden devaluation of the currency as occurred in Mexico in 1994 or in East Asia in 1997.

Fourth, when a currency union exists, countries can no longer use competitive devaluations as part of their economic policy. Competitive devaluations occur when countries deliberately devalue their currency in order to increase demand for their exports. Countries that do not devalue will see their exports fall as their goods become uncompetitive. Other countries are then tempted to devalue in response to the initial devaluation setting off a chain reaction.

This happened during the 1930s when countries went off the gold standard to boost their own economies. Eventually, every country had gone off the gold standard and devalued their currency so that each country ended up back where they had started. Similarly, when most East Asian countries' currencies devalued in 1997, but the currencies of Hong Kong and China did not, exports from Hong Kong and China became uncompetitive. A single currency would eliminate this problem.

Fifth, a single currency encourages competition because it becomes easier to compare prices. This will be one of the primary benefits of the introduction of the Euro to Europe. Individuals and firms can now compare costs in the same currency throughout continental Europe in order to buy goods at the lowest possible cost. Low cost producers will have the incentive to market their product to a wider market knowing that they can increase their customer base because of their superior prices. If someone sees that a bar of soap costs 4 French Francs in Paris and 30 Belgian Francs in Brussels, the price in Paris is lower, but this is not as obvious as if the price were 70 cents in Paris and 80 cents in

Brussels. Although no one would travel to Paris to buy the cheaper bar of soap, over time competition will lower the price in Brussels.

Sixth, because the Central Bank which oversees the currency union is not controlled by a single government, it will be easier for the Central Bank to focus on its primary objective-to control prices and fight inflation. Although the trend throughout the world is for greater Central Bank independence in order to achieve price stability, central banks remain under the indirect control of government. The government that created the central bank can change the bank's powers and independence whenever it wants. The ideal central bank is both independent and accountable. A supranational central bank could maintain its independence while remaining accountable to government oversight.

The currency union could work both in favor of and against the central bank. A supranational central bank would not be free from political influence. This problem can be seen in the compromise that occurred when the first president of the European Central Bank was appointed. Because of pressure from the French, the first ECB president was appointed to only a four-year, rather than an eight-year, term after which he will "voluntarily" resign. This compromise was reached because the French wanted greater political control over the European Central Bank, and the Germans wanted greater independence.

On the other hand, if the central bank fails to control inflation, countries can always opt out of the currency union and go back to having their own domestic central bank. This threat can place pressure on the central bank to follow a policy of price stabilization. Because of Germany's experience with hyperinflation in the 1920s, Germany has long had a fear of price instability, and they have been adamant that the primary goal of the European Central Bank should be price stability.

As this section has detailed, there are many economic benefits to introducing a single currency because a single currency makes it easier to carry out economic transactions. This is the basic reason why money replaced barter as the basis for exchange several millennia ago, and it is also the reason why historically the world has moved toward a single currency whenever this move was politically feasible. Nevertheless, there are drawbacks to having a single currency, and these will be discussed in the next section.

The Economic Costs of a Eurodollar

Although there are many economic benefits from a single currency, there are also costs. The primary benefits of a single currency are microeconomic. The single currency enables individuals and businesses to carry out economic transactions more efficiently. There are also macroeconomic benefits from having a single currency. A single currency encourages international trade, and reduces the disruptions that result from currency fluctuations.

On the other hand, most of the costs of having a single currency are macroeconomic or political. The macroeconomic costs of exchange rates occur because a devaluation affects the price of all internationally traded goods, producing nationwide effects whenever the currency changes its value. Since large economic changes can affect elections, there are potential political costs as well.

Governments benefit from having a single currency within their own borders. The currency gives the government greater control over the economy, but if the country joins a currency union, it loses this control. The country becomes part of a currency union over which they have no control producing a loss of political and economic power. If the currency the country shares a currency that collapses, politicians must bear the cost, even if they had no control over the collapse of the currency. So currency union provides microeconomic benefits, but macroeconomic and political costs. This is why there is a strong correlation between political boundaries and currency areas. Let's analyze what the costs of a single currency would be.

First, a single currency forces a country to forgo an independent monetary policy. After the currency union begins, the country's monetary policy is determined by the supranational central bank and not by the domestic central bank. Though this produces a loss of economic sovereignty, some might argue that this could prove beneficial because having a central bank that is independent of ill-advised political influence can increase the effectiveness of monetary policy. If a nation is part of a currency union, the central bank cannot tailor its monetary policies to target that nation. On the other hand, if a national economy is growing too rapidly, or if it is in a recession, the central bank's ability to change the money supply or interest rates to reduce the severity of the recession or to restrain inflation is reduced.

If the United States consisted of 50 separate countries, each with its own central bank, and if Texas was in a slump while California was booming, the central bank of each state could change interest rates and the money supply to produce the appropriate solution. Since the United States has a common currency, regional monetary adjustments cannot be made. Instead, the United States would have to turn to fiscal policy to redress this problem.

This is why the theory of optimal currency areas emphasizes the importance of flexible prices, labor mobility and fiscal transfers. When monetary and exchange rate policy cannot adjust to differences in the economic activity between regions, prices, labor and fiscal policy must make the adjustments for them.

On the other hand, because flexible prices and labor mobility become more important when a currency union exists, governments have more incentive to make markets work more efficiently because governments can no longer rely on monetary policy to smooth out fluctuations in the business cycle. When a currency union is introduced, the cost of putting up structural barriers in labor and consumer markets becomes even costlier. The incentives to encourage competition can be one of the unintended consequences of a currency union.

A second effect of the currency union is that there will be less regional differentiation. The economy of a region of the country that is dependent on farm goods passes through its economic cycles at different times than a regional economy that depends on oil or on financial services. Different currencies would allow these regions more freedom to time their asynchronous business cycles through changes in the exchange rate.

Because prices are similar throughout the currency union, and because a single currency favors economies of scale, economic homogenization will result from the currency union. Interest rates and prices will be similar throughout most of the currency area. The Federal Reserve in the United States cannot lower interest rates in one part of the United States which is in a recession while simultaneously raising interest rates in another part of the country which is booming. Similarly, traded goods have roughly the same prices throughout the United States. Only goods such as real estate, which cannot be traded, will vary substantially in price from one part of the country to the other.

This example shows the primary benefit of having exchange rates for different economic regions. When there are different currencies, exchange rates can supplant other forms of economic adjustments. It is much easier to devalue the currency than to lower everyone's wages in order to make a country more competitive and increase exports. A single currency also removes the central bank's ability to use the exchange rate to influence the business cycle.

There are also political costs to a currency area. Electoral success and political support depend upon a strong economy. If the economy is facing a problem of unemployment, inflation or a recession, the government is expected to do something. If the government loses its monetary policy tool, politicians are limited to using fiscal policy to influence the macroeconomy.

In short, the primary costs of a single currency are macroeconomic and political. The government can use exchange rates and interest rates in order to influence the behavior of the economy, but the introduction of a single currency removes these economic tools. Clearly, a single currency has both costs and benefits, but the primary question is, do the overall benefits of a single currency exceed the costs?

The Economics of a Single Currency

To repeat, the primary benefits of a single currency are microeconomic. The existence of a single currency forces firms to be more price competitive, transaction costs are reduced, future prices can be set in a single currency without worrying about exchange rate fluctuations, and there can be greater price stability. The primary costs of a single currency are macroeconomic. There is a loss of independent monetary policy, exchange rates and interest rates can no longer be used to influence the business cycle, and economic regional differentiation is reduced. How would these costs and benefits apply to a currency union between the United States and Europe?

The primary question is whether a single currency for the United States and Europe would be more efficient than multiple currencies. It could very well be that a single currency would work for the United States, but not for the Untied States and Europe. Or it could be that Europe would benefit from a currency union at the expense of the United States, or vice versa.

Historically, the primary factor determining the existence of currency areas has been political boundaries rather than regional economic integration. There are several countries, such as Italy and China, which have diverse regional economies, but which share a single currency for political, rather than economic, reasons. Is the national economy worse off because its regional economies share a single currency? Would the United States, China and India be better off with one currency or with several currencies?

In both India and China (as well as Italy, Germany and other national economies), it is questionable whether multiple currencies would have improved national economic performance. Political chaos between the wars in China, or socialistic, inward-looking policies in India and China after the war had more to do with these countries' lack of economic growth than the imposition of a single currency. Although some economists have argued that northern and southern Italy would benefit from separate currencies, there is no evidence that southern Italy would be better off today if it had a separate currency from the north.

In fact, one could argue that national currencies are a cost imposed upon economies by governments in order to maintain their power. It would be difficult to argue that the former Soviet Union is better off with 15 currencies in 1998 than with one currency in 1988. A Commonwealth of Independent States central bank that was independent of political influence would have reduced the monetary chaos that has persisted in some former Soviet republics since the Soviet Union was dissolved. Removing the government's control over the currency, as has been done in Estonia, reduces the government's influence over the economy, and in the long run this can be beneficial.

For this reason, many economists question how much the government, or even central banks, should control interest rates and exchange rates to influence the economy. In contrast to some Keynesian economists who feel that losing control over monetary policy would be a cost to society, some neoclassical economists question the wisdom of using activist monetary policy to influence the business cycle. If a single currency were introduced for the United States and Europe, political influence over monetary policy would be reduced, and the influence of financial markets would increase. Some economists would see this as a beneficial result of a single currency in and of itself.

Supporters of a universal currency could argue that a government that wants to control its currency will also want to control other parts of its economy. It is no coincidence that Argentina gave up control over its currency by linking the Peso to the Dollar at the same time that Argentina began liberalizing and privatizing its economy, reducing the government's influence over the entire economy. Argentina made this change because the military had controlled both society and the economy in stifling detail and ended up mismanaging both.

But what about a currency union for the United States and Europe? It is impossible to know the exact economic (much less social or political) impact of introducing a single currency. Most historical evidence provides information only on currencies within a country's borders, though some multinational currency unions, such as the Latin Union in the 1800s and the CFA Franc in Africa today have met with success. Yet, there is little evidence that the costs of a currency union have exceeded the benefits. It would seem absurd for the United States to introduce different currencies in each of its fifty states.

Some would argue that main the difference between a currency union for the United States and a currency union for the United States and Europe would be the inability to use fiscal transfers to offset asynchronous regional economic cycles between the United States and Europe. However, no fiscal transfer mechanism existed in nineteenth century America to alleviate regional economic differences, yet a single currency succeeded. The only examples in United States history of multiple currencies are colonial times when separate currencies existed or each colony (the Massachusetts Shilling differed in value form the Pennsylvania Shilling) and during the civil war. But there is little evidence that the United States was better off with multiple currencies than with one currency.

Most of the costs of a single currency would occur in making the adjustment from having multiple currencies into having a single currency, as Europe has discovered in the past few years. There is little if any evidence that, barring a major political or economic crisis, such as the outbreak of World War I, once a single currency has been established within a national or international region, there would be any tendency to move back to a system of multiple exchange rates.

This provides some evidence that the microeconomic benefits of a single currency probably exceed the macroeconomic costs, and that the United States and Europe would benefit from sharing a single currency. Political, and not economic costs, have been the primary barrier to introducing a single multinational currency. This is as true of Europe in the 1990s as it will be in the United States and Europe in the 2000s.

Moreover, having a single international currency could spur economic reform in other areas of the economy, and would further improve economic trade and growth. In Europe, the determination with which governments have committed themselves to encouraging the free inter-EEC movement of labor, capital and goods, as well as introducing a single currency, has been in sharp contrast with their determination to maintain many of the domestic structural barriers that exist in domestic labor, agricultural and import markets. The preoccupation with Europe-wide market reforms may have enabled European governments to avoid making many of the structural reforms which are currently needed.

Another benefit is that the introduction of a single currency would give individuals and corporations greater economic choice. The single currency would encourage trade which could in turn place pressure on governments to reduce the barriers to trade which exist between countries, and force governments to reduce structural barriers to trade within their own borders. Multiple currencies and trade barriers can help domestic companies to maintain their market power, but as these barriers fall, these companies' market power will be reduced, enhancing competition. The market reforms that will inevitably follow from the introduction of a single currency should be included in the list of benefits that a Eurodollar would provide.

Conclusion

It is impossible to fully measure the impact of introducing a single currency for Europe and the United States. Monumental structural changes will often lead to results that were unexpected because no one is capable of thinking through the ripple effects of a change of this nature. The currency reform would inevitably lead to structural, market and trade reforms as well as introducing financial and economic change. Although there would be costs in the process of change, over the long run, the economic and political benefits of a single currency clearly exceed the costs.

This article has looked at the economic aspects of introducing a single currency for the United States and Europe. An analysis of the political and financial aspects of this change is provided in other articles in this series. The final article provides a timetable that explains how the adjustment to a single currency for the United State and Europe can be made.

35. How will the E.C.U. be utilized by the Soviet Union to rebuild their economy and maintain their military buildup?

In November 1990, President Gorbachev devalued the Russian ruble and sold 22 billion in gold bullion. The value is now 1/10th its prior vale. The tying of the ruble to the E.C.U. is essential to Soviet economic rejuvenation and continued military expenditures. This is the next great economic event to happen between the E.C. and the U.S.S.R. With Soviet citizens the greatest 'savers' on earth, with no products to spend it on and no banking system, this will bring tremendous wealth to Soviet peoples, quell revolution, and continue to supply capital for exponential military buildup. Mr. Grant Jeffrey documents in his latest book, Messiah: "War in the Middle East and the Road to Armageddon", the Soviets have numerical superiority in every class of military hardware and men, to the U.S.A. and allies.

Table 35-1

WEAPON TYPE	RUSSIA OUTSPENDS THE U.S.A.
Submarine Launched ICBMs	3.5 to 1
Battle Tanks	3.8 to 1
Surface-to-Air Missiles	6.4 to 1
Self-propelled artillery	8.6 to 1

Russia has deployed the new Topol-M missiles that can be moved on a flatbed trailer and targeted with a single 50 megaton warhead. It is mobile enough to park in your driveway. Russia has built a Typhoon Class nuclear submarine that is much bigger and quieter that our nuclear submarines and can carry many more missiles. They claim that they are untraceable. They have continued to build at a rate of roughly one new submarine every seven weeks.

The lastest version of the Russian Sukoy combat jet is far superior, in the latest airshows, to any of our latest tactical fighter jets. Numerical superiority in their army divisions, navy ships, ICBMs, submarines, fighter and bomber aircraft, etc. raise a serious doubt as to whether the United States could indeed prevent a Russian lead alliance from takeover of the Middle East, especially with a neutralized or openly co-operative Europe.

The Beast Dictator - Russian Ruler

36. **How will the nations attack Israel in the End Times and when will this occur?**

A Prophecy Against Gog

Ezekiel 38:1- 23

1 And the word of the LORD came unto me, saying,

2 Son of man, set thy face against Gog, the land of Magog **[Russia of Moscow and Tubolsk],** *the chief prince of Meshech and Tubal, and prophesy against him,*

3 And say, Thus saith the Lord GOD; Behold, I [am] against thee, O Gog, the chief prince of Meshech and Tubal: . **[leader of Russia]**

4 And I will turn thee back, and put hooks into thy jaws, and I will bring thee forth, and all thine army, horses and horsemen, all of them clothed with all sorts [of armour, even] a great company [with] bucklers and shields, all of them handling swords: **[The Assyrian Empire put a hook in the lower lip or tongue of its captives. It will draw the Russians and all their allies down on the Mideast oil, captive to it for military and industrial development.]**

5 Persia **[Iran, Iraq, and Afganistan]**, *Ethiopia, and Libya* **[Ethiopia and Libya]** *with them; all of them with shield and helmet:*

6 Gomer **[Germany, Austria, Hungary, Czechoslovakia]**, *and all his bands; the house of Togarmah of the north quarters* **[Latvia, Lithuania, Estonia, Byelorussia]** *from, and all his bands: [and] many people with thee.* **[Many allies with Russia, including many Islamic allies]**

7 Be thou prepared, and prepare for thyself, thou, and all thy company that are assembled unto thee, and be thou a guard unto them. **[Russia will have the chief chain of military command in this invasion.]**

8 After many days thou shalt be visited: in the latter years thou shalt come into the land [that is] brought back from the sword, [and is] gathered out of many people, against the mountains of Israel **[The second and final exodus will have occurred and all Jews who will be led by circumstance or the Holy Spirit, will return to the land of Israel following several wars with its neighbours.]**, *which have been always waste: but it is brought forth out of the nations, and they shall dwell safely all of them. .* **[The peace that will be present at the time of the attack will be a false peace, sealed by a peace treaty sponsored by the New World Order goverment.]**

9 Thou shalt ascend and come like a storm, thou shalt be like a cloud to cover the land, thou, and all thy bands, and many people with thee.

10 Thus saith the Lord GOD; It shall also come to pass, [that] at the same time shall things come into thy mind, and thou shalt think an evil thought:

11 And thou shalt say, I will go up to the land of unwalled villages; I will go to them that are at rest, that dwell safely, all of them dwelling without walls, and having neither bars nor gates,

12 To take a spoil, and to take a prey; to turn thine hand upon the desolate places [that are now] inhabited, and upon the people [that are] gathered out of the nations, which have gotten cattle and goods, that dwell in the midst of the land.

13 Sheba, and Dedan, and the merchants of Tarshish, **[Yemen, Jordan, and Spain; representing the Oil Producing Mideast and European Nations]**, *with all the young lions thereof, shall say unto thee, Art thou come to take a spoil? hast thou gathered thy company to take a prey? to carry away silver and gold, to take away cattle and goods, to take a great spoil?*

14 Therefore, son of man, prophesy and say unto Gog, Thus saith the Lord GOD; In that day when my people of Israel dwelleth safely, shalt thou not know [it]?

15 And thou shalt come from thy place out of the north parts **[Moscow is directly North of Jerusalem]**, *thou, and many people with thee, all of them riding upon horses, a great company, and a mighty army:*

16 And thou shalt come up against my people of Israel, as a cloud to cover the land **[A vast multinational invasion force will be lead by Russia in the Last Days.]**; *it shall be in the latter days, and I will bring thee against my land, that the heathen may know me, when I shall be sanctified in thee, O Gog, before their eyes.* **[Jesus will return for the Second and last time, to reward the righteous in Christ Jesus, and to judge the wicked at this time.]**

17 Thus saith the Lord GOD; [Art] thou he of whom I have spoken in old time by my servants the prophets of Israel, which prophesied in those days [many] years that I would bring thee against them?

[Are you not the Beast dictator or Antichrist spoken of by all the Prophets?]

18 And it shall come to pass at the same time when Gog shall come against the land of Israel, saith the Lord GOD, [that] my fury shall come up in my face.

19 For in my jealousy [and] in the fire of my wrath have I spoken, Surely in that day there shall be a great shaking in the land of Israel; **[This will be the time of the Great Earth Upheaval at the day of the Lord.]**

20 So that the fishes of the sea, and the fowls of the heaven, and the beasts of the field, and all creeping things that creep upon the earth, and all the men that [are] upon the face of the earth, shall shake at my presence and the mountains shall be thrown down, and the steep places shall fall, **[This will be the greatest earthquake in Man's History on Earth, and will affect every living creature on the planet.]**, *and every wall shall fall to the ground.* **[Every mountain will crumble on earth and every building on earth will fall down.]**

21 And I will call for a sword against him throughout all my mountains, saith the Lord GOD: every man's sword shall be against his brother.

22 And I will plead against him with pestilence and with blood; and I will rain upon him, and upon his bands, and upon the many people that [are] with him, an overflowing rain, and great hailstones, fire, and brimstone. **[Radioactive rain will fall on his troops and these nations.]**

23 Thus will I magnify myself, and sanctify myself; and I will be known in the eyes of many nations, and they shall know that I [am] the LORD. **[This is the world-wide, visible to every eye, return of the King of Kings and Lord of Lords in Judgment.]**

Ezekiel 39:1- 29

1 Therefore, thou son of man, prophesy against Gog, and say, Thus saith the Lord GOD; Behold, I [am] against thee, O Gog, the chief prince of Meshech and Tubal:

2 And I will turn thee back, and leave but the sixth part of thee, and will cause thee to come up from the north parts, and will bring thee upon the mountains of Israel:

3 And I will smite thy bow out of thy left hand, and will cause thine arrows to fall out of thy right hand. **[When Russia leads many nations, God will destroy them utterly, war machines and the many nations will assemble against Israel.]**

4 Thou shalt fall upon the mountains of Israel, thou, and all thy bands, and the people that [is] with thee: I will give thee unto the ravenous birds of every sort, and [to] the beasts of the field to be devoured.

5 Thou shalt fall upon the open field **[Thermonuclear incineration in the battlefield of Armageddon!]:** *for I have spoken [it], saith the Lord GOD.*

6 And I will send a fire on Magog, and among them that dwell carelessly in the isles **[You will be destroyed by a nuclear attack and fall in the open field of battle.]***: and they shall know that I [am] the LORD.* **[Long range ICBMs will strike Russia and and its allies and the continental North America and all its allies.]**

7 So will I make my holy name known in the midst of my people Israel; and I will not [let them] pollute my holy name any more: and the heathen shall know that I [am] the LORD, the Holy One in Israel. **[All the nations of the world will know that I, Jesus, will return in Judgment and Mercy.]**

8 Behold, it is come, and it is done, saith the Lord GOD; this [is] the day whereof I have spoken. . **[This is the Day of Judgment or Rosh Ha Shanah, The Day of the Eternal, the Day of the Lord, The Day of the Almighty!]**

9 And they that dwell in the cities of Israel shall go forth **[Under the divine protection of the Lord, the saved, both Believing Jews and Gentiles will survive and live in the land of Israel.]**, *and shall set on fire and burn the weapons, both the shields and* *the bucklers, the bows and the arrows, and the handstaves, and the spears, and they shall burn them with fire seven years:*

10 So that they shall take no wood out of the field, neither cut down [any] out of the forests; for they shall burn the weapons with fire: and they shall spoil those that spoiled them, and rob those that robbed them, saith the Lord GOD.

11 And it shall come to pass in that day, [that] I will give unto Gog a place there of graves in Israel, the valley of the passengers on the east of the sea: and it shall stop the [noses] of the passengers: and there shall they bury Gog and all his multitude: and they shall call [it] The valley of Hamongog. **[The saints will not be able to travel east from Haifa through the Valley of Meggido but will be blocked by the radioactive fallout of the nuclear attack on the many armies buried there.]**

12 And seven months shall the house of Israel be burying of them, that they may cleanse the land.

13 Yea, all the people of the land shall bury [them]; and it shall be to them a renown the day that I shall be glorified, saith the Lord GOD.

14 And they shall sever out men of continual employment, passing through the land to bury with the passengers those that remain upon the face of the earth, to cleanse it: after the end of seven months shall they search.

15 And the passengers [that] pass through the land, when [any] seeth a man's bone, then shall he set up a sign by it, till the buriers have buried it in the valley of Hamongog.

16 And also the name of the city [shall be] Hamonah. **[There will be those employed to cleanse the land of the radioactive bones left after the nuclear attack against the armies that fall at the battles of Armageddon. After seven literal months, there will be those who go throughout the land and detect the radioactive dead's bones. Others will be employed to bury**

these bones in the Valley of Harmon Gog.] *Thus shall they cleanse the land.*

17 And, thou son of man, thus saith the Lord GOD; Speak unto every feathered fowl, and to every beast of the field, Assemble yourselves, and come; gather yourselves on every side to my sacrifice that I do sacrifice for you, [even] a great sacrifice upon the mountains of Israel, that ye may eat flesh, and drink blood.

18 Ye shall eat the flesh of the mighty, and drink the blood of the princes of the earth, of rams, of lambs, and of goats, of bullocks, all of them fatlings of Bashan.

19 And ye shall eat fat till ye be full, and drink blood till ye be drunken, of my sacrifice which I have sacrificed for you.

20 Thus ye shall be filled at my table with horses and chariots, with mighty men, and with all men of war, saith the Lord GOD. **[The Lord is in control. He will bring the armies together for the battle of Armageddon, and there in North Israel, will destroy these invading armies. The wild animals will eat their flesh as beasts of carrion.]**

21 And I will set my glory among the heathen, and all the heathen shall see my judgment that I have executed, and my hand that I have laid upon them.

22 So the house of Israel shall know that I [am] the LORD their God from that day and forward. **[Jesus will fight the battle for Israel. All the nations will know that the Lord has defended the House of Israel.]**

23 And the heathen shall know that the house of Israel went into captivity for their iniquity: because they trespassed against me, therefore hid I my face from them, and gave them into the hand of their enemies: so fell they all by the sword. **[Israel went into exile because they sinned against the Lord.]**

24 According to their uncleanness and according to their transgressions have I done unto them, and hid my face from them.

25 Therefore thus saith the Lord GOD; Now will I bring again the captivity of Jacob, and have mercy upon the whole house of Israel, and will be jealous for my holy name;

26 After that they have borne their shame, and all their trespasses whereby they have trespassed against me, when they dwelt safely in their land, and none made [them] afraid.

27 When I have brought them again from the people, and gathered them out of their enemies' lands, and am sanctified in them in the sight of many nations; **[The Lord will bring back all the people of Israel with the second Exodus.]**

28 Then shall they know that I [am] the LORD their God, which caused them to be led into captivity among the heathen: but I have gathered them unto their own land, and have left none of them any more there. **[The day that Jesus will return will be one of the seven Memorial Feasts given in Lev 22. The former 'rain', represented by the First Coming, fulfilled the first four feast of the Spring. The latter 'rain', will be fulfilled by the Second Coming. This will be fulfilled by the Three Feasts of Trumpets, Atonement, and Tabernacles. Jesus will return on the first of these, the Feast of Trumpets. All the Saved Jews and Christians will be brought into the Land of Israel and will dwell safely in the land forever!]**

29 Neither will I hide my face any more from them: for I have poured out my spirit upon the house of Israel, saith the Lord GOD. **[At that time the nations of the world will know Jesus is the Lord their God. Jesus will not hide His face from the Jews, for He will pour out his Spirit on Believing Jews and Gentiles to reconcile the two divisions of His body. By this means He will unseal the words of all the prophets for the end of the Age.]**

A Prophecy Against Gog

The War of Gog and Magog and the War of Armageddon are the same battle. The invasion of Israel by Russia and allies is the same war as that of the battle of the end of the Age, and the War of Gog and Magog (Gog and Magog refers to Russia). <u>God is a God of order, simplicity and understanding, not disorder and confusion.</u> According to Ezekiel, Russia will be both military arms supplier and leader of the invasion force against the Northern Territories of Israel. **[see Q. #37 for the list of nation allied with Russia]** They will descend like a cloud upon the nation of Israel.

Exactly three and a half years after the peace treaty between the Beast of the New World Government and Israel, it will be broken. As all three battles are one, the leader of this New World Government will be the leader of Russia. **[Jewish calendar year of 360 days]** Daniel 9:27, prophesies the Beast breaking this treaty, midway through the last seven years, the time of Jacob's Trouble. Peace will be only apparent but not real. Jews and Arabs will be forced into a compromise agreement that neither will accept in their hearts. This Treaty and the dedication of the tabernacle to occur on the Feast of Tabernacles will signal the first day of the last seven years.

Every previous tabernacle or temple was dedicated on the Feast of Tabernacles.

In line with the New World Order Timetable, the former U.S.S.R. and the U.S.A. have sponsored conjoint peace negotiations between Israel and all of its Arab neighbours. Both sides have been forced to the negotiating table. Managing the U.S. side of these first stages is the very capable James Baker, a member of the New World Order organization, the C.F.R. or Council on Foreign Relations. Gorbachev and Yeltsin, his old colleague and political 'nemesis', both use New World Order terminology in their Perestroika and post coup rhetoric. Its is very evident that they are all illuminated masons, both in their goals and methods.

Prophecy tells us that when this false peace is proclaimed, the Antichrist will take over the world and herald seven terrible years of tribulation. The first half will be a false peace and prosperity and the second will be 666, the first six seals, trumpets and vials of the wrath of Satan.

1 Thessalonians 5:1-7

1 But of the times and the seasons, brethren, ye have no need that I write unto you.

2 For yourselves know perfectly that the day of the Lord so cometh as a thief in the night. **[It will come upon those who do not watch as a thief, but not to Christians who are present at the unsealing of Revelation and the book of Daniel.]**

3 For when they shall say, Peace and safety; then sudden destruction cometh upon them, as travail upon a woman with child; and they shall not escape. **[The false peace of the New World Order will be signalled to the world by the false Arab-Israeli Peace Treaty. Those who accept this false peace will be under judgment and they will be destroyed by a series of terrible disasters to afflict the earth, which occur more and more terrible and frequent until Jesus returns for the second, and last time, for Believing Jews and Gentiles, his church.]**

4 But ye, brethren, are not in darkness, that that day should overtake you as a thief.

5 Ye are all the children of light, and the children of the day: we are not of the night, nor of darkness. **[Believers are enlightened by the Holy Spirit in prophetic unsealing of the Word, the Bible. His people will show the way at the time of the End, by the annointed prophets of God for this season, measured against the Word and tested in prayer.]**

6 Therefore let us not sleep, as [do] others; but let us watch and be sober.

7 For they that sleep sleep in the night; and they that be drunken are drunken in the night.

Jacque Delore, President of the European Parliament has stated in 1990, to the media, "There is no European Community without stability in the Middle East. Without stability, there is not secure oil supply to Europe." Oil is the lifeblood of the United States of Europe. The baited reckless moves of the dictator Saddam Hussein, on August 2nd, 1990, proved the absolute necessity of an Arab-Israeli Peace Treaty to the existence of a United European Empire. The New World Order has a serious stake in securing such a peace to allow the greatness of this empire to rise to world dominance.

The West is dependent on Middle Eastern oil. The U.S.A. obtains only 7 percent of its oil from the Middle East. Canada imports an even smaller proportion than the United States. Japan has been currently estimated to import 73 percent plus from the Mideast, and for this reason, has undertaken to build the world's most extensive network of breader reactors to produce energy, in world history. Europe's imports are close behind with about two thirds of its requirements fulfilled with Mideast crude. Although Britain has its own reserves, it has had to share them with the other E.C. members, and is therefore also dependant on oil from here as well.

Israel is the only element in the equation preventing a Russian sponsored Arab oil dictatorship.

Ezekiel 38:11-13

11 And thou shalt say, I will go up to the land of unwalled villages; I will go to them that are at rest, that dwell safely, all of them dwelling without walls, and having neither bars nor gates, **[This is the United States, the Unwalled Nation of Spiritual Israel. The attack will occur after a peace treaty with the New World Order and the nation of Israel.]**

12 To take a spoil, and to take a prey; to turn thine hand upon the desolate places [that are now] inhabited, and upon the people [that are] gathered out of the nations, which have gotten cattle and goods, that dwell in the midst of the land. **[When the Second Exodus has occurred, and all the people have returned to Israel, then Russia and allies within the New World Order will turn to attack America, the only obstruction to Russian world domination.]**

13 Sheba, and Dedan, and the merchants of Tarshish, with all the young lions thereof, shall say unto thee, Art thou come to take a spoil? hast thou gathered thy company to take a prey? to carry away silver and gold, to take away cattle and goods, to take a great spoil? **[Saudi Arabia, and the other Arab Oil Kingdoms, Jordan and Spain (representing the European Community), will all diplomatically protest the Russian sponsored invasion of America. They will question the motives, and ask if it is Russian imperial control of the World Oil Reserves that is its motivation.]**

The Russian leader will believe at the Time of the End that he must destroy Israel to seize control of the world via control of the world's oil reserves. The Arab oil sheikdoms, Europe and the West will make idle accusations only and will have no stomach for military retaliation. Russia will believe that hatred of the Jews will stir the West to abandon them to Russian sponsored Islamic annihilation. The "War of Gog and Magog" will bring Russia down upon Israel, enslaved in its need for oil, as surely as the ancient Assyrians put hooks in the jaws of their captives. The empire that will result will be the last **Empire of Clay and Iron**. Oil and manufacturing capacity will be as **Clay** to build a New World Industrial revolution. This program of building a sustainable world will be enforced with the **Iron** of military force and the one world electronic currency through the Mark of the Beast Empire, placed on the forehead and right hand with a bar code.

The last seven years of history are divided into 84 months of 30 days each according to the Jewish Calendar. The false Arab-Israeli Peace, sealed by the leader of the New World Order, Russia, will start the last seven years on the Feast of Tabernacles. Only through this Peace could the Jewish dream of the Temple Sacrifice occur again, initiated on the same day as the First and Second Jewish Temples. Most Jews find the idea of a Jewish Temple co-habiting the Temple mount with a Pagan shrine that is built where the Temple has always been placed since it took up permanent residence during the reign of King David.

Daniel prophesied the breaking of this Islamic/Palestinian-Israeli Peace Treaty will occur at exactly halfway through the 42 month term of its duration. The prophet's words in Revelation are clear that Believers, both Jew and Gentile will prophesy of this time of terrible tribulation for 1,260 days, and with the Mark of the Beast and the start of the war and the invasion of Israel, there will be a terrible holocaust that will pale the Holocaust of the Second World War. Passover will mark this beginning of the great time of tribulation to come upon the whole world, the same time when our Lord was crucified.

The Christians who heed the words of this prophecy will receive a blessing to witness to the world the truth of the Will of God. This will be like the ark of the time of Noah, that when the flood came the eight were saved. Carrying forth the nature of the Lord's supernatural protection, John's words in Revelation 12 show that by this means the church will be taken care of for exactly 1,260 days, the time of the rule of the Beast. This brings us to day 2,520, the Feast of Rosh Hashanah, the feast of the last trumpet blast, when the Lord will return for his bride, the Church, with power and great glory and all the world will know in the sight of many nations, that He, Jesus, is King of Kings, and Lord of Lords.

37. Which modern nations will attack Israel in the end times?

Table 37-1

Nations that Attack Israel at Armageddon or the Battle of Gog and Magog (Eze. 38:1-6)

Ancient Nations	*Modern Nations*
Gog and Magog	Russia
Meshech and Tubal	Moscow and Tubolsk
Persia Iran, Iraq, Afghanistan	Same Nations Today
Ethiopia	Ethiopia and Sudan
Askenaz	Czekslovakia
Gomer Eastern Europe	Austria and Germany
Togarmah	The Baltic States
"Many nations with you."	Various allied nations

Ezekiel 38 and 39 show that the nations that will attack Israel in the end time is led and armed by Russia, the head of the USSR and includes the cities of Moscow and Tobolsk. Persia is included which includes Iran, parts of Iraq, Afghanistan. Ethiopia and the Sudan are included, as is Libya. Gomer which are the East European nations such as East Germany, and the Slavic countries of Czechoslovakia, Hungary, Rumania, are included. Togarmah of the north country which includes the Baltic States. The many other nations include various other nations included within the hundred plus nations in the Euro Russian Empire.

38. What will the West's first response be to the invasion?

Europe's first answer will only be a diplomatic protest.

Ezekiel 38:13: Sheba, and Dedan, and the merchants of Tarshish, with all the young lions thereof, shall say unto thee, Art thou come to take a spoil? hast thou gathered thy company to take a prey? to carry away silver and gold, to take away cattle and goods, to take a great spoil?

The nations of the United Kingdom, coastal Europe, including the countries of Great Britain, United States, Canada and possibly commonwealth nations will diplomatically protest the invasion to apparently take great loot or wealth. The most likely great wealth within Israel such as the Dead Sea will not only be its agricultural and technological wealth, but also the oil that will be found in the area called the Boot of Asher, territory in the Valley of Megiddo, south of Haifa. This will be dealt with later in regard to the Nation of Israel and its specific prophecies regarding oil in the Middle East. Above all prizes, the Russian greed for world oil control by elimination of Israel, will be foremost.

39. (a) Why is Egypt absent from the roll-call of attacking nations?
  (b) What will happen to Egypt and Syria when Iraq and Russia attack?

(a) Of great importance is the absence of Egypt, as Egyptians have signed a peace treaty with Israelis March 26, 1979. Israel gave back the Sinai and its oil fields to Egypt. Most recently the U.S.A. forgave $7 billion in national debts to the U.S.A. in January 1991. The Egyptian and other Desert Storm Arab allies fought against Iraq and Saddam.

(b) In Daniel 11:40, Egypt is referred to as the King of the South. Egypt is thus the lead Arab ally against Iraq and its Arab allies. Egypt will thus be on the side of the U.S.A. and Israel. However, as Daniel 11:42 states, Iraq will attack and temporarily invade many countries, including part of Israel and including Egypt.

Daniel 11: 40-45

40 And at the time of the end [**of the Age**] *shall the king of the south* [**Egypt**] *push at him: and the king of the north* [**American occupation forces!**] *shall come against him* [**The Russian Beast Dictator**] *like a whirlwind* [**open a lightning 2nd line of battle**], *with chariots, and with horsemen, and with many ships* [**tanks and armoured personnel carriers**]; *and he shall enter into the countries, and shall overflow and pass over.*

41 *He shall enter also into the glorious land* [**Israel**], *and many [countries] shall be overthrown:* [**Middle Eastern Oil Producing Countries**] *but these shall escape out of his hand, [even] Edom, and Moab, and the chief of the children of Ammon.* [**Jordan will be delivered from the Russian and Islamic Invasion!**]

42 *He shall stretch forth his hand also upon the countries:* [**He will attack other countries just as Saddam has attacked Kuwait, i.e. Arab oil producers.**] *and the land of Egypt shall not escape.* [**Egypt will fall to the Russian and Islamic Invasion Force!**]

43 *But he shall have power over the treasures of gold and of silver, and over all the precious things of Egypt: and the Libyans and the Ethiopians [shall be] at his steps.*

44 *But tidings out of the east and out of the north shall trouble him: therefore he shall go forth with great fury to destroy, and utterly to make away many.* [**Russia and the Islamic Allies will overrun all the surrounding oil producing countries!**]

45 *And he shall plant the tabernacles of his palace between the seas in the glorious holy mountain* [**Mount Moriah in Jerusalem!**]; *yet he shall come to his end, and none shall help him.*

40. How will Europe try to produce a false Prophet or Messiah acceptable to the Jews and who is he likely to be?

The masons will be in control of the world economy. The European Economic Community will be lead by a false prophet or messiah. Their Masonic leader will be claiming Jewish decent in the Davidic line through the tribe of Judah. All the kings of Europe and Russia, including our current Queen of England and her son, Prince Charles, claim to be of Merovignian blood. (reference to Holy Blood and the Holy Grail and The Messianic Legacy - Baigent, Leigh, Lincoln, Corgi Books)

The authors of the two books *The Holy Blood and the Holy Grail,* and *The Messianic Legacy,* Michael Baigent, Richard Leigh and Henry Lincoln, claim that Freemasons at the top level believe in a European Royal blood line. They document that the pagan cult of Freemasons claims that Jesus did not die on the cross, but was taken to Marseilles, France area with his wife, Mary of Migdal or Mary Magdalene and their children. The Royal line of the Franks and later the Merovingian line was the proposed result. From the current royalty on the throne in Europe to the royal clans of Scotland, all claim this bloodline, from Jesus.

Jesus said that his people would not accept him coming in his father's name but would accept the beast dictator, as he comes in peace, in the end times coming in his own name. This explains the Jews accepting a European leader who will establish the Arab-Israeli Peace Treaty, and usher in an Age of Peace.

East Germany is the thirteenth member of the E.C. and thus has subdued one of the former horns, West Germany. According to Daniel 7:9, two other current E.C. members will be absorbed into the E.C. growing New German nation. This will be an attempt to resurrect the Austro-Hungarian Empire with these two nations previously led during the Hapsburg-Holy Roman Empire by Merovingian bloodline descendants. This would include all the descendants of Gomer in the roll call of nations to attack Israel with the former U.S.S.R. (See Ezekiel 38:1-6, Question #37)

Illuminated world Masonism will not be happy with the arrangement made with America and the New World Order and US military domination as quoted in:

Revelation 17:16-18,

> *16 And the ten horns which thou sawest upon the beast, these shall hate the whore, and shall make her desolate and naked, and shall eat her flesh, and burn her with fire.* **[America will be attacked with nuclear weapons and burnt with fire!]**
>
> *17 For God hath put in their hearts to fulfil his will, and to agree, and give their kingdom unto the beast, until the words of God shall be fulfilled.*
>
> *18 And the woman which thou sawest is that great city, which reigneth over the kings of the earth.* **[America is the the Daughter of Babylon in Revelation 18 and also referred as the Whore Babylon, for it claims to be a Christian Nation but indeed is Masonic and Satanic in its essence; therefore, is reserved for fire.]**

This reference is directly to this Russian-Eurasian empire led by these ten strong nations that hate the New Age Messiah and look forward to a Davidic king. They will; therefore, attack using the religion of the Babylonian New Age religious system and the false messiah while taking over the control of the oil in the world with a concerted multi-national attack and doublecross against the oil-producing Arab nations of the Middle East.

Dreams and Visions:

In October 1991, I was standing in my kitchen with Pastor Clyde Williamson of the Kerith Connection, from Toronto. His ministry was bringing Jews back to Israel, especially from Russia. Michelle, my wife, and Pastor Williamson stood in a circle. After praise and worship, the power of the Holy Spirit came on me and in an instant, the angel Gabriel took me to Jerusalem. He took me to the Via Dolorosa, and walked me in the spirit up to a man. He told me his name was Nicola Saliba, and that I would soon leave with Pastor Williamson with my wife and we would meet this man and he would show us important things that I must tell God's people.

Then as Gabriel had me standing on the Temple Mount and we stood observing the Cohens assembling the lights at night and erecting the Tabernacle of Moses beside the Dome of the Rock and the Mosque of Omar. Gabriel stood by as they quickly assembled. He told me to take note for this was the first event of the last seven years and the start of the Time of Jacob's Trouble. In time I would be revealed that they did this of their own wisdom, and not by the will and power of God. I was overwhelmed with the oppression of that moment on the Temple Mount and a feeling of terror and grief!

Again, just as rapidly, I stood in the circle holding hands. When I told the story of my vision and the name of Nicola Saliba, Clyde immediately told us that we would leave in the next few days for Israel. We did!

After several days on call, and little sleep and less on the El Al flight from Toronto, Canada, we arrived at Ben Gurion airport. When my foot touched the ground, I heard an audible voice, "You are now standing on American soil, for the anointing of Israel to bring the gospel to the world has fallen on America. Their fates are One!" I knew I had heard the Voice of the God!

Prayer started immediately on arrival at Tom Hess's House of Prayer on the top of the Mount of Olives. We were all exhausted. That night, Michelle woke me and shook me over and over again to arise and pray as she knew that we must leave immediately. I passed out repeatedly.

Finally, I prayed, and God said, "Why did you not listen to your wife right away! Get up now and dress, and without a warning go to Tel Aviv and pray, and I will send my angel Gabriel to tell you to come back to Jerusalem. Then you will meet

Nicola Saliba and he will show you things that you must tell My People!" We prayed for three days, face down on the floor of our room.

Friday morning, the angel Gabriel came in a vision and shouted, "Get up and bring your wife in hast to Jerusalem!" So we left and entered the Old City of Jerusalem. My bad sense of direction lead us into the Islamic-Arab quarter. After a frightening incident of not giving enough bakshish or alms and the apparent danger of travel in this section sunk in, we argued while walking out into the Jewish quarter. A man walked up to us and said, I know you must be Christians, for I can see the Shekinah!

He then took us to the Church of the Holy Sepulcher, where he was the master marble mason rebuilding the church. After a private tour, he took us to a private room high in the church where the Greek Orthodox monks had something special, that he said the Holy Spirit said we must see. Up a winding stairway, marked with crosses of the Knights Templar, we stood in front of a marble pedestal with a glass case with the silver boots and spurs of Godfrey de Bouillon. This was the leader of the First Crusade, who fathered all the Kings and Queens of Europe and all the Czars of Russia. Their horrible blasphemy was that they had the Bloodline right to rule the world, through the line of Jesus and Mary Magdalene. When I looked on the case, I heard again the audible voice of God, "Take note and remember the things said here today. You must tell the people of this abomination, and their plans to rule the world in the time of Jacob's trouble." Clinton and Bush, recent Presidents, are in this line through King Edward IV.

41. **How will Russia take over control of the world and when will this happen?**

The head of Russia will be the Beast Dictator or **Antichrist,** who for the last three and a half years of the seven-year period, will rule the earth. The Russian invasion of the Middle East will allow the takeover of Arab countries as well as most of Israel sparing parts of Jordan only, to set up a Palestinian state.

The Russian doublecross will allow the head of Russia to become world dictator by controlling the Middle Eastern oil with Russia as the current leading oil producer then in control of all the Middle Eastern oil.

Russia is now not a significant oil exporter as of June 1992. Within several years 'hooks will draw the Russian bear down to take a spoil from the Middle East – its oil.' As Russia's oil runs out in the mid 90's as it rushes to market communism, God will allow 'hooks' to be put in its jaws to draw it down to attack Israel.

42. How will America, Babylon the Great be destroyed and how will the world respond?

This is the destruction of America by nuclear war that makes it uninhabitable by humans. All the cargoes listed in Rev. 18: 11-13 are an extensive list of tradeable commodities available at the time of John's writing Revelation. In Rev. 18: 15 it states that all these things are sold to America for wealth. This wealth is based on oil. America or Babylon the Great, will be destroyed in one hour, and the merchants who became wealthy will weep and mourn at the destruction of the oil wealth of America.

In Revelation 18 we see the falling of Babylon the Great. (Ref. to Q. #).

Revelation 18:8-24

8 Therefore shall her plagues come in one day, death, and mourning, and famine; and she shall be utterly burned with fire **[nuclear attack]***: for strong [is] the Lord God who judgeth her.*

9 And the kings of the earth, who have committed fornication and lived deliciously with her, shall bewail her, and lament for her, when they shall see the smoke of her burning,

10 Standing afar off for the fear of her torment, saying, Alas, alas, that great city Babylon, that mighty city! **[The Nuclear Destruction of New York City!]** *for in one hour is thy judgment come.*

11 And the merchants of the earth shall weep and mourn over her; for no man buyeth their merchandise any more:

12 The merchandise of gold, and silver, and precious stones, and of pearls, and fine linen, and purple, and silk, and scarlet, and all thine wood, and all manner vessels of ivory, and all manner vessels of most precious wood, and of brass, and iron, and marble,

13 And cinnamon, and odours, and ointments, and frankincense, and wine, and oil, and fine flour, and wheat, and beasts, and sheep, and horses, and chariots, and slaves, and souls of men.

14 And the fruits that thy soul lusted after are departed from thee, and all things which were dainty and goodly are departed from thee, and thou shalt find them no more at all.

15 The merchants of these things, which were made rich by her, shall stand afar off for the fear of her torment, weeping and wailing,

16 And saying, Alas, alas, that great city, that was clothed in fine linen, and purple, and scarlet, and decked with gold, and precious stones, and pearls!

17 For in one hour so great riches is come to nought. **[mourning a loss The New Your Stock Exchange]** *And every shipmaster, and all the company in ships, and sailors, and as many as trade by sea, stood afar off,*

18 And cried when they saw the smoke of her burning, saying, What [city is] like unto this great city!

19 And they cast dust on their heads, and cried, weeping and wailing, saying, Alas, alas, that great city, wherein were made rich all that had ships in the sea by reason of her costliness! for in one hour is she made desolate.

20 Rejoice over her, [thou] heaven, and [ye] holy apostles and prophets; for God hath avenged you on her.

21 And a mighty angel took up a stone like a great millstone, and cast [it] into the sea, saying, Thus with violence shall that great city Babylon be thrown down, and shall be found no more at all.

22 And the voice of harpers, and musicians, and of pipers, and trumpeters, shall be heard no more at all in thee; and no craftsman, of whatsoever craft [he be], shall be found any more in thee; and the sound of a millstone shall be heard no more at all in thee;

23 And the light of a candle shall shine no more at all in thee; and the voice of the bridegroom and of the bride shall be heard no more at all in thee: for thy merchants were the great men of the earth; for by thy sorceries were all nations deceived.

24 And in her was found the blood of prophets, and of saints, and of all that were slain upon the earth.

Jeremiah 6:14

14 They have healed also the hurt [of the daughter] of my people slightly, saying, Peace, peace; when [there is] no peace.

1 Thessalonians 5:3

3 For when they shall say, Peace and safety; then sudden destruction cometh upon them, as travail upon a woman with child; and they shall not escape.

Genesis 3

1 Now the serpent was more subtle than any beast of the field which the LORD God had made. And he said unto the woman, Yea, hath God said, Ye shall not eat of every tree of the garden?

2 And the woman said unto the serpent, We may eat of the fruit of the trees of the garden:

3 But of the fruit of the tree which [is] in the midst of the garden, God hath said, Ye shall not eat of it, neither shall ye touch it, lest

ye die. **[STOP PRAYER AND DIRECTION FROM GOD'S HOLY SPIRIT!]**

4 And the serpent said unto the woman, Ye shall not surely die:

5 For God doth know that in the day ye eat thereof, then your eyes shall be opened, and ye shall be as gods, knowing good and evil.

During the first three and one-half years, there will be great economic prosperity for America or the Harlot Spiritual Israel as it rides upon the Beast empire Euro-Asia. The Beast Empire and its member nations will hate American Christian Evangelism and fear the revolution internally will turn her back to become once again a Christian Nation ruled by the will of God.

43. What is the mystery Babylon and how does it control the world?

It is the occultic resurrected religion of ancient Babylon. It is the Illuminated Sons of Satan that control world-wide business, and will set up the New World Order and the New Age End-Time EcoSocialist Communist Religion of the False Prophet.

The Hindu-Buddhist ideas portrayed through the New Age Movement are based on reincarnation, magic, and demonic spirit guidance and manifestation. Down through the ages these evil religious beliefs have been in Eastern mystic religions. They have since the time of Solomon's Temple been represented by Masonism, the self-proclaimed super-religion.

Today Mormonism is this same Masonic paganism shrouded in Christian terms that have had their true meaning twisted. At the heart of the religion of Babylon the Great is mother goddess worship, started by Nimrod and his wife Semiramis. They initiated the godhead of Jah-Bal-On of world-wide Masonism. The current Masonic movement, and witchcraft throughout the ages have very similar gods, ceremonies, penalties and beliefs.

There are, therefore, two main streams of the New Age Movement. The first being the one with the occult emphasis, primarily based on eastern mysticism and having its roots in ancient Babylon. The second stream of thought is that of the humanistic emphasis where they believe in humankind's unlimited potential. Both streams end up with the same end with the worship of man.

The 'Gaia' phenomenon is named after a Greek mother goddess of the earth. Scientists refer to the term in supposed scientific discussions.

World-wide Royal Arch Masonism is in control of the world economy. Through international banking, the Council on Foreign Relations, the International Monetary Fund or I.M.F., the United Nations, and Council on Security and Co-operation in Europe, C.S.C.E., Illuminated Royal Arch Masonism controls the world's economy.

2 Thessalonians 2:9-12

9 [Even him], whose coming is after the working of Satan with all power and signs and lying wonders,

10 And with all deceivableness of unrighteousness in them that perish; because they received not the love of the truth, that they might be saved.

11 And for this cause God shall send them strong delusion, that they should believe a lie:

12 That they all might be damned who believed not the truth, but had pleasure in unrighteousness.

Genesis 3:4-5

4 And the serpent said unto the woman, Ye shall not surely die:

5 For God doth know that in the day ye eat thereof, then your eyes shall be opened, and ye shall be as gods, knowing good and evil.

Matthew 24:5

> 5 For many shall come in my name, saying, I am Christ; and shall deceive many.

Matthew 24:23-28

> 23 Then if any man shall say unto you, Lo, here [is] Christ, or there; believe [it] not.
>
> 24 For there shall arise false Christs, and false prophets, and shall shew great signs and wonders; insomuch that, if [it were] possible, they shall deceive the very elect.
>
> 25 Behold, I have told you before.
>
> 26 Wherefore if they shall say unto you, Behold, he is in the desert; go not forth: behold, [he is] in the secret chambers; believe [it] not.
>
> 27 For as the lightning cometh out of the east, and shineth even unto the west; so shall also the coming of the Son of man be.
>
> 28 For wheresoever the carcase is [spiritually dead person], there will the eagles be gathered together.

44. What shall happen to this Babylonian mother-goddess 'Christ-within' creation worship religious system?

The resurrected Roman Empire will be the 7th Kingdom to be ruled by the religion of Babylon, Masonism and its newer forms of New Ageism. The ten kingdoms of the world proposed by the Club of Rome will destroy this Mystery Babylon religious system when the eighth kingdom of the Beast dictator is set up. This will occur with the communist takeover of Europe by Russia and its allies, starting in the middle of the seven years.

America will fall with the communist takeover of the Middle East at half way through to the seven year period. Just as the woman who sat upon the tiger and was eaten in a familiar poem, the prostitute of mystery Babylon or America will ride

upon the tiger for forty-two months and then be burned alive and eaten by the Beast Empire in the final conflict.

These events will follow the Passover with the five month UN sponsored Russian and allied occupation of Arab countries, East Jerusalem and the occupied territories. This will be an apparent move by World Masonism to stabilize the Middle East. (See Fig. 23-1) At that time there will be a gathering of military forces from the Russia and Europe as the Beast Empire of Rev 13:1 converge on north Israel for the battle to End the Age. [RED] America fresh from a Revolution will return to fight at the Battle of Armageddon, as the salvation of the nation of Israel. [BLUE] The Kings of the East, China and India, etc., will converge with a total of 200 million troops in all three armed forces. [YELLOW]

Revelation 13-14-17:

14 And deceiveth them that dwell on the earth by [the means of] those miracles which he had power to do in the sight of the beast; saying to them that dwell on the earth, that they should make an image to the beast, which had the wound by a sword, and did live.

15 And he had power to give life unto the image of the beast, that the image of the beast should both speak, and cause that as many as would not worship the image of the beast should be killed.

16 And he causeth all, both small and great, rich and poor, free and bond, to receive a mark in their right hand, or in their foreheads:

17 And that no man might buy or sell, save he that had the mark, or the name of the beast, or the number of his name. **[universal identicode]**

45. What are the three main signposts of the end of the age?

The three main sign posts of the end of the age are: 1) The nation Israel has returned in 1948. 2) The revived Roman Empire, or seventh kingdom, will be resurrected in 1992 with January 1, 1999-2002 EURO currency union. 3) The rebuilding of Babylon which has been undertaken by Saddam Hussein.

46. What is the most rapidly growing religion in the Mideast?

Islamic fundamentalism is the most rapidly growing religion on earth in these later days. This occurs in the 10-40 window, the least evangelized area on Earth.

Islam is a counter-religion to reverse the account of what happens with Isaac and Ishmael. In the Moslem account, Ishmael is considered the covenant child and the land of promise given to Isaac and his descendents is therefore given to the descendents Ishmael. This would, of course, make void the lineage from Jesus to be the Messiah. The faith of Islam is a direct attack on Judeo-Christian beliefs with Ishmael replacing Isaac and Mohammed replacing Jesus.

The holy war or Jihad is the most dangerous element of Islam today, with the faith of Islam willing to use war or terrorism to convert the rest of the world to its faith. With the increasing importance of oil and the vast majority of easily obtainable oil in the Middle East, this is being used as the fuel to forward the Islamic fundamentalist resurrection of the ancient Empire of Babylon.

The current war in the Gulf is not with just Saddam and Iraq. It is now with Islam, in the past eight years since the Desert Storm campaign, the 25 nations of Islam now are fused together with a common enemy. It is the United States. We are now facing a well-armed Islam with the Islamic bomb capable of striking US soil with the help of technologies that were provided by President Clinton. Now the satellite targeting technologies given China, enter Islam via Pakistan and Iran, cosigners of the 1989 treaty with China for mutual defense. We are indeed on the march toward Armageddon with the May 4th, 1999 deadline looming and the prospect with a trigger-happy Israel standing between Mutual Assured Annihilation and a peace described as "A Cup of Trembling!".

47. What is the identity of the empire of the Antichrist?

This fourth empire as described by Daniel 7:7-9 is the resurrected Roman empire. It is through this kingdom that the leader will force the rest of the world to accept the Mark of the Beast. C.F.R. territories #2-W. Europe, #5-former USSR, & #7-Middle East will be taken up in the month of the Bear, Russia as the Empire of Clay and Iron is consolidated. The other seven world territories as laid out by the Club of Rome (Q. #34), will be crushed underfoot or obey the policies of this dictatorship.

The Empire of the Beast Kingdom is a United States of Euro-Asia. The Western leg was the Holy Roman Empire and the Eastern leg was the Byzantine Empire. This implies that the Berlin wall must fall, which has. It also implies that Western Europe or the E.C. must unite with the Eastern Bloc countries to reconstitute the two legs of the ancient Roman Empire. Out of a united Euro-Soviet Empire will the ruler come that will destroy the city of Jerusalem and the Tabernacle. We see this in:

Daniel 9:26

> *26 And after threescore and two weeks shall Messiah be cut off, but not for himself: and the people of the prince* **[Gog]** *that shall come shall destroy the city and the sanctuary* **[Russia and allies will destroy the city of Jerusalem and the New Tabernacle of the Peace Treaty]***; and the end thereof [shall be] with a flood, and unto the end of the war desolations are determined.*

The Bible tells us in **Ezekiel 38: 19-20, Ezekiel 38:23, Ezekiel 39:11, 17-19, 21-22,** that when Israel is attacked by Russia and its allies, then God will no longer hide his face from Israel and he will display his glory among the nations.

Ezekiel 38: 19-20

19 For in my jealousy [and] in the fire of my wrath have I spoken, Surely in that day there shall be a great shaking in the land of Israel; **[world-wide megaquake]**

20 So that the fishes of the sea, and the fowls of the heaven, and the beasts of the field, and all creeping things that creep upon the earth, and all the men that [are] upon the face of the earth, shall shake at my presence, and the mountains shall be thrown down, and the steep places shall fall, and every wall shall fall to the ground. **[Every city on earth will crumble with a world-wide megaquake.]**

Ezekiel 38:23

23 Thus will I magnify myself, and sanctify myself; and I will be known in the eyes of many nations, and they shall know that I [am] the LORD.

Ezekiel 39:11, 17-19, 21-22

11 And it shall come to pass in that day, [that] I will give unto Gog a place there of graves in Israel, the valley of the passengers on the east of the sea: and it shall stop the [noses] of the passengers: and there shall they bury Gog and all his multitude: and they shall call [it] The valley of Hamongog.

17 And, thou son of man, thus saith the Lord GOD; Speak unto every feathered fowl, and to every beast of the field, Assemble yourselves, and come; gather yourselves on every side to my sacrifice that I do sacrifice for you, [even] a great sacrifice upon the mountains of Israel, that ye may eat flesh, and drink blood.

18 Ye shall eat the flesh of the mighty, and drink the blood of the princes of the earth, of rams, of lambs, and of goats, of bullocks, all of them fatlings of Bashan.

19 And ye shall eat fat till ye be full, and drink blood till ye be drunken, of my sacrifice which I have sacrificed for you.

21 And I will set my glory among the heathen, and all the heathen shall see my judgment that I have executed, and my hand that I have laid upon them.

22 So the house of Israel shall know that I [am] the LORD their God from that day and forward.

This is when God allows the **one great earthquake** that is described in **Ezekiel 38:20**. This identifies the beast dictator as the leader of the former Soviet Union, the ruler of Russia, that makes possible the Arab-Israeli Peace Treaty.

At halfway through the seven years of 360 days, the Communist atheists try to destroy America and invade Europe and the Mideast to take over Arab oil countries and attack at North Israel, Jerusalem.

Zechariah 14:2

2 For I will gather all nations **[UN peace keeping force take over East Jerusalem, the Temple Mount, and occupied territories]** *against Jerusalem to battle; and the city shall be taken* **[East Jerusalem]**, *and the houses rifled* **[Soviet and Islamic-Arab armies steal goods and destroy property of primarily Russian Jews in the occupied territories and East Jerusalem]**, *and the women ravished* **[ultimate anti-Semitism in retaliation for an Israeli military counterattack on Iraq]**.*; and half of the city shall go forth into captivity* **[All the Christian and Jewish occupants of Jerusalem will be removed from the city!]**, *and the residue of the people* **[Moslems]** *shall not be cut off from the city.*

The United Nations is a platform to allow a U.N. force to be able to gather all nations to fight against it. It or its replacement from a New World Parliament will ultimately send in the armies gathered at the battle of Armageddon, or Gog and Magog.

The Jewish resistance to Land for Peace, the giving up the occupied territories and East Jerusalem, will be in vain. The New World Order Government will enforce a peace upon Israel, that will not only give up the occupied territories, but allow a Jewish Tabernacle to co-habit the Temple Mount with the pagan shrine of the Islamic third holies shrine, the Dome of the Rock.

Daniel 7:7-9

> 7 *After this I saw in the night visions, and behold a fourth beast, dreadful and terrible, and strong exceedingly; and it had great iron teeth: it devoured and brake in pieces, and stamped the residue with the feet of it: and it [was] diverse from all the beasts that [were] before it; and it had ten horns.* **[This is the Resurrected Roman Empire]**
>
> 8 *I considered the horns, and, behold, there came up among them another little horn, before whom there were three of the first horns plucked up by the roots: and, behold, in this horn [were] eyes like the eyes of man, and a mouth speaking great things.* **[This is the Empire of the Dictator Beast the Euro-Asian Empire, the joined European Community Nations with the Eastern Block Nations of the Former Soviet Socialist Republics]**
>
> 9 *I beheld till the thrones were cast down, and the Ancient of days did sit, whose garment [was] white as snow, and the hair of his head like the pure wool: his throne [was like] the fiery flame, [and] his wheels [as] burning fire.*

> **As we see after the resurrection of the Roman Empire in the end times which must last a little while, as explained again in Daniel 7:23. The fourth beast is a fourth kingdom that will appear on earth. It will be different from all the other kingdoms and will devour the nations of the whole earth, trampling them down and crushing them. The ten horns are ten political leaders of the ten economic-political territories of the plan of the Club of Rome.**

After them another political leader will rise different from the earlier ones, on a platform of world peace as the new President of the United States of Euro-Asia. This is the Antichrist, Beast Dictator, the Russian leader spoken of in Ezekiel 38-39.

Daniel 7:24-27

24 And the ten horns out of this kingdom [are] ten kings [that] shall arise: and another shall rise after them; and he shall be diverse from the first, and he shall subdue three kings., **[He will take over three world kingdoms, Western Europe, Soviet Union and Middle East, by economic domination with the Mark of the Beast from America and the EURO dollar.]**

25 And he shall speak [great] words against the most High, and shall wear out the saints of the most High, and think to change times and laws **[persecute Gentile and Jewish Believers]**.: *and they shall be given into his hand until a time and times and the dividing of time.* **[He will persecute 1,260 days.]**

26 But the judgment shall sit, and they shall take away his dominion, to consume and to destroy [it] unto the end.

27 And the kingdom and dominion, and the greatness of the kingdom under the whole heaven, shall be given to the people of the saints of the most High, whose kingdom [is] an everlasting kingdom, and all dominions shall serve and obey him. **[The eternal reign of Jesus in a New Heaven and New Earth]**

Jesus will return after a nuclear war in the Middle East to rule and reign for eternity in a united New Heaven and Earth.

48. How will Russia, leading the Soviet Union, gain the economic power to support the end times military that will dominate the world?

Soviet goods are of such poor quality that foreign money from exports is impossible to fuel the Soviet economy. Much of the Soviets import obligations are paid in German marks or Japanese yen, which are paid for 50 percent by the sale of oil and 50 percent by sale of arms to foreign countries. Russian dependency is expressed by Gorbachev's recent request for $250 billion in loans or loan guarantees over five years, nearly one million U.S. dollars per Soviet citizen. Boris Yeltsin has continued those requests for ongoing Western aid.

The poor response from the G7 summit in July '91 precipitated the 'supposed' military coup of Aug. 19-21, 91. All eight men were 'hand-picked' by Mikhail Gorbachev, albeit some were hardliners. Six years of Perestroika and Glasnost have not cut but has multiplied military hardware output. Mr. Gorbachev was head of the K.G.B., Mr. Yazov of the military, Mr. Curchykov of the K.G.B. and Mr. Pavlov of the government suddenly lost face and soon all eight were like 'hunted fugitives'. Gorbachev now was resurrected by his political rival-come-ally Mr. Boris Yeltsin, and Gorbachev achieved moral justification for a purge and important moral and political support from the Soviet public. Mr. Gorbachev's apparent exit from active Soviet politics has been to continue to spread 'disinformation' about the true nature of the shadow powers in continuing of the Unified States of the former Soviet Union. He has done this through lucrative and influential articles he has put forth from his private institute in Moscow and freelanced in such renouned papers as the New York Times.

After the August 3, 1991 coup and the takeover of the now Confederation of Independent States, Mr. Boris Yeltsin as head of Russia has been able to obtain $24 billion in currency stabilization funds from the International Monetary Fund, and a guarantee of three per cent assets when Russia and the Soviet, former republic, join the I.M.F. These are but preliminary plans to join the Russian ruble to the European Currency Unit which will become the currency standard for the new European economic super giant set to take effect December 31, 1992. The Russian ruble tied to the European Currency Unit would make it a very stable currency and attract tremendous amounts of investment to support the growth of its huge military machine.

Long before the apparent collapse of the U.S.S.R., in the last five years of power Mr. Gorbachev has spent $50 billion on double-hulled titanium Typhoon-class nuclear submarines. Each submarine costs approximately two and one-half billion dollars, and carries 200 missiles capable of 50 independently targeted warheads. The total Russian arsenal of 100 submarines of this type, holds ransom 10,000 cities with a potential of a first nuclear strike. (Ref. Pagan Invasion Video Series - Preview of the Antichrist - Matriciani)

The scheme is like this, "If you don't give me money, I'll have a dangerous civil war on you!" This charade is an attempt to convince the West that the Soviets are serious; all 'media fluff'. The threat of 15 republics having civil wars with nuclear weapons and starving masses, gives a clear scenario to the Western mind, "Cough up the Cash 'George' or no New World Order", starting with an Arab-Israeli treaty to stabilize world oil prices, for Europe and the world economy. The Soviets are the top chess masters for good reason.

During the Gulf War the Soviets had thousands of military advisors present in Iraq assisting with the war, and at their eight joint military bases with Iraq. They supplied most of the weaponry and technology to Iraq as well as satellite intelligence information during the war. Communications have even been interrupted directly between Saddam Hussein and Gorbachev, and Gorbachev notified Saddam of both the air and ground war within minutes of conversations with President George Bush. During that war, the Soviets had 220,000 troops at the Soviet-Turkish border ready to invade should the 200,000 Turkish troops at the Turkish-Iraqi border enter northern Iraq. Behind those Russian troops were tactical nuclear weapons as identified by American spy satellites. Gorbachev is playing at global brinkmanship at the same time has bargained for a New World Order with the economic engine of Europe directly tied to the Soviet Union to assure Russia's continued world dominance as the creator of the greatest machine of military destruction in history.

Mr. Gorbachev, as of June 1991, has requested 'most favoured nation' status with the G7 nations with respect to trade, one hundred plus billion dollars of aid to Russia over five years to maintain Perestroika and Glasnost. They also requested status at the next G7 Summit meetings in July '91. With the U.S. and NATO they have plans for treaties to remove all Western conventional troops and limit and reduce all Western nuclear weapons in the European theatre, to be signed by the end of July '91.

The Russian policy from the time of Peter the Great of two steps backwards and one step forward shows that the Russian approach toward advancing, a goal of taking over the world. It is like the hammer in the flag of the Russian Empire drawing back first and then driving forward. Glasnosts have happened on five previous occasions when the Russian Empire opened to accept western technology and monetary aid and then further expand its borders and consume other nations in its communist empire. Its goal to conquer the world has not changed.

49. What role does the ruler of Russia have in the end times?

We have another player in the end times, in the king who exalts himself, in

Daniel 11:36-45

36 And the king shall do according to his will; and he shall exalt himself, and magnify himself above every god, and shall speak

marvellous things against the God of gods, and shall prosper till the indignation be accomplished: for that that is determined shall be done.

37 Neither shall he regard the God of his fathers, nor the desire of women **[Tammuz, later Baal, the fertility god and a symbol for one of the Masonic Trinitarian Godhead!]**, *nor regard any god* **[he will be an atheist]**: *for he shall magnify himself above all.* **[He will be a self-worshiping atheist fascist dictator.]**

38 But in his estate shall he honour the God of forces **[He will honor the military power that arms him, the Russians and its Soviet allies]**: *and a god whom his fathers knew not shall he honour with gold, and silver, and with precious stones, and pleasant things.*

39 Thus shall he do in the most strong holds with a strange god, whom he shall acknowledge [and] increase with glory: and he shall cause them to rule over many, and shall divide the land for gain.

40 And at the time of the end shall the king of the south push at him: and the king of the north shall come against him like a whirlwind, with chariots, and with horsemen, and with many ships; and he shall enter into the countries, and shall overflow and pass over.

41 He shall enter also into the glorious land, and many [countries] shall be overthrown: but these shall escape out of his hand, [even] Edom, and Moab, and the chief of the children of Ammon.

42 He shall stretch forth his hand also upon the countries: and the land of Egypt shall not escape.

43 But he shall have power over the treasures of gold and of silver, and over all the precious things of Egypt: and the Libyans and the Ethiopians [shall be] at his steps. **[He will make his allies in control of Arab oil wealth and raise the world oil price. He will with Russian-European Combined Military**

forces, invade Saudi Arabia, Kuwait again, the Emirates, Bahrain and Quatar and will redistribute the oil territory, lands and religious cities.]

44 But tidings out of the east and out of the north shall trouble him: therefore he shall go forth with great fury to destroy, and utterly to make away many.

45 And he shall plant the tabernacles of his palace between the seas in the glorious holy mountain; yet he shall come to his end, and none shall help him.

Hosne Mubarak was told of this Neo Babylon Plan, cooked up by Gorbachev and the K.G.B. at an Arab Summit meeting in the late '80's. It was reported in <u>Newsweek, January 28, 1991, page 17</u>. Mr. Saddam Hussein approached Mr. Mubarak with this plan. Iraq would get most of the east of Saudi Arabia and the oil, Jordan would get the Holy cities of Mecca and Medina. Syria would receive the northern provinces. South Yemen would get the southern provinces split up with Egypt. In one fell swoop, on a weekend there would be a New Babylon in Modern Times and no "staging ground" for U.S. and allied troops during the Gulf War.

Daniel 11:40-45

40 And at the time of the end shall the king of the south push at him: and the king of the north shall come against him like a whirlwind, with chariots, and with horsemen, and with many ships; and he shall enter into the countries, and shall overflow and pass over.

41 He shall enter also into the glorious land, and many [countries] shall be overthrown: but these shall escape out of his hand, [even] Edom, and Moab, and the chief of the children of Ammon.

42 He shall stretch forth his hand also upon the countries: and the land of Egypt shall not escape.

43 But he shall have power over the treasures of gold and of silver, and over all the precious things of Egypt: and the Libyans and the Ethiopians [shall be] at his steps.

44 But tidings out of the east and out of the north shall trouble him: therefore he shall go forth with great fury to destroy, and utterly to make away many.

45 And he shall plant the tabernacles of his palace between the seas in the glorious holy mountain; yet he shall come to his end, and none shall help him.

He is the same as the other horn of Daniel 8: 9-14

9 And out of one of them came forth a little horn **[out of one of the four divisions of the third kingdom, that of the Goat or Alexander the Great's (Mede's) Kingdom, will the stern faced king of Daniel 8:23 and Daniel 11:36-46.],** *which waxed exceeding great, toward the south, and toward the east, and toward the pleasant [land].* **[It took over North Israel, and Jerusalem (at least East Jerusalem and the Temple Mount) and also the Jewish Temple.]**

10 And it waxed great, [even] to the host of heaven; and it cast down [some] of the host and of the stars to the ground, and stamped upon them.

11 Yea, he magnified [himself] even to the prince of the host, and by him the daily [sacrifice] was taken away, and the place of his sanctuary was cast down.

12 And an host was given [him] against the daily [sacrifice] by reason of transgression, and it cast down the truth to the ground; and it practised, and prospered.

13 Then I heard one saint speaking, and another saint said unto that certain [saint] which spake, How long [shall be] the vision [concerning] the daily [sacrifice], and the transgression of desolation, to give both the sanctuary and the host to be trodden under foot? **[How long would it take for Russia to stop the** daily sacrifice through the United Nations and invade and take over East Jerusalem and the Temple Mount until the Temple rededication is completed again at Jesus' coming?]

14 And he said unto me, Unto two thousand and three hundred days; then shall the sanctuary be cleansed. **[From the Temple sacrifice is stopped by Iraq through the U.N. until Jesus returns to reconsecrate the sanctuary, there will be 1,150 days, i.e. 2,300 evenings and mornings, sacrifices. New Age ideas have turned people away from God. By rebelling from God, he gives over the Temple and many of the Jewish Temple Priests are killed along with many other Jews. This will be yet another Holocaust.]**

Daniel 8: 23-26:

23 And in the latter time of their kingdom **[at the end of the Age]**, *when the transgressors are come to the full* **[the New Age Christian Church is in full blossom at the End Times]**, *a king of fierce countenance* **[Russian Leader]**, *and understanding dark sentences, shall stand up.*

24 And his power shall be mighty, but not by his own power **[Russian and European military armaments!]**: *and he shall destroy wonderfully [brilliant criminal mastermind], and shall prosper, and practise, and shall destroy the mighty and the holy people.* **[He will destroy America and her allies as well as Israeli military attempting to come against him.]**

25 And through his policy also he shall cause craft to prosper in his hand; and he shall magnify [himself] in his heart, and by peace shall destroy many **[He will deceive many when he signs the seven-year peace treaty with Israel and later breaks it as part of his plan, with the Russian leader!]**: *he shall also stand up against the Prince of princes; but he shall be broken without hand.* **[Jesus will destroy this Russian leader himself.]**

26 And the vision of the evening and the morning which was told [is] true: wherefore shut thou up the vision; for it [shall be] for many days.. [There will be 1,150 days from the termination of the sacrifice on the Temple mount, until the Day of the Lord!]

50. How will Russia destroy and subdue the surrounding nations?

The astounding devastation that he may wreak will be related to the nuclear weapons potential and supergun that he has developed. Nuclear material has been obtained from mining in northern Iraq. He has use of centrifuges and possibly nuclear reactors to generate fissionable material and a delivery system of the super gun developed by Gerald Bull, a Canadian Ballistics scientist. The U.N. nuclear investigations team has been repeatedly been prevented from examining caluronics equipment for refining uranium.

Two years since the Gulf War has been over, the breakup of the Soviet Union has resulted in bargain prices for high tech Soviet weapons of mass destruction, including nuclear weapons and delivery systems, etc. The countries of the Islamic fundamentalist oil producing Middle Eastern States have purchased literally billions of dollars in these doomsday tools of Satan.

As a political leader Mr. Hussein has won the political battle while losing the military war. After the invasion of Kuwait, and expulsion by a multinational force, he continues to survive and develop his nerve gas, the super gun, nuclear and other weapons of mass destruction such as the fuel-air explosion, as powerful as small nuclear weapons. (Ref. G. Jeff Messiah Ch. 3).

The New World Order of Mr. George Bush, President of the United States, and Comrade President Mikhail Gorbachev has been outlined in **"PERESTROIKA - New Thinking for Our Country and The World."** It clearly shows the philosophical basis for a plan by the Soviet Union to take over the world. Mr. Hussein could not have contemplated an Iraqi war without full Soviet-backed planning, military and strategic aid from Mr. Gorbachev.

51. What role has Russia in the plans of Saddam Hussein to take over the Arab oil producing countries?

As Grant Jeffrey details on page 105 of his book, **Messiah. - War in the Middle East and The Road to Armageddon**, we must review his observations of the 'Gorbachev's Gambit'.

Newsweek, January 28, 1991, page 17 details a meeting between President Saddam Hussein, and President Hosni Mubarak of Egypt. Saddam approached Mubarak at the conclusion of an Arab League meeting. Saddam invited Egypt to jointly invade Saudi Arabia, Kuwait, Bahrain, and the United Arab Emirates.

The 'Plan' was developed by a joint Soviet-Iraqi military strategic planning based in Iraq since 1978, by the cunningly evil Uri Andropov. Gorbachev had to be personally involved in carrying out the plan. Communications between Presidents Bush and Gorbachev were quickly followed by a hasty call to Saddam by Gorbachev, monitored by U.S. intelligence, warning 24 hours in advance of the Desert Storm Air War. This gave Saddam precious time to hide his weapons systems of mass destruction, both nuclear and non-nuclear, i.e. biological, chemical and 'fuel-air explosive'. When Bush again warned the Soviets of the Land War Phase, the U.S. President kept the phone line tied up and only gave Saddam one-half hour to ready for the assault.

52. When will the former Soviet Union open fully to the gospel? How long will this last?

With the August 19, 1991 apparent three-day abortive coup by communist hardliners, the purge to remove Stalinistic restrictions on religious expression marked the beginning of 'full' opening of the Soviet Union to the gospel. This is not to say that Glasnost has not over eight years been seen as a miraculous opening. The coup and political resurrection of Gorbachev has been difficult to grasp but opens an unprecedented window of opportunity. Christians will be able to get Bibles, video, audio and other tools and teachers into the Soviet Union. We know that this time is short, however, for

Russia as an armourer and leader of the Soviet Union will attack Israel during the last 3-1/2 years of this age.

Ralph Mann of the Mission Possible Foundation, and author of the book **Glasnost - Gateway to World Revival**, chronicles the dilemma of diversity of the Soviet Empire. The history of the suffering Christian Church and the lack of real improvement of true religious freedom in the USSR. However, the time has come when religious freedoms are opening both to Christian evangelization and to the false religions and false New Age Movement. Many Jews have returned from Russia to Israel in the start of last and greatest Exodus.

Jeremiah 16:14-16

14 Therefore, behold, the days come, saith the LORD, that it shall no more be said, The LORD liveth, that brought up the children of Israel out of the land of Egypt;

15 But, The LORD liveth, that brought up the children of Israel from the land of the north, and from all the lands whither he had driven them: and I will bring them again into their land that I gave unto their fathers.

16 Behold, I will send for many fishers, saith the LORD, and they shall fish them **[fishers = ministers of the gospel]**; *and after will I send for many hunters* **[hunters = New Age ministers of the Shamballah, they create a Holocaust for Jews and Christians]**, *and they shall hunt them from every mountain, and from every hill, and out of the holes of the rocks.*

More Jews will return from the Soviet Union to Israel in the second and greatest Exodus. The apparent end to communism and increasing Soviet anti-Semitism will force all Jews who can leave, to leave the Soviet Union. Many will settle in Israel, U.S.A., Canada and other western countries. The return of the Jews from Russia is the last thing Orthodox Jews know will precede the seven years of Jacob's trouble, the tribulation and the return of their Messiah at the end of this period.

Referring to the quotation from Jeremiah 16:14-16, we see in verse 16 that God will first send forth the fishermen. When Jesus called forth his apostles as fishers of men, he meant that he would bring the gospel to Jews through Christian gentiles and Believing Jews. It is after this that God will allow the sending forth of the hunters which to anti-Semitism and the New Age Movement will drive all Jews to seek refuge and return to their homeland, Israel, and to places of refuge, protected by spiritual Israel, the church or body of believers.

Dreams and Visions:

In a vision in September 98, I saw the Russians encouraging Christians to help all the Jews to return to Israel. They plotted to make sure most returned to Israel so that they would come down and kill them all once and for all in the land of Israel. This is the evil plot that Russia and allies has in mind when they come down on the land of Israel, as described in Ezekiel 38.

I saw many Jews and Christians taken captive and executed, with the Russian and Islamic invasion and the taking of Jerusalem and Israel. Those who heeded the warnings of the prophets of the END were carried to safety to the wings of a great eagle, North and South America to places of refuge, as I looked down upon the Earth. They who believed the Christians who came to their rescue became believers in Jesus. Thus a remnant of the nation of Israel will be saved from the next holocaust.

53. How long will this door to Soviet revival be open?

This door will be opened fully for only a little as we shall see it will last only 1,260 days after the Islamic-Israeli peace treaty when the sacrifice will be abolished. As Daniel 11:40-41 says, Egypt described as the King of the South will try to engage Iraq or modern Babylon militarily. At this point the USSR and allies, especially Iraq, will come down to apparently attack the Arab States allied with the U.S.A., and will take over the countries of the

Middle East to control Middle Eastern oil. The unknown time before the Peace Treaty plus 1,260 days, will be open for free spreading of the Gospel to the former Soviet Union. (Fig. 23-1).

54. How will the Russian led invasion of the Middle East proceed?

The attacking nations are catalogued in Ezekiel 38:1-6, double crosses detailed in Daniel 11:40-43 and Ezekiel 30:3-5. This invasion ends with Ezekiel 39:5 with a description that explains in modern terms a nuclear exchange with soldiers falling in the open field.

Ezekiel 38:1-6

1 And the word of the LORD came unto me, saying,

2 Son of man, set thy face against Gog, the land of Magog, the chief prince of Meshech and Tubal, and prophesy against him,

3 And say, Thus saith the Lord GOD; Behold, I [am] against thee, O Gog, the chief prince of Meshech and Tubal:

4 And I will turn thee back, and put hooks into thy jaws, and I will bring thee forth, and all thine army, horses and horsemen, all of them clothed with all sorts [of armour, even] a great company [with] bucklers and shields, all of them handling swords:

5 Persia, Ethiopia, and Libya with them; all of them with shield and helmet:

6 Gomer, and all his bands; the house of Togarmah of the north quarters, and all his bands: [and] many people with thee.

Daniel 11:40-43

40 And at the time of the end shall the king of the south **[Egypt]** *push at him: and the king of the north* **[America and allies]** *shall come against him like a whirlwind, with chariots, and with horsemen, and with many ships; and he shall enter into the countries, and shall overflow and pass over.*

41 He shall enter also into the glorious land **[Israel]**, *and many [countries] shall be overthrown: but these shall escape out of his hand, [even] Edom, and Moab, and the chief of the children of Ammon.*

42 He shall stretch forth his hand also upon the countries: and the land of Egypt shall not escape.

43 But he shall have power over the treasures of gold and of silver, and over all the precious things of Egypt: and the Libyans and the Ethiopians [shall be] at his steps.

Ezekiel 30:3-5

3 For the day [is] near, even the day of the LORD [is] near, a cloudy day; it shall be the time of the heathen.

4 And the sword shall come upon Egypt, and great pain shall be in Ethiopia, when the slain shall fall in Egypt, and they shall take away her multitude, and her foundations shall be broken down.

5 Ethiopia, and Libya, and Lydia, and all the mingled people, and Chub, and the men of the land that is in league, shall fall with them by the sword.

> *Cush and Put, Lydia and all Arabia, Libya and the people of the covenant land will fall by the sword along with Egypt.* **[Neo-Babylonian Kingdom will rise in the Last Days, to include all the Islamic nations that make a pact to destroy Israel!]**

Ezekiel 39:5-7

5 Thou shalt fall upon the open field: for I have spoken [it], saith the Lord GOD. **[The nuclear attack on Russian troops and allies shows battlefield nuclear weapons attacks making them fall in the open field. God affirms how certain this is.]**

6 And I will send a fire on Magog, and among them that dwell carelessly in the isles **[Russia-Europe and allies & Eastern** and Western European allies]: *and they shall know that I [am] the LORD.*

7 So will I make my holy name known in the midst of my people Israel; and I will not [let them] pollute my holy name any more: and the heathen shall know that I [am] the LORD, the Holy One in Israel. . **[At the time of the Soviet invasion, the Lord will show all the nations that he is the Holy One in Israel. This will occur at the Second Coming, at the 7th or Last Trumpet.]**

Joel 2:20

20 But I will remove far off from you the northern [army], **[Russia and allies]** *and will drive him into a land barren and desolate, with his face toward the east sea,* **[Dead Sea]** *and his hinder part toward the utmost sea* **[Mediterranean Sea] [Amphibious assault via Haifa at the mouth of the Valley of Meggido]***, and his stink shall come up, and his ill savour shall come up, because he hath done great things.*

Ezekiel 38: 5-6

5 Persia, Ethiopia, and Libya with them; all of them with shield and helmet:

6 Gomer, and all his bands; the house of Togarmah of the north quarters, and all his bands: [and] many people with thee.

[See Q. #37]
[THE REVIVED EASTERN AND WESTERN ROMAN EMPIRE]
[Fully eighty-five per cent of the troops will die from the invading countries as they invade north Israel.]

Ezekiel 39:2

2 And I will turn thee back, and leave but the sixth part of thee, and will cause thee to come up from the north parts, and will bring thee upon the mountains of Israel: **[Russia and allies will be brought down like captives of ancient Assyria with hooks** in the noses or lower lips, pulled along by the 'maddening wine' of oil]

(Dr. Whiteford's research was presented to the Second International Conference on the United Nations and World Peace, Seattle, 14 April 1989.)

55. a) What will happen in the day of the Lord?

The Great Earthquake of Ezekiel 38: 18-20 will happen on the Day of the Lord. His wrath shall be poured out at <u>the last trumpet</u>.

The great earthquake of:

Ezekiel 38:18-23

> *18 And it shall come to pass at the same time when Gog* **[Russia and allies]** *shall come against the land of Israel, saith the Lord GOD, [that] my fury shall come up in my face.* **[Day of the Lord's wrath at the Last Trumpet.]**
>
> *19 For in my jealousy [and] in the fire of my wrath have I spoken, Surely in that day there shall be a great shaking in the land of Israel;* **[Nuclear War triggered Megaquake.]**
>
> *20 So that the fishes of the sea, and the fowls of the heaven, and the beasts of the field, and all creeping things that creep upon the earth, and all the men that [are] upon the face of the earth, shall shake at my presence, and the mountains shall be thrown down, and the steep places shall fall, and every wall shall fall to the ground.*
>
> *21 And I will call for a sword against him* **[God will summon a nuclear attack against the military forces of the multinational army attacking Israel from the North, lead by Russia.]** *throughout all my mountains, saith the Lord GOD: every man's sword shall be against his brother.*
>
> *22 And I will plead against him with pestilence and with blood; and I will rain upon him, and upon his bands, and upon the many*

people that [are] with him, an overflowing rain, and great hailstones, fire, and brimstone.

23 Thus will I magnify myself, and sanctify myself; and I will be known in the eyes of many nations, and they shall know that I [am] the LORD.

A professor from the University of New Brunswick, Dr. Gary T. Whiteford, Ph. D., has shown very extensive research indicating a direct relationship between underground nuclear testing and great earthquakes that have occurred over the past thirty years. [See Q. # 54]

How much greater would the earthquakes released be that would result from a nuclear war involving many nations? It was obvious that every wall falls to the ground due to the magnitude of this earthquake, that the judgments involve rain, 120-pound hailstones, burning sulfur, all signs of a nuclear attack. Terrible winds producing 100-pound hailstones referred to elsewhere in the Bible occur on the day of the Lord's wrath. This will be the ultimate proof in that God will make himself known in the sight of many nations that he is the Lord of the Earth. It is to come at the time when Jesus returns as a warrior king to take over the throne of Israel and the world. This event occurs only at the end of the seven years, and at the end of the three and one-half year period of tribulation. As seen in Fig. 23-1, it coincides with the Feast of Trumpets on the 2,520th day at the exact end of seven years, 360 each. This is the Feast of Trumpets and the moment of God's final wrath which is a spiritual judgment detailed in Revelation 11:18.

The great earthquake is the one final earthquake which is so great that it occurs at the end of the tribulation. The invading nations of the end of the tribulation are the nations of the beast dictator, i.e. the Russio-Eurasian Empire, which will not only take over Europe, but the Middle East as well and become dictator of the world. The unholy alliance between the Russian leader and Soviet allies and the leader of Iraq will scheme to control world oil, money and military power and take over the world.

The Lord will send fire on Magog or the USSR and on those who dwell in safety in the coastlands from Ezekiel 39:6. This includes the countries such as Britain, the United States, Canada, etc. We see from the exact timing that this occurs at the time of God's wrath which is at the end of tribulation when Russia and its allies attack Israel.

55. b) When will Iraq attack and invade neighbouring countries?

Ezekiel 29: 9-12

> 9 And the land of Egypt shall be desolate and waste; and they shall know that I [am] the LORD: because he hath said, The river [is] mine, and I have made [it].
>
> 10 Behold, therefore I [am] against thee, and against thy rivers, and I will make the land of Egypt utterly waste [and] desolate, from the tower of Syene **[Aswan]** even unto the border of Ethiopia.
>
> 11 No foot of man shall pass through it, nor foot of beast shall pass through it, neither shall it be inhabited forty years. **[It will be radioactive]**
>
> 12 And I will make the land of Egypt desolate in the midst of the countries [that are] desolate, and her cities among the cities [that are] laid waste shall be desolate forty years: **[Due to radioactivity, chemical and biological weapons' residue used by Iraq/Russia etc. on Egypt.]** and I will scatter the Egyptians among the nations, and will disperse them through the countries.

Egypt's southern regions will be destroyed by a nuclear attack from Russia and Islamic allies and that no one can pass through land for forty years. The positive end will be the settling of the upper Nile delta with the Egyptians gathered from the nations to which they are scattered.

Ezekiel 29:13-14

> *13 Yet thus saith the Lord GOD; At the end of forty years will I gather the Egyptians from the people whither they were scattered:*
>
> *14 And I will bring again the captivity of Egypt, and will cause them to return [into] the land of Pathros, into the land of their habitation; and they shall be there a base kingdom.*

We see that Israel is not included in this list as the attack, which will occur on the Passover, will pass over the Nation of Israel because God had supernaturally protected the nation and they utilize sophisticated anti-missile defences devised before and after the Gulf War. The other Arab countries burned by the nuclear attack from Iraq and Russia, etc., include Jordan, Syria, Kuwait, Saudi Arabia, Yemen, Lebanon, northern Iraq and Iran. They are listed in Jeremiah chapters 49 and 50, and also Ezekiel chapters 25 to 32. The cruel ruler sent against Egypt in the end times is the Russian ruler, who will destroy the southern cities of Egypt to be desolate 40 years.

Ezekiel 30: 24-26

> *24 And I will strengthen the arms of the king of Babylon* **[Iraq]**, *and put my sword in his hand: but I will break Pharaoh's arms* **[Egypt]**, *and he shall groan before him with the groanings of a deadly wounded [man].*
>
> *25 But I will strengthen the arms of the king of Babylon* **[Military forces of Iraq]**, *and the arms of Pharaoh shall fall down* **[Egyptian military weakness and internal revolt]**; *and they shall know that I [am] the LORD, when I shall put my sword into the hand of the king of Babylon, and he shall stretch it out upon the land of Egypt.*
>
> *26 And I will scatter the Egyptians among the nations, and disperse them among the countries; and they shall know that I [am] the LORD.*

56. Do we have proof that the Ezekiel tablets are unaltered from ancient times?

The recent discovery of the Ezekiel tablets dating back 2,700 years confirms the authenticity of the book of Ezekiel. A Jewish oral tradition dating from the time of Ezekiel and written down in the 1840's by a Jewish Rabbi was called Vilna Gaon (Refer Grant Jeffrey, "Armageddon...", p. 106). It states, "When the Russians and their Allies come through the Bosporus into the Mediterranean, put on your Sabbath clothes for the Messiah is coming to save Israel."

Mr. David Allen Lewis in his book, "Prophecy 2000", quotes a friend of his, Yehuda Oppenheim, as having examined the Ezekiel tablets of marble and basalt. He feels that these are not a copy but the direct, original book of Ezekiel from the hands of the prophet.

To Take A Spoil

57. Why would Israel be invaded by the Russia and allies?

The motive will be to plunder great wealth.

Ezekiel 38:10-12

> *10 Thus saith the Lord GOD; It shall also come to pass, [that] at the same time shall things come into thy mind, and thou shalt think an evil thought:*
>
> *11 And thou shalt say, I will go up to the land of unwalled villages* **[After a peace treaty and deceived by the man of peace, the leader of Russia. America is the land of unwalled villages!]**; *I will go to them that are at rest, that dwell safely, all of them dwelling without walls, and having neither bars nor gates,* **[This states the circumstances of the attack on America!]**
>
> *12 To take a spoil, and to take a prey; to turn thine hand upon the desolate places [that are now] inhabited, and upon the people [that are] gathered out of the nations* **[All of the people**

of America, who have come from all over the world to seek freedom!], *which have gotten cattle and goods, that dwell in the midst of the land.*

What great wealth is in the Middle East but oil! Secondly, Israel is at the center of the navel of the earth, a land bridge between Europe, Africa and Asia positioned strategically for world military domination. To take the strategic nation of Israel, America must simultaneously be attacked.

Later we will review specific prophecies related to the oil present in Israel and the importance of Israel in relationship to countering the Russian dominance in the Middle East by the United States of America, Canada and European nations. Israel has vast oil reserves and also nuclear and conventional military strategic counters to Russian invasion of the Middle East. Therefore, a key nation to be removed from obstructing the Russian plans for world domination, is Israel.

58. What is the composition and characteristics of the final empire of clay and iron of Daniel 2:33?

The final empire combines the military power of the Soviets [**iron**] with the economic power of Germany and the European Community and the oil resource countries of the Middle East [**clay**]. The Empire that Jesus would destroy would include the four world-wide kingdoms of gold, silver, brass and iron, and the toes of mixed iron and clay. This would include the Japethite nations of Magog, Mechech and Tubal to comprise the West and Central U.S.S.R. nations. It would also be composed of the nations of Iraq, Iran, Greece, Ethiopia, including the eastern Sudan, Libya, Ukraine and the adjacent nations of the Western Former U.S.S.R., and the Slavic nations of Southwestern Former U.S.S.R. such as Yugoslavia, Romania, and eastern Turkey. These are the same nations mentioned by the prophet Daniel in the second chapter and in Ezekiel, chapter thirty-eight. Gomer also contains the country of Germany, through the son Ashkenaz. Comparing this territorial map with that of the Club of Rome ten world economic-political kingdoms, we see that kingdoms two, five, and seven are taken over by the Beast and are ruled from the middle of the last seven years until the End of the Age. (From Foreign Affairs the Journal of the C.F.R.)

Revelation 13: 1-18

1 And I stood upon the sand of the sea, **[Empire]** *and saw a beast rise up out of the sea,* **[the chaos of nations]** *having seven heads and ten horns, and upon his horns ten crowns, and upon his heads the name of blasphemy.* **[The resurrected UnHoly Roman Empire of Masonic Blasphemy; all the royalty of Europe and Russia who claim to be bloodline decendants from Jesus and Mary Magdalene, through Godfrey de Bouillon. The world is divided up into ten territories by the Council on Foreign Relations into ten geopolitical regions!]**

2 And the beast which I saw was like unto a leopard, and his feet were as [the feet] of a bear, and his mouth as the mouth of a lion: and the dragon **[America directed by Satanic Masonism]** *gave him his power, and his seat, and great authority.*

3 And I saw one of his heads as it were wounded to death; and his deadly wound was healed: and all the world wondered after the beast.

4 And they worshipped the dragon which gave power unto the beast: and they worshipped the beast, saying, Who [is] like unto the beast? who is able to make war with him? **[Who can make war with the New World Order!]**

5 And there was given unto him a mouth speaking great things and blasphemies; and power was given unto him to continue forty [and] two months. **[His power is time limited to 3-1/2 years on the Jewish calendar or 1,260 days!]**

6 And he opened his mouth in blasphemy against God, to blaspheme his name, and his tabernacle, and them that dwell in heaven. **[The Masonic NWO will blaspheme the Tabernacle in Jerusalem and stop the sacrifice on the Temple Mount!]**

7 And it was given unto him to make war with the saints, and to overcome them: and power was given him over all kindreds, and tongues, and nations. **[Jewish and Christian Believers will be martyred by the N.W.O.!]**

8 And all that dwell upon the earth shall worship him, whose names are not written in the book of life of the Lamb slain from the foundation of the world.

9 If any man have an ear, let him hear.

10 He that leadeth into captivity shall go into captivity: he that killeth with the sword must be killed with the sword. **[Christians will revolt – some will be executed – some will fight and die in the civil war in America and other countries!]** *Here is the patience and the faith of the saints.*

11 And I beheld another beast coming up out of the earth; and he had two horns like a lamb, and he spake as a dragon. **[America is this second beast that will enforce the Mark of the Beast!]**

12 And he exerciseth all the power of the first beast before him, and causeth the earth and them which dwell therein to worship the first beast, whose deadly wound was healed.

13 And he doeth great wonders, so that he maketh fire come down from heaven on the earth in the sight of men, **[America's superior Star Wars weaponry will enforce the Mark on the whole world!]**

14 And deceiveth them that dwell on the earth by [the means of] those miracles which he had power to do in the sight of the beast; saying to them that dwell on the earth, that they should make an image to the beast, which had the wound by a sword, and did live.

15 And he had power to give life unto the image of the beast, that the image of the beast should both speak, and cause that as many as would not worship the image of the beast should be killed.

16 And he causeth all, both small and great, rich and poor, free and bond, to receive a mark in their right hand, or in their foreheads: **[The Mark of the Beast Year/Month/Day:Mesh Bar Code -Sector --/Subsector- -/ and Local Subsector--:DNA Fingerprint - - - - - -, 6/6/6. The Iridium Project in Denver, Colorado is the location from which this system will be based for the world!]**

17 And that no man might buy or sell, save he that had the mark, or the name of the beast, or the number of his name. **[All other means of exchange will be outlawed!]**

18 Here is wisdom. Let him that hath understanding count the number of the beast: for it is the number of a man; and his number [is] Six hundred threescore [and] six.

The beast of Revelation 13:1 represents the same beast as Revelation 17:11, which is the **eighth successive secular empire.** William Goetz explains these successive empires in his book "Economy to Come", as Assyria, Egypt, Babylon, Medo-Persia, Greece, Rome and the United States of Europe is the seventh. The eighth empire is the New World Order Government, that at the midpoint of the last seven years, it will take over the seventh empire based on the economic domination of The United States of Europe. The prophet Daniel explains in Daniel 7:24, that the dictator of this final empire will take over three of the world's final economic-political kingdoms. The Club of Rome, a Masonic New World Order Organization, published in 1970, its plan for this ten kingdom New World Order Government. Based on the Masonic prophet, Albert Pike's 1860 Royal Arch Masonic Bible, "Morals and Dogma", foretold of such a ten kingdom world government with three of these kingdoms taken over by the Antichrist, at the End of the Age. These are The United States of Europe and the Oil Nations of the Middle East after a Militarily Unified Russian Lead Former Soviet East Block Alliance. The leader of Russia will be that coming world dictator.

Revelation 17:9-18

9 And here [is] the mind which hath wisdom. The seven heads are seven mountains, on which the woman sitteth.

10 And there are seven kings: [These are seven secular empires.] *five are fallen, and one is, [and] the other is not yet come; and when he cometh, he must continue a short space.* **[The first five-world secular kingdoms have fallen. The current one is Rome. Resurrected Rome is to come at the time of the End, but will only last for a little while.]**

11 And the beast that was, and is not, even he is the eighth, and is of the seven, and goeth into perdition.

12 And the ten horns which thou sawest are ten kings, which have received no kingdom as yet; but receive power as kings one hour with the beast.

13 These have one mind, and shall give their power and strength unto the beast.

14 These shall make war with the Lamb, and the Lamb shall overcome them: for he is Lord of lords, and King of kings: and they that are with him [are] called, and chosen, and faithful.

15 And he saith unto me, The waters which thou sawest, where the whore sitteth, are peoples, and multitudes, and nations, and tongues.

16 And the ten horns which thou sawest upon the beast, these shall hate the whore, and shall make her desolate and naked, and shall eat her flesh, and burn her with fire.

17 For God hath put in their hearts to fulfil his will, and to agree, and give their kingdom unto the beast, until the words of God shall be fulfilled.

18 And the woman which thou sawest is that great city, which reigneth over the kings of the earth. **[This is America, the daughter of Babylon the Great!]**

The eighth king is the take-over in the middle of the seven-year period by the beast of Russia in collusion with the King of Iraq to control the world economy and to dominate the world with Russia's military machine. We can therefore see that the composition of the Beast Empire will include all of the above kingdoms of Assyria, Egypt, Babylon, Medo-Persia, Greece, Rome. The military power of Russia and its allies will be considered the nations of Iron, and the economic power of Germany as head of a United Europe and the oil-producing resources of the Middle East as the Nations of Clay. They will not hold together, nor will the tenuous alliance between New Age Masonism and Communist Secular Atheism. Is it not fitting that the God of Abraham, Isaac, and Jacob will allow Secular Atheism to destroy all of the Abomination Religions on earth originating from ancient Babylon. He will then come in Power and Glory to destroy the ruler of Secular Communist Atheism, with his Holy ones.

59. How long will the authority of the Antichrist Empire of the Fourth Reich last?

His period of authority will be for forty-two months or 1,260 days and therefore it shows that the Russians take over the European economy in the middle of the seven year period. The second beast is a false prophet who would eventually be accepted by the Jews as Messiah.

This will result in Russian invasion of the middle east after the King of Iraq stands in the Dome of the Rock. Russia will seize three of the ten world kingdoms with capitulation of the E.C. Nations and control of the world oil reserve in Neo-Babylon via Iraq's nuclear attack on Arab neighbours. This beast 'out of the earth' made all people on earth worship the resurrected Nazi German-based New Age Socialism of the European Economic community. All inhabitants of Earth will be forced to take the Mark of the Beast., by the False Prophet U.S. President. This is a microchip mark in their right hand and/or forehead, a universal databank identicode.

60. Who is the current enforcer of the New World Order?

The enforcer of the New World Order at our current time is none other than the President of the United States of America under the authority of the United Nations. To illustrate, the war of Desert Storm with the U.N. coalition against Iraq was not so much a war against an evil aggressor but a war to establish the moral right and military will to enforce U.N. decisions.

With the U.S.A. and Soviet Union co-operating, nothing could prevent the New World Order from enforcing peace. This kind of peace is a form of government enforced by a U.S. lead G-7 country U.N. with economic and military backing from all the great industrial nations, U.S.A. and allies, former Soviet Nations, European Community, and Japan and Eastern rim nations.

America = Mystery Babylon!
Pogo: "I have seen the enemy and the enemy is us!"

Revelation 3:17-18

17 Because thou sayest, I am rich, and increased with goods, and have need of nothing; and knowest not that thou art wretched, and miserable, and poor, and blind, and naked:

18 I counsel thee to buy of me gold tried in the fire, that thou mayest be rich; and white raiment, that thou mayest be clothed, and [that] the shame of thy nakedness do not appear; and anoint thine eyes with eyesalve, that thou mayest see.

Revelation 10:4

And when the seven thunders had uttered their voices, I was about to write: and I heard a voice from heaven saying unto me, Seal up those things which the seven thunders uttered, and write them not.

Revelation 10:9

> *And I went unto the angel, and said unto him, Give me the little book. And he said unto me, Take [it], and eat it up; and it shall make thy belly bitter, but it shall be in thy mouth sweet as honey.*

> The scroll will be eaten, digested and become part of the end time Christians. Its sweetness is a blessed hope that Jesus will return at the end of these crisis, but its bitterness is the awful judgments to come upon the earth with the ultimate judgment to many fellow men of eternal second death in the lake of fire separated from God for eternity.

American President = False Prophet!
"There is no profit like a false prophet!"

Revelation 16:13

> *13 And I saw three unclean spirits like frogs [come] out of the mouth of the dragon, and out of the mouth of the beast, and out of the mouth of the false prophet.* **[The Religion of the New World Order Will Be the Ancient Babylonian Recycling-Reincarnation Lie Presented as the Earth Charters 18 Commandments for a New Sustainable Planet!]**

Jeremiah 28:13-16

> *13 Go and tell Hananiah, saying, Thus saith the LORD; Thou hast broken the yokes of wood; but thou shalt make for them yokes of iron.*

> *14 For thus saith the LORD of hosts, the God of Israel; I have put a yoke of iron upon the neck of all these nations, that they may serve Nebuchadnezzar king of Babylon; and they shall serve him: and I have given him the beasts of the field also.*

> *15 Then said the prophet Jeremiah unto Hananiah the prophet, Hear now, Hananiah; The LORD hath not sent thee; but thou makest this people to trust in a lie.*

16 Therefore thus saith the LORD; Behold, I will cast thee from off the face of the earth: this year thou shalt die, because thou hast taught rebellion against the LORD.

Dreams and Visions:
January 2nd, 1999

In the middle of the night, the angel Gabriel came to me. He announced that he was sent to correct a serious error in what I was thinking about the world leader that would be the False Prophet.

In an instant I stood in the Oval Office of the White House in Washington, but I could not make out the face or the voice of the president as he sat at his Presidential desk. The content of the conversation to the Russian leader was as follows: "We are now prepared for the contingency of implementing the National Implantable Identification, but I would be most appreciative if you will commit to at least 500,000 Russian troops via the United Nations, to quell any resistance from the civilian American population!"

In a flash, I stood with him outside on the lawn in front of the Washington Monument. The President was on a platform, with many secret service men about watching security.

To my dismay, I heard him say: "My American brothers and sisters and citizens of our tiny and fragile planet Earth, I address you with a response to the grave news of the world-wide recent environmental catastrophe ... Today I am adopting the Earth Charter that has been ratified by the United Nations, and requesting that all citizens take to heart the chance to change the face of our history. I ask you, as President, to join with me and ask what you can do to save our world as we open the pages of the New Millennium. All citizens have been asked to recycle, and to minimize their consumption of energy. Preservation of our open spaces and parks, and the heritage of clean air, water are a legacy we must pledge to preserve not only for future generations but for all life forms on our planet. Just as President Kennedy announced that we were up to the challenge of the voyage to the moon, it will be one step for America, and one giant leap for the salvation of the Earth, our mother planet.

Tomorrow, I ask that all citizens will report in an orderly fashion for a more secure national identification. This final step in our phased-in National ID program will assure peace and security for all our citizens. Violence in our streets and theft will end. Illegal sales of drugs will be removed from the dangerous hearts of our inner cities. Medical care and social security will take a major leap forward. This new ID Chip will make the chances of a medical mistaken identity impossible that would result in the death of a loved one.

The rights of all minorities in our great nation will be guaranteed: the right to live in a clean and safe world, free from drugs, violence and the oppression of poverty.

Join me in a call to peace and security, that will end the troubles that came at the outset of this New Millennium with Y2K, terrorism and the proliferation of weapons of mass destruction.

This is a time to personally agree with me in an oath to save our Nation and our planet. Resolve with me, your President, to join in creating a New World Order, one based on not only the brotherhood of all men but of all life forms on Earth. This is the challenge I ask you to meet tomorrow, as we witness to the whole world. May our example, and our determination to save our nation and our world prepare us for the challenges of this Golden Millennium!"

61. Why is the re-unification of Germany so important to end times creation of the final Empire of Clay and Iron?

The link between these two great empires of the European United States and Soviet State is Germany. In 1990, we've seen reunification of Germany, and cheap labour from eastern bloc countries was available to world wide investments. All is set in motion for Frankfurt, German banks, to control the world economy.

The need to modernize and resurrect and restructure the broken USSR economy as mentioned by President Mikhail Gorbachev was the payoff in the deal made between the U.S.A. and the USSR and European countries to allow East Germany to become unified with the West. Notably all other Russian countries have been prevented from leaving. The European economic community is unified in Daniel 7:24, the seventh kingdom, the European unification. The eighth kingdom of the Russio-Eurasian Empire or of Revelation 17:9-11, subdues three Monarchy kingdoms or countries, kingdoms within the ten kingdom world government.

On reviewing Gorbachev's book, "PERESTROIKA - New Thinking for Our Country and the World", he deals with the issue of Europe's opportunities in Chapter 6, from page 190 to 209. It is very clear from Mr. Gorbachev's policy that he was behind the German unification and was pushing for disarmament and direct economic links between the unified European currency and the Russian ruble. All these events have occurred, the latest being the $24 billion from the International Monetary Fund to back the Russian ruble as of April '91, and a mechanism to control the number of rubles in circulation.

Once the E.C.U. or European Currency Unit becomes established as a currency standard for Europe after December 31, 1992, they will be moved to directly tie the Russian ruble to the European Currency Unit, and to open up E.C. membership for eastern bloc countries including Russia. With the vast majority of investment dollars approximately 82 per cent through Frankfurt bank to the

Eastern Bloc countries this provides the economic infrastructure for Russia to continue its military expansion and plans for a takeover of the seventh empire of the European community halfway through the seven-year period.

62. Who is the Dictator Beast of the New World Order?

The dictator beast of Revelation 13: 1-10 of the New World Order leader of Russia referred to in Ezekiel 38 and 39. He enforces the world's economic system based on the Trilateral Commission, set up by the world Royal Arch Masons under the Illuminati based on the United States, Japan and Europe as a center of the world economy. This occurs under the co-operation of the Russians to enforce the Arab States to agree to a peace treaty with Israel. The purpose is to stabilize the oil supply to Europe to stabilize the world's economy. The E.F.T., Electronic Fund Transfer technology, and the enforcement of the New World Order by the U.S.A. will thus exclude all Christians from commerce.

Beast Empire = E+W Europe+Middle East!
"Nero, can you play that tune again!"

Revelation 13:1-10

1 And I stood upon the sand of the sea, and saw a beast rise up out of the sea, having seven heads and ten horns, and upon his horns ten crowns, and upon his heads the name of blasphemy.

2 And the beast which I saw was like unto a leopard, and his feet were as [the feet] of a bear, and his mouth as the mouth of a lion: and the dragon gave him his power, and his seat, and great authority.

3 And I saw one of his heads as it were wounded to death; and his deadly wound was healed: and all the world wondered after the beast.

4 And they worshipped the dragon which gave power unto the beast: and they worshipped the beast, saying, Who [is] like unto the beast? who is able to make war with him?

5 And there was given unto him a mouth speaking great things and blasphemies; and power was given unto him to continue forty [and] two months.

6 And he opened his mouth in blasphemy against God, to blaspheme his name, and his tabernacle, and them that dwell in heaven.

7 And it was given unto him to make war with the saints, and to overcome them: and power was given him over all kindreds, and tongues, and nations.

8 And all that dwell upon the earth shall worship him, whose names are not written in the book of life of the Lamb slain from the foundation of the world.

9 If any man have an ear, let him hear.

10 He that leadeth into captivity shall go into captivity: he that killeth with the sword must be killed with the sword. Here is the patience and the faith of the saints.

63. What is the origin of the word New World Order?

The 'New World Order' is a translation of the Latin term Novas Order Seclorum, from the U.S. Federal Reserve note, or dollar. It is the name of the Illuminati set up in 1726 and the latest organization formed by Royal Arch Masons to control the world economy. Mr. George Bush joined the Masons while at Yale University and became a member of the Skull and Bones Ivy-league Fraternity. Mr. Gorbachev likewise uses terms which indicate that he has Masonic roots as well, including the term "New World Order" repeated numerous times, and his brand of socialism in his book "PERESTROIKA--" is none other than New Age Marxist-Leninist Communism. Although each has different definitions of their New Age philosophy of creating a Utopia, both

Mr. Bush and Mr. Gorbachev have been working closely at creating the New World Order with greater economic and military co-operation demonstrated by the Gulf War, unification of Germany, and the welding together of the nation-states of Europe into the seventh empire - the United States of Europe.

64. How did Nazism forewarn of the New World Order and the Rise of the Beast Empire of Clay and Iron?

Masons controlled the German National Party which later became the Nazi Party. Therefore, German Nationalist Masons outlawed Masonry and purged all those who would not accept their political ideals for development of the Aryan civilization based on New Age philosophies. Those Masons that were not executed or killed were imprisoned. After the war Masonism regained economic and political control of Germany. Examination of the flag of East Germany before unification, shows clearly the combination of the Soviet symbols of the hammer and sickle with the symbols of Masonism - the square and compass.

It is well known that Nazism is identical in all of its viewpoints with the development of the Aryans and the mysticism of Hindu Aryanism is confirmed by the finding of 1,000 Tibetan monks in Berlin during the World War II Russian invasion of the city. The explanation is that Hitler was a Hindu Buddhist swami and that there were direct ties to eastern mysticism that ruled the policy of elimination of Jews. As we see the reunification of Germany the rise of Neo-Nazism and intolerance shows that the identical elements are present.

It appears that the conditioning, however, is much more effective with mass media such as television and radio and mass communications hasn't prepared the populace of not only Germany, but all of the western countries to accept New Age philosophy as infiltrated through everything from education to religion and science. The European psyche (sp.) has been particularly tuned to this. We are indeed on the verge of the Fourth

Reich with the economic power of Germany and the military power of a resurrected Russian-Germanic empire.

65. How has the United Stated co-operated with the development of United States as world economic enforcer?

Lenin staged the counter revolution with the Bolshevics against a popularly elected legal government, supported by the Rockefellers in 1917. $10,000,000.00 of arms were sent from New York harbour to help the Bolshevic revolution. In the early '70's the U.S.A. sponsored the setting up of the bank of Russia and later the bank of China. It is obvious that the United States has acted as the world economic enforcer.

As we shall see, the Bretton-Woods plan which served until the early seventies basically used the United States as the world currency base. Since that time the U. S. has continued to be the economic and military enforcer and has been instrumental in development of the Tri-lateral Commission supporting the United Nations, development of the International Monetary Fund and World Bank and setting up major bank branches in other third world countries as well as the communist world. The Tri-lateral Commission, sponsored by the United States and set up by the Illuminati Masons, now moves quickly toward stabilization with the development of a European United States of Europe balanced against the United States and its trading allies, as well as Japan and its eastern rim Asian allies. As demonstrated in the Gulf War, the United States is still the only country capable of mobilizing a large force and striking against the significant armed forces of the fourth largest size in the world prior to the Gulf War.

66. Who is the God of Masonism?

The God of Masonism is Jahbulon or Jahweh, creator God of Israel, Baal the Assyrian fertility God and Osiris the Egyptian God of death and the underworld. They thus elevate Satan to be equivalent to God and make no difference between good and evil, but serve both.

The God of Masonism is therefore a composite God made of the creator God, Jahweh, of ancient Israel, and the destroyer, Satan. Satan assumes the creative role as the fertility god as the interaction between the creative force of Jahweh and the destructive force of Satan. This is no different than any of the other forms of eastern mysticism such as Ying and Yang in China, or RaMaat in the Arab World, that is Ra symbolizing the sun god or creation and Maat signifying the destroyer. By becoming masters of good works and in the service of evil for good ends, world Masonism attempts to worship man and elevates him to Godhood by obtaining such mastery. These are no different than the forces of Star Wars of the good force and the dark force. They were manipulated by the Jedi masters. The most reliable thing about the New Age is that there is nothing new since the initial lie in Genesis, but the packaging has been updated.

67. How does a Mason view good works and the mastery of both good and evil? What are the identity of the two Babylons of the end times?

Masonic Shriners set up burn units and orthopaedic units. Masons try to collect good works to enter the grand lodge in the heavenlies. Salvation is therefore not by grace, but by works. Masonism is in direct opposition to the gospel, in that exaltation of self, as Jesus Christ said, would result in destruction, but whosoever would humble himself before Jesus would be exalted.

There will be two Babylons in the End Times. The first Babylon, the Beast of Seven Heads and ten horns, is Mystery Babylon, world Royal Arch Masonism and the New Age Religious Movement controlling the world economy with the United States leading the U.N. as being enforcer. The second is Babylon the Great, the resurrection of the ancient Babylonian Empire based on oil, wealth, and military power. This is the Empire from which the holy war against Israel is launched and later results in the Russian invasion and takeover of the Arab and Moslem oil producing states.

The New Age Movement based at the Tara Centre in California is behind such a Moslem fundamentalist as their New Age Matreya, the messiah for the New Age. The Babylonish economic power of Royal Arch Masonism are trying to place a Davidic-line Jew from European royalty onto the throne of Emperor of a new Holy Roman Empire which would come in direct conflict with not only Babylon the Great, the resurrected ancient Babylonian empire based on oil, but Mystery Babylon the New Age religious system will ride its back. The Beast of Seven Heads and ten horns will destroy Babylon the Great and Mystery Babylon. It is at the time when the Beast Dictator of Russia takes over Europe, that the Great Persecution will commence against the Christian, both Jew and Gentile, within the territory of his combined three kingdoms.

Revelation 17:15-18

15 And he saith unto me, The waters which thou sawest, where the whore sitteth, are peoples, and multitudes, and nations, and tongues.

16 And the ten horns which thou sawest upon the beast, these shall hate the whore, and shall make her desolate and naked, and shall eat her flesh, and burn her with fire.

17 For God hath put in their hearts to fulfil his will, and to agree, and give their kingdom unto the beast, until the words of God shall be fulfilled.

18 And the woman which thou sawest is that great city, which reigneth over the kings of the earth.

The Beast or head of Russia, will hate America, Mystery Babylon and Spiritual Israel. This is what will cause hooks to be placed in jaws of Russia as the military leader of this alliance. God will bring it down to take over control of the Middle East and destroy Babylon, and to persecute and destroy the Babylonian religious system. Masonism believes in European domination of the world through their Davidic-line king.

68. What are the military events which have occurred in the Middle East at the middle of the Tribulation?

These events start in the middle of the seven year period with Egypt, Arab and American Allies pushing militarily against an increasingly aggressive Iraq, with Russian and allied support. This later results in an Iraqi-Arab Moslem/Russian alliance taking over the nations of the Middle East with Russian help and armaments. The Russian/Iraqi alliance will camp and surround Jerusalem in the middle of the seven years and the half of the population who are Jews and Christians will be removed, persecuted, and executed over a 1,260-day period.

Zechariah 14:2-5

2 For I will gather all nations against Jerusalem to battle; and the city shall be taken, and the houses rifled, and the women ravished; and half of the city shall go forth into captivity, and the residue of the people shall not be cut off from the city. **[When Russian backed Iraq enters Jerusalem, then the Western half of the population will be Jews or Christians, and will be removed from the city and taken back captive just as king Nebuchadnezzar did to ancient Israel.]**

3 Then shall the LORD go forth, and fight against those nations, as when he fought in the day of battle.

4 And his feet shall stand in that day upon the mount of Olives, which [is] before Jerusalem on the east, and the mount of Olives shall cleave in the midst thereof toward the east and toward the west, [and there shall be] a very great valley; and half of the mountain shall remove toward the north, and half of it toward the south. **[God himself will fight for the nation of Israel and his spiritual people of Israel, Christians both Jew and**

Gentile. The Great Earthquake is the one great quake that will end the Age and time for man on the old Earth.]

5 And ye shall flee [to] the valley of the mountains; for the valley of the mountains shall reach unto Azal: yea, ye shall flee, like as ye fled from before the earthquake in the days of Uzziah king of Judah: and the LORD my God shall come, [and] all the saints with thee. **[This is the time for the THE SIGN OF JESUS COMING with his Holy Ones. This is time time of the Rapture of all those left alive till the Coming of the LORD.]**

69. What is the identity of the nation of Harlot Babylon and what is its ultimate fate?

Dreams and Visions:

In October 1998, after a busy office, I was praying and reading in Jeremiah. Suddenly, I was taken in the spirit by the angel Gabriel to the Parliament of Europe in Strasbourg, France. There he told me to observe the meeting that was happening with eighteen representatives of the European Union around a large board table. In the center, there was a silver challis and they passed a short, approximately 18 inch, silver sword with a golden handle to all the members at the table and swore a blood oath by cutting their right thumb and marking the blood on the right ear after bleeding into the challis with blood mixed with wine. They came together in worship of Satan and setup his kingdom on earth. They also swore to destroy America.

"By the blood of Hiram and the enlightenment of Osiris, I do pledge to the most excellent and illuminated One, to carry forth my pledge and duty to the New Order of the Ages. By my blood and with this sign, I seal my honor to do all that we have purposed here today, on pain of death by disembowelment and having my heart wrenched from my bosom. So say the Noble Knights of the Order."

I was completely overwhelmed that countries we consider our allies would scheme to destroy our nation in order to set up the New World Order. I asked the angel when, and he again had me turn my attention to the debate as to when America would be attacked. They all came to one accord to destroy America when the EURO Dollar was completely in control of the European Economy and the all of the Illuminated Sons had removed their wealth from America and the US Stock Market into the European Banking System. Thus the sign were set and the plot hatched to destroy America when this evil plot has been brought to the fullness, and not a day earlier.

Exodus 28:15-68

15 But it shall come to pass, if thou wilt not hearken unto the voice of the LORD thy God, to observe to do all his commandments and his statutes which I command thee this day; that all these curses shall come upon thee, and overtake thee:

16 Cursed [shalt] thou [be] in the city, and cursed [shalt] thou [be] in the field.

17 Cursed [shall be] thy basket and thy store.

18 Cursed [shall be] the fruit of thy body, and the fruit of thy land, the increase of thy kine, and the flocks of thy sheep.

19 Cursed [shalt] thou [be] when thou comest in, and cursed [shalt] thou [be] when thou goest out.

20 The LORD shall send upon thee cursing, vexation, and rebuke, in all that thou settest thine hand unto for to do, until thou be destroyed, and until thou perish quickly; because of the wickedness of thy doings, whereby thou hast forsaken me.

21 The LORD shall make the pestilence cleave unto thee, until he have consumed thee from off the land, whither thou goest to possess it.

22 The LORD shall smite thee with a consumption, and with a fever, and with an inflammation, and with an extreme burning, and with the sword, and with blasting, and with mildew; and they shall pursue thee until thou perish.

23 And thy heaven that [is] over thy head shall be brass, and the earth that is under thee [shall be] iron.

24 The LORD shall make the rain of thy land powder and dust: from heaven shall it come down upon thee, until thou be destroyed.

25 The LORD shall cause thee to be smitten before thine enemies: thou shalt go out one way against them, and flee seven ways before them: and shalt be removed into all the kingdoms of the earth.

26 And thy carcase shall be meat unto all fowls of the air, and unto the beasts of the earth, and no man shall fray [them] away.

27 The LORD will smite thee with the botch of Egypt, and with the emerods, and with the scab, and with the itch, whereof thou canst not be healed.

28 The LORD shall smite thee with madness, and blindness, and astonishment of heart:

29 And thou shalt grope at noonday, as the blind gropeth in darkness, and thou shalt not prosper in thy ways: and thou shalt be only oppressed and spoiled evermore, and no man shall save [thee].

30 Thou shalt betroth a wife, and another man shall lie with her: thou shalt build an house, and thou shalt not dwell therein: thou shalt plant a vineyard, and shalt not gather the grapes thereof.

31 Thine ox [shall be] slain before thine eyes, and thou shalt not eat thereof: thine ass [shall be] violently taken away from before thy face, and shall not be restored to thee: thy sheep [shall be] given unto thine enemies, and thou shalt have none to rescue [them].

32 Thy sons and thy daughters [shall be] given unto another people, and thine eyes shall look, and fail [with longing] for

them all the day long: and [there shall be] no might in thine hand.

33 The fruit of thy land, and all thy labours, shall a nation which thou knowest not eat up; and thou shalt be only oppressed and crushed alway:

34 So that thou shalt be mad for the sight of thine eyes which thou shalt see.

35 The LORD shall smite thee in the knees, and in the legs, with a sore botch that cannot be healed, from the sole of thy foot unto the top of thy head.

36 The LORD shall bring thee, and thy king which thou shalt set over thee, unto a nation which neither thou nor thy fathers have known; and there shalt thou serve other gods, wood and stone.

37 And thou shalt become an astonishment, a proverb, and a byword, among all nations whither the LORD shall lead thee.

38 Thou shalt carry much seed out into the field, and shalt gather [but] little in; for the locust shall consume it.

39 Thou shalt plant vineyards, and dress [them], but shalt neither drink [of] the wine, nor gather [the grapes]; for the worms shall eat them.

40 Thou shalt have olive trees throughout all thy coasts, but thou shalt not anoint [thyself] with the oil; for thine olive shall cast [his fruit].

41 Thou shalt beget sons and daughters, but thou shalt not enjoy them; for they shall go into captivity.

42 All thy trees and fruit of thy land shall the locust consume.

43 The stranger that [is] within thee shall get up above thee very high; and thou shalt come down very low.

44 He shall lend to thee, and thou shalt not lend to him: he shall be the head, and thou shalt be the tail.

45 Moreover all these curses shall come upon thee, and shall pursue thee, and overtake thee, till thou be destroyed; because

thou hearkenedst not unto the voice of the LORD thy God, to keep his commandments and his statutes which he commanded thee:

46 And they shall be upon thee for a sign and for a wonder, and upon thy seed for ever.

47 Because thou servedst not the LORD thy God with joyfulness, and with gladness of heart, for the abundance of all [things];

48 Therefore shalt thou serve thine enemies which the LORD shall send against thee, in hunger, and in thirst, and in nakedness, and in want of all [things]: and he shall put a yoke of iron upon thy neck, until he have destroyed thee.

49 The LORD shall bring a nation against thee from far, from the end of the earth, [as swift] as the eagle flieth; a nation whose tongue thou shalt not understand;

50 A nation of fierce countenance, which shall not regard the person of the old, nor shew favour to the young:

51 And he shall eat the fruit of thy cattle, and the fruit of thy land, until thou be destroyed: which [also] shall not leave thee [either] corn, wine, or oil, [or] the increase of thy kine, or flocks of thy sheep, until he have destroyed thee.

52 And he shall besiege thee in all thy gates, until thy high and fenced walls come down, wherein thou trustedst, throughout all thy land: and he shall besiege thee in all thy gates throughout all thy land, which the LORD thy God hath given thee.

53 And thou shalt eat the fruit of thine own body, the flesh of thy sons and of thy daughters, which the LORD thy God hath given thee, in the siege, and in the straitness, wherewith thine enemies shall distress thee:

54 [So that] the man [that is] tender among you, and very delicate, his eye shall be evil toward his brother, and toward the wife of his bosom, and toward the remnant of his children which he shall leave:

55 So that he will not give to any of them of the flesh of his children whom he shall eat: because he hath nothing left him in the siege, and in the straitness, wherewith thine enemies shall distress thee in all thy gates.

56 The tender and delicate woman among you, which would not adventure to set the sole of her foot upon the ground for delicateness and tenderness, her eye shall be evil toward the husband of her bosom, and toward her son, and toward her daughter,

57 And toward her young one that cometh out from between her feet, and toward her children which she shall bear: for she shall eat them for want of all [things] secretly in the siege and straitness, wherewith thine enemy shall distress thee in thy gates.

58 If thou wilt not observe to do all the words of this law that are written in this book, that thou mayest fear this glorious and fearful name, THE LORD THY GOD;

59 Then the LORD will make thy plagues wonderful, and the plagues of thy seed, [even] great plagues, and of long continuance, and sore sicknesses, and of long continuance.

60 Moreover he will bring upon thee all the diseases of Egypt, which thou wast afraid of; and they shall cleave unto thee.

61 Also every sickness, and every plague, which [is] not written in the book of this law, them will the LORD bring upon thee, until thou be destroyed.

62 And ye shall be left few in number, whereas ye were as the stars of heaven for multitude; because thou wouldest not obey the voice of the LORD thy God.

63 And it shall come to pass, [that] as the LORD rejoiced over you to do you good, and to multiply you; so the LORD will rejoice over you to destroy you, and to bring you to nought; and ye shall be plucked from off the land whither thou goest to possess it.

64 And the LORD shall scatter thee among all people, from the one end of the earth even unto the other; and there thou shalt serve other gods, which neither thou nor thy fathers have known, [even] wood and stone.

65 And among these nations shalt thou find no ease, neither shall the sole of thy foot have rest: but the LORD shall give thee there a trembling heart, and failing of eyes, and sorrow of mind:

66 And thy life shall hang in doubt before thee; and thou shalt fear day and night, and shalt have none assurance of thy life:

67 In the morning thou shalt say, Would God it were even! and at even thou shalt say, Would God it were morning! for the fear of thine heart wherewith thou shalt fear, and for the sight of thine eyes which thou shalt see.

68 And the LORD shall bring thee into Egypt again with ships, by the way whereof I spake unto thee, Thou shalt see it no more again: and there ye shall be sold unto your enemies for bondmen and bondwomen, and no man shall buy [you].

Isaiah 13:1-9

1 The burden of Babylon, which Isaiah the son of Amoz did see.

2 Lift ye up a banner upon the high mountain **[Jesus crucifixion on Golgotha]**, *exalt the voice unto them, shake the hand, that they may go into the gates of the nobles.*

3 I have commanded my sanctified ones, I have also called my mighty ones for mine anger, [even] them that rejoice in my highness.

4 The noise of a multitude in the mountains, like as of a great people; a tumultuous noise of the kingdoms of nations gathered together: the LORD of hosts mustereth the host of the battle.

5 They come from a far country, from the end of heaven, [even] the LORD, and the weapons of his indignation, to destroy the whole land.

6 Howl ye; for the day of the LORD [is] at hand; it shall come as a destruction from the Almighty.

7 Therefore shall all hands be faint, and every man's heart shall melt:

8 And they shall be afraid: pangs and sorrows shall take hold of them; they shall be in pain as a woman that travaileth: they shall be amazed one at another; their faces [shall be as] flames. **[Radiation effects on the bowel and radiation burns to the faces of the victims of nuclear attack!]**

9 Behold, the day of the LORD cometh, cruel both with wrath and fierce anger, to lay the land desolate: and he shall destroy the sinners thereof out of it.

Isaiah 13:19-22

19 And Babylon, the glory of kingdoms, the beauty of the Chaldees' excellency, shall be as when God overthrew Sodom and Gomorrah. **[Nuclear Holocaust!]**

20 It shall never be inhabited, neither shall it be dwelt in from generation to generation: neither shall the Arabian pitch tent there; neither shall the shepherds make their fold there. **[It will be uninhabitable for humans.]**

21 But wild beasts of the desert shall lie there; and their houses shall be full of doleful creatures; and owls shall dwell there, and satyrs shall dance there.

22 And the wild beasts of the islands shall cry in their desolate houses, and dragons in [their] pleasant palaces: and her time [is] near to come, and her days shall not be prolonged.

Revelation 17:3-6

3 So he carried me away in the spirit into the wilderness: and I saw a woman **[woman = Mystery Babylon, America]** *sit upon a scarlet coloured beast, full of names of blasphemy, having seven heads and ten horns.*

4 And the woman was arrayed in purple and scarlet colour, **[World Masonism in its many forms, and the New Age World Religion, that will arise from this Prostitute.]** *and decked with gold and precious stones and pearls, having a golden cup in her hand full of abominations and filthiness of her fornication:*

5 And upon her forehead [was] a name written, MYSTERY, BABYLON THE GREAT, THE MOTHER OF HARLOTS AND ABOMINATIONS OF THE EARTH.

6 And I saw the woman drunken with the blood of the saints, and with the blood of the martyrs of Jesus: and when I saw her, I wondered with great admiration. **[The New Age Religion of the New World Government, will persecute and put to death many Christians.]**

From Revelation 15 to 18 it is this economic center, America and the New York Stock Exchange in particular which has prostitute itself by denying the Christian foundations of America, and has become worse that the pagan nations of the world.

This is further confirmed by the tremendous amount of trade identified in Revelation 18 and the continuing reference to the nations of the earth becoming drunk with the wine of her excessive luxuries. This wine is, of course, the money which makes the modern world drunk with wealth and power.

The ultimate judgment will be total destruction to the point of uninhabitability of America. Jeremiah 51:6-10, shows how the nations have drunk the wine [false wealth of the Masonic Controlled New York Stock Exchange] and have gone mad. The context is the same as Revelation 18:2-3 and identifies Babylon the Great with America, modern Babylon. It shows clearly in Revelation 18:8, that America will be the victims of a nuclear holocaust. (See Question 58).

70. When will the Babylon Empire rise to great prominence on the world scene?

According to ***Zechariah 5:5-11***

> *5 Then the angel that talked with me went forth, and said unto me, Lift up now thine eyes, and see what [is] this that goeth forth.*
>
> *6 And I said, What [is] it? And he said, This [is] an ephah that goeth forth. He said moreover, This [is] their resemblance through all the earth.*
>
> *7 And, behold, there was lifted up a talent of lead: and this [is] a woman that sitteth in the midst of the ephah.*
>
> *8 And he said, This [is] wickedness. And he cast it into the midst of the ephah; and he cast the weight of lead upon the mouth thereof.*
>
> *9 Then lifted I up mine eyes, and looked, and, behold, there came out two women, and the wind [was] in their wings; for they had wings like the wings of a stork: and they lifted up the ephah between the earth and the heaven.*
>
> *10 Then said I to the angel that talked with me, Whither do these bear the ephah?*
>
> *11 And he said unto me, To build it an house in the land of Shinar: and it shall be established, and set there upon her own base.* **[Temple to Marduk built by Saddam in Babylon]**

It will occur when a temple is built in the land of Shinar in the city of ancient Babylon. This has now been done by the dictator Saddam Hussein who survived a great devastating war from a coalition of almost thirty nations.

Saddam Hussein or the Iraqi leader to follow will be used by the Russians for controlling the Middle Eastern oil. The Russians and allies will come down from the north in a double cross and as prophesied in Revelation 17:16. Russian and allies will burn

Babylon with fire and depopulate and plunder the Arab countries. Simultaneous with the destruction of Mystery Babylon, or the New Age Movement, will be the destruction of Babylon the Great, the Neo-Babylonian Empire.

71. How will Iraq rise to military dominance in the Middle East?

The Ram of Daniel 8:9 is the fourth part of the splintered kingdom of Alexander the Great, the Medo-Persian Empire. The stern-faced king of Daniel 8:23 is clearly the leader of Iraq, currently Saddam Hussein or his successor. In Daniel 8:24, he will become powerful by another military power, also clearly primarily Russian.

Saddam's ploy is to unify the Arab mentality, to retaliate the infidel invasion of the Middle East. U.S. and allied presence is considered an invasion of the Holy Lands according to Islam. [26-71A, 13-71A]

72. How will Moslems unite for the last great Jihad?

This stern-faced king will set up his court at the Temple Mount in Jerusalem from Daniel 11:45. The city of Jerusalem will thus be destroyed by Moslems and the temple sanctuary where reinstituted Jewish sacrifices will be performed will be destroyed. The leader of Shiite Islam, the Imam-Mahdi, will claim to be the Messiah and set up worship of himself as the Messiah to the Islamic fundamentalists and world-wide New Agers.

Islam will sweep across the third world. This religious center will be set up in the Mosque of Omar, or Dome of the Rock, and as the false Moslem New Age Messiah leads the next and last Moslem holy war or Jihad. This will start on the Feast of Purim when Haman tried during the Medo-Persian Empire to destroy all Jews from the face of the Earth. It is this event that will force the hand of the Russians to be pulled down upon the Middle East to to fight against total Neo-Babylonian control of world oil under an Islamic

Oil-New Age Messianic Kingdom. This Imam-Mahdi results in the desolation or removal of the remaining population of Jews and Christians in West Jerusalem, and will result in the eventual doublecross by Russians and take over of all the Arab countries.

73. Why must Babylon fall under Saddam Hussein, the Iraqi leader, or King?

Jeremiah 51:49

49 As Babylon [hath caused] the slain of Israel to fall, **[Iraq will be destroyed for destroying Israel]**, *so at Babylon shall fall the slain of all the earth.* **[Armageddon will result from oil and Iraq]**

Babylon must fall because so many Jews have been slain in reborn Israel. Only since 1948 could this prophecy come true. Further in Jeremiah 51:49, it goes on to state that the slain in all the earth have fallen in the battle of the end of the age (Armageddon) because of what they have done to Iraq or Babylon the Great. Many other verses from the Bible will seal the fate of modern day Iraq.

Jeremiah 50:46

46 At the noise of the taking of Babylon the earth is moved, and the cry is heard among the nations. **[the great earth upheaval]**

Jeremiah 51:7

7 Babylon [hath been] a golden cup in the LORD'S hand, that made all the earth drunken: the nations have drunken of her wine; therefore the nations are mad.

Jeremiah 51:24

24 And I will render unto Babylon and to all the inhabitants of Chaldea all their evil that they have done in Zion in your sight, saith the LORD. **[God will avenge the destruction of Israel]**

Jeremiah 50:29

> 29 Call together the archers against Babylon: all ye that bend the bow, camp against it round about; let none thereof escape: recompense her according to her work; according to all that she hath done, do unto her: for she hath been proud against the LORD, against the Holy One of Israel.
>
> 30 Therefore shall her young men fall in the streets, and all her men of war shall be cut off in that day, saith the LORD.

Jeremiah 50:41

> 41 Behold, a people shall come from the north, and a great nation, and many kings shall be raised up from the coasts of the earth. **[U.S.A. and allies]**

The uproar among the nations is of course over oil as *Isaiah, 13:3-22 prophesied,*

> 3 I have commanded my sanctified ones, I have also called my mighty ones for mine anger, [even] them that rejoice in my highness. **[Nations that side with Israel, i.e. Christian Nations]**
>
> 4 The noise of a multitude in the mountains, like as of a great people; a tumultuous noise of the kingdoms of nations gathered together: the LORD of hosts mustereth the host of the battle.
>
> 5 They come from a far country, from the end of heaven, [even] the LORD, and the weapons of his indignation, to destroy the whole land.
>
> 6 Howl ye; for the day of the LORD [is] at hand; it shall come as a destruction from the Almighty.
>
> 7 Therefore shall all hands be faint, and every man's heart shall melt:
>
> 8 And they shall be afraid: pangs and sorrows shall take hold of them; they shall be in pain as a woman that travaileth **[radiation abdominal pain]**: they shall be amazed one at another; their faces [shall be as] flames. **[radiation facial burns]**

9 Behold, the day of the LORD cometh, cruel both with wrath and fierce anger, to lay the land desolate: and he shall destroy the sinners thereof out of it. **[nuclear desolation]**

10 For the stars of heaven and the constellations thereof shall not give their light: the sun shall be darkened in his going forth, and the moon shall not cause her light to shine. **[fallout/smoke clouds block out the stars and the sun]**

11 And I will punish the world for [their] evil, and the wicked for their iniquity; and I will cause the arrogancy of the proud to cease, and will lay low the haughtiness of the terrible.

12 I will make a man more precious than fine gold; even a man than the golden wedge of Ophir. **[Man will be as rare as the eight that survived the flood at the Time of Noah].**

13 Therefore I will shake the heavens, and the earth shall remove out of her place, in the wrath of the LORD of hosts, and in the day of his fierce anger. **[The Great Earth Upheaval]**

14 And it shall be as the chased roe, and as a sheep that no man taketh up: they shall every man turn to his own people, and flee every one into his own land.

15 Every one that is found shall be thrust through; and every one that is joined [unto them] shall fall by the sword.

16 Their children also shall be dashed to pieces before their eyes; their houses shall be spoiled, and their wives ravished.

17 Behold, I will stir up the Medes against them, which shall not regard silver; and [as for] gold, they shall not delight in it. **[The Kurds, ancient allies of Persia.]**

18 [Their] bows also shall dash the young men to pieces; and they shall have no pity on the fruit of the womb; their eye shall not spare children.

19 And Babylon, the glory of kingdoms, the beauty of the Chaldees' excellency, shall be as when God overthrew Sodom and Gomorrah. **[Nuclear desolation.]**

20 It shall never be inhabited, neither shall it be dwelt in from generation to generation: neither shall the Arabian pitch tent there; neither shall the shepherds make their fold there.

21 But wild beasts of the desert shall lie there; and their houses shall be full of doleful creatures; and owls shall dwell there, and satyrs shall dance there.

22 And the wild beasts of the islands shall cry in their desolate houses, and dragons in [their] pleasant palaces: and her time [is] near to come, and her days shall not be prolonged.

74. What is the role of the Kurds in the ultimate destruction of Iraq?

There is also a prophecy that the Medes will turn and attack Iraq. The people of the Medes are the Kurds.

Isaiah 13:17-22

17 Behold, I will stir up the Medes against them, which shall not regard silver; and [as for] gold, they shall not delight in it.

18 [Their] bows also shall dash the young men to pieces; and they shall have no pity on the fruit of the womb; their eye shall not spare children.

19 And Babylon, the glory of kingdoms, the beauty of the Chaldees' excellency, shall be as when God overthrew Sodom and Gomorrah.

20 It shall never be inhabited, neither shall it be dwelt in from generation to generation: neither shall the Arabian pitch tent there; neither shall the shepherds make their fold there.

21 But wild beasts of the desert shall lie there; and their houses shall be full of doleful creatures; and owls shall dwell there, and satyrs shall dance there.

22 And the wild beasts of the islands shall cry in their desolate houses, and dragons in [their] pleasant palaces: and her time [is] near to come, and her days shall not be prolonged.

The people of Kurdistan (potential nation) have a population of approximately 22 to 25 million, which include areas of Northern Iraq, Turkey, Iran and the Southern USSR. The Kurds are Moslems, but are not Arabs, and will attack Iraq.

This is similar to the period in which the Medes joined the Babylons to defeat Syria in 612-609 B.C., but later united with Cyrus the Persian to conquer Babylon in 539. As a result we see, eventually, the turning of fundamentalist Moslem nations against the more modern Moslem nations that reject the Imam-Mahdi and we see a battle in which Iran or Persia and the Kurds again will attack and destroy Babylon.

75. What will ultimately happen between the U.S.A. and Israel versus the Russian Lead Resurrected Roman Empire and Arab allies, and when will Babylon the Great ultimately be destroyed?

At day 1,260 there will be an attack by the Russia, Iraq and Islamic allies America and an attempted attack on Israel.

Ultimately, as the forces gather for the battle of Armageddon in the second half of the seven years, these will all culminate however in a three-way nuclear exchange between the kings of the east which include the communist countries such as China and the Moslem countries as well as most probably Japan, the Euro-Russian empire, and the last of the three nations groups will be the United States and its allies.

Jeremiah 25:26

> "...And all the kings of the north, far and near, one with another, and - all the kingdoms of the world, which are upon the face of the earth: and the king of Sheshach shall drink after them. [Sheshach is a cryptogram for Babylon. The Leader of Iraq has a nuclear war proof underground palace. America is the Daughter of Babylon the Great and will be the last to drink the cup of destruction.]

The probable reason for destruction of the Arab oil producing states last is because of the great importance of oil to the world economy. As shown by the tremendous ecological and economic devastation caused by attacks on oil well-heads and supply depots during the Desert Storm counter attack against Iraq after Iraq invaded Kuwait August 2, 1990. Mystery Babylon, America, will therefore be destroyed in one day as Revelation 18 and elsewhere demonstrates, and this will be the 2,520th day after the peace treaty has been signed between the Arabs and Jews. The destruction will come as Sodom and Gomorrah by a nuclear attack making Iraq uninhabitable.

Chapter 3

ARMAGEDDON: SEALS, TRUMPET AND VIAL JUDGMENTS

76. What is the relationship between the sixth and seventh seals of Revelation 6?

The sixth and seventh seals will have a great earthquake happen at the end of the sixth and seventh seals. The seventh seals start on day 1,260 at the Feast of Passover and ends in the great earthquake, at the Feast of Trumpets, or Rosh Hashanah, at day 2,520. The seventh seal is the spiritual judgment occurring simultaneously in heaven on this day ends simultaneously with the great earth upheaval, resulting from a world-wide nuclear holocaust.

The seven trumpets judgments parallel seven vial judgments which have similar plagues occur simultaneously on the earth. The first to fifth trumpets and vials occur on the same day as the first woe, at the Feast of Passover in the middle of the seven years, on day 1,260. The sixth trumpet and vial and the second woe occurs on day 1,415. From the prophet Daniel 8:13-14, there will be 1,150 days from the temple falling until it is rededicated on the New Earth. Exactly 1,150 days back from the 2,565th day, the 17th of Heshvan, brings us to the 1,415th day, five thirty day-months after the end of Passover week of the middle of the last seven years. The significance of this five months is that it corresponds exactly to the Revelation 9 prophecy of a five month invasion Middle Eastern Arab nations. The seventh trumpet and vial and the third woe, occur on the Feast of Trumpets, at day 2,520, on the day of the nuclear world-wide holocaust. (See Fig. 76-1)

Daniel 12:9-12

9 And he said, Go thy way, Daniel: for the words [are] closed up and sealed till the time of the end.

10 Many shall be purified, and made white, and tried; but the wicked shall do wickedly: and none of the wicked shall understand; but the wise shall understand.

11 And from the time [that] the daily [sacrifice] shall be taken away, and the abomination that maketh desolate set up, [there shall be] a thousand two hundred and ninety days.

12 Blessed [is] he that waiteth, and cometh to the thousand three hundred and five and thirty days.

Figure 76-1

Day	Event Feast	Jewish
1	Peace Treaty & Tabernacle Sacrifice Abomination of Desolation	Tabernacles (Sukkot)
1,230	Temple Sacrifice is Stopped	Purim
1,260	Beast Empire - NWO- United E&W Europe Israel & America Attacked	Passover
1,415	Islamic Takeover of the Temple Mount [The 2,300 evening and morning sacrifices & later the temple is cleansed on day 2,565.]	Dan 12:12 Dan 8:14
2,520	3-Way Attack World Nuclear War	Trumpets (Rosh Hashanah)
2,565	The Saved Survivors Enter the Kingdom	17th Heshvan Dan 12:12 Noah Emerges From the Ark

77. When is the timing for the first nuclear attack or first woe during the Tribulation?

It is a time in winter according to Revelation 6:13 and Zechariah 14:6. It is a time when the Jewish law is in effect as the Sabbath prevents any movement beyond 1,000 paces. There is a warning for women that have babies that they are breast feeding for they will have great distress. During this time Babylon the Great Neo Babylonian Empire is attacking with help from Russia with nuclear weapons and conventional weapons.

Revelation 8:7-12

7 The first angel sounded, and there followed hail and fire mingled with blood, **[nuclear attack]** *and they were cast upon the earth: and the third part of trees was burnt up,* **[nuclear firestorm]** *and all green grass was burnt up.* **[world-wide ozone depletion from ice crystal clouds and dust particles catalyzing the Chlorine Monoxide reaction to destroy the protective ozone layer!]**

8 And the second angel sounded, and as it were a great mountain burning with fire was cast into the sea: and the third part of the sea became blood;

9 And the third part of the creatures which were in the sea, and had life, died; and the third part of the ships were destroyed. **["mushroom" fallout 'mountain' clouds fall into the ocean]**

10 And the third angel sounded, and there fell a great star from heaven, burning as it were a lamp **[torch = rocket ICBM]**, *and it fell upon the third part of the rivers, and upon the fountains of waters;*

11 And the name of the star is called Wormwood: and the third part of the waters became **[wormwood = Chernobyl in Russian Ukranian]**; *and many men died of the waters, because they were made bitter.* **[freshwater poisoned by radioactive fallout]**

12 And the fourth angel sounded, and the third part of the sun was smitten, and the third part of the moon, and the third part of the stars; so as the third part of them was darkened, and the day shone not for a third part of it, and the night likewise.

Revelation 9:18

18 By these three was the third part of men killed, by the fire, and by the smoke, and by the brimstone, which issued out of their mouths.

In Revelation 8:7, there is nuclear exchange with one-third of the trees burned up and the ozone layer is destroyed so that all the grassy plants are destroyed world-wide by short wave ultra-violet radiation. This is the first trumpet and the first vial in Revelation 8:7 and Revelation 16:1-2. As we see in figure 77-1, the first nuclear exchange occurs on day 1,260 during the Passover and Jerusalem is passed over for seven days because of its anti-missile system and divine protection. [Q# 58]

Figure 77-1

1st Woe		2nd Woe		3rd Woe	End of Age
Seals 1-5		Seal 6		Seal 7	Jeshua's
Trumpets 1-5		Trumpet 6		Trumpet 7	Eternal
Vials 1-5		Vial 6		Vial 7	Reign in
Woe 1		Woe 2		Woe 3	the New Jerusalem on Earth
Day 1,230 Purim	Day 1,260 Passover	Day 1,265 End of Feast of Unleavened Bread	Day 1,415 3 Armies Gathering for the Battle of Armageddon	Day 2,520 Feast of Trumpets	Day 2,565 17th of Heshvan
Temple Sacrifice Stopped	Occupation of America and Israel			3 Way Nuclear War	Temple is Consecrated
	144,000 Israelites Sealed (Christians)				
	Gentile/Jewish Believers				

78. What will happen during this attack?

This takes place when the Russians attack the Middle East and Babylon the Great – America with the Islamic Nations around Israel. A United Eastern and Western Europe under Russian leadership.

Israel, surrounded with Islamic nations with nuclear weapons, and backed into a corner with no margin for a conventional defense, will resort to a policy of rapid nuclear strike of all Islamic capitals within 3,000 miles of Jerusalem. When the conventional forces surround Israel in a Jihad, Israel will strike out and in a thermonuclear flash on Passover, destroy their tormentors and bring the Russians and the United Nations troops down upon the Middle East and the oil of the region will be in the firm Russian Bear's grip. The world will then be locked in a battle focusing on Northern Israel, in the Valley of Decision, Armageddon!!

79. To what extent will radioactivity poison fresh and salt water and kill life on earth? How much of the fresh water on earth will be radioactive and undrinkable?

The second trumpet sees a great mountain thrown into the sea in Revelation 8:9, "... a third of the living creatures in the sea died, and a third of the ships were destroyed." This occurs just as the first trumpet cause radiation burns similar to the plague of sores in Egypt in Exodus 9:10-11. The second trumpet causes one-third of all salt water creatures and one-third of the ships to be destroyed while the second vial of Revelation 16:3 described the same mountain falling in salt water and all of the creatures in the sea being destroyed. The vial judgments referred to specific judgments against the Beast Dictator's Kingdom and the trumpet judgments against the world.

Downwind of the Middle East is the Indian Ocean. The Moslem countries and the Kings of the East including China, Japan, etc., which will eventually come and invade the Middle East during the battle of Armageddon, partly due to this ecocatastrophe.

The expanding industry of China and the current economy of Japan are very dependent on Middle Eastern oil. Japan currently gets 73% of its oil from the Middle East Gulf States, and with the downward environmentalist political pressure to reduce local nuclear power generation, happening at the middle of the seven-year period, the Kings of the East will have a vested interest in invading and controlling the Middle East, for economical control and environmental motives.

As the plankton die in the oceans, as nuclear winter accelerates ozone depletion, ultraviolet light turns the ocean literally red. It is well known that when phyto-plankton die, from the damage due to the upper ocean from ultra-violet UVB radiation, they become red in color. The oceans will become red just as the Nile river was turned to blood during one of the plagues in which Moses tried to convince Pharoah to let the Israelites go. (Exodus 7:17-21).

The third trumpet is again referring to this great mountain as a star called wormwood, i.e. Chernobyl in Russian, Revelation 8:10-22. One-third of our fresh water on earth is also contaminated with radio-activity. As down wind of the Indian Ocean and the Middle East, the jet stream would carry high into the atmosphere radio-active fall out which would circle the earth and affect one-third of the fresh drinking water. This is a third vial of Revelation 16:4-7, and Iraq, the Kingdom of Babylon, has given blood i.e. radioactivity to drink just as Egypt was given blood to drink during the plagues Moses sent on Egypt for not letting God's people go. (Exodus, 7:17-21) In that plague Moses turned the Nile into blood.

80. Would high atmospheric fallout disturb sunlight and starlight and moonlight and therefore adversely affect crops world wide?

It is noted that the firestorm would affect those without the mark of God, and that this firestorm would cause a great darkness upon the throne of the Beast, and as the kingdom was plunged into darkness, strongly suggests an attack on an oil-producing nation with the resulting firestorm blotting out the sun completely, as compared to high atmospheric fallout and dust particles blotting out one-third of the day and one-third of the night for other nations on earth.

The fourth trumpet Revelation 8:12-13 is the blotting out of one-third of the day and one-third of the stars and moon at night by world-wide high atmospheric dust particles and clouds created by the nuclear attack on the Middle East, U.S., allied Arab countries primarily by Iraq with the help of the Russians. Just preceding this fourth trumpet will be the vial which resulted from the nuclear firestorm, and the scorching heat which effects those without the mark of God. The darkness is similar to Exodus 10:21-23, in which Moses was commanded by God to send a plague of darkness on Egypt.

The Three Woes

81. Who leads the five-month invasion found in Revelation 9?

Three Woes = Last 3-1/2 yrs @ Feasts!
"It always get dark before it gets really black!"

Revelation 8:13

13 And I beheld, and heard an angel flying through the midst of heaven, saying with a loud voice, Woe, woe, woe, to the inhabiters of the earth by reason of the other voices of the trumpet of the three angels, which are yet to sound!

The first through fifth trumpet and first through fifth vial are the same as the first woe and all speak about the same event from a different prophetic perspective. The first woe of Revelation 9:11 is an invading army led by Abbadon, the name of the angel of the Abyss or Satan which is the name given to call upon at death to seventeenth level Masons of the Scottish Rite. [Webber 17th Level of Masonism].

The Moslems have been looking for their Imam Mahdi, reincarnate Apollonys (Abaddon). He is the one who has the right, according to Moslems, to lead them into the holy war that will begin a new age on earth and destroy the infidels. The first woe is a conventional occupation force following a nuclear attack that lasts for a period of five months. As it will only affect those who do not have the seal of God, it must therefore be an occupation force of a Moslem nation. It will be a most predictable response of Iraq after rebuilding its armament and seeing the extremist Moslem nations rise up with an Imam Mahdi about to declare a holy war.

A similar situation occurred under the Ayatullah during the Iran/Iraq war but on a much bigger scale. It is obvious that he does utilize nuclear weapons against these countries and they receive radiation burns.

Revelation 9: 1-6

> *1 And the fifth angel sounded, and I saw a star* **[Satan]** *fall from heaven unto the earth: and to him was given the key of the bottomless pit.*
>
> *2 And he opened the bottomless pit; and there arose a smoke out of the pit, as the smoke of a great furnace; and the sun and the air were darkened by reason of the smoke of the pit.* **[nuclear war was the result]**
>
> *3 And there came out of the smoke locusts upon the earth: and unto them was given power, as the scorpions of the earth have power.*
>
> *4 And it was commanded them that they should not hurt the grass of the earth, neither any green thing, neither any tree; but only those men which have not the seal of God in their foreheads.* **[deceive those that will take the Mark of the Beast]**
>
> *5 And to them it was given that they should not kill them, but that they should be tormented five months: and their torment [was] as*

the torment of a scorpion, when he striketh a man. **[Force upon them the Mark of the Beast]**

6 And in those days shall men seek death, and shall not find it; and shall desire to die, and death shall flee from them.

The first five trumpets start at day 1,260. The angel flying in the mid-air, Revelation 14:6-7, is the fifth angel and heralds in the first woe. Refer to Figure 77-1. The fifth trumpet and vial are the first woe, therefore start on day 1,260 and go for 150 days of the invasion of locusts or the U.N. Peace Keeping Force which occupies America and West Jerusalem Jerusalem and the occupied territories. The Arab nations will also be occupied by this force and will suffer from radiation burns at the same time Israel will be protected by its Star Wars anti-missile defence system. The rocket anti-ICBM was developed with 80% U.S. funding in conjunction with the country of South Africa. [Broadcast on the CBC program, "The Journal" in 1991.]

82. What events follow this nuclear Iraqi attack against its Moslem enemies?

The second woe which is Revelation 9: 13-16, is the three-way counter attack which includes the sixth vial and trumpet, on day 1,415.

Revelation 9:13-16

13 And the sixth angel sounded, and I heard a voice from the four horns of the golden altar which is before God,

14 Saying to the sixth angel which had the trumpet, Loose the four angels which are bound in the great river Euphrates.

15 And the four angels were loosed, which were prepared for an hour, and a day, and a month, and a year, for to slay the third part of men.

16 And the number of the army of the horsemen [were] two hundred thousand thousand: and I heard the number of them.

This represents both the Russian invasion and involves the gathering of troops from Communist China and the Kings of the East as well as other Arab countries to converge on north Israel. The color of their breast plates utilizes the color red for the Russian Allied Socialist-Communists, blue for the United States and allies and yellow for the Moslem and Communist countries of the Kings of the East to include Japan and the Asian rim countries.

The plagues described in Revelation 9:18, represented by fire, smoke and sulphur, are the same as the colors noted above. Fire means nuclear fire, smoke means radio active dust and smoke debris and the sulphur represents radiation burns.

Revelation 10:7-10

7 But in the days of the voice of the seventh angel, when he shall begin to sound, the mystery of God should be finished, as he hath declared to his servants the prophets.

8 And the voice which I heard from heaven spake unto me again, and said, Go [and] take the little book which is open in the hand of the angel which standeth upon the sea and upon the earth.

9 And I went unto the angel, and said unto him, Give me the little book. And he said unto me, Take [it], and eat it up; and it shall make thy belly bitter, but it shall be in thy mouth sweet as honey.

10 And I took the little book out of the angel's hand, and ate it up; and it was in my mouth sweet as honey: and as soon as I had eaten it, my belly was bitter.

What the prophet John sees here is military helicopters with anti-tank missiles and laser guided bombs and jets such as the A-10 tank killer with high tech weapon systems. This will be followed five months later by the gathering of troops for the battle of Armageddon, with a Soviet counter attack with conventional forces.

Day 1,415 is the day on which the United Nations' troops have withdrawn and Iraq takes over control of the territory of West

Jerusalem and removes half the population as King Nebahedezzar did. Saddam Hussein has sworn to do as prophecied.

Zechariah 14:2-3

> 2 For I will gather all nations against Jerusalem to battle; and the city shall be taken, and the houses rifled, and the women ravished; and half of the city shall go forth into captivity, and the residue of the people shall not be cut off from the city.
>
> 3 Then shall the LORD go forth, and fight against those nations, as when he fought in the day of battle.

Revelation 9:13-19 describes the next phase of the attack with the ingathering of the three major armies described above, under the three different colors. This will start on day 1,415 and continue until the final nuclear exchange on day 2,520, the Feast of Trumpets. This is very significant as it is the last trump that signifies the resurrection of the church, at the hour of thermonuclear exchange.

83. Why will the oil bearing state of Babylon or Iraq be the last to fall during the Tribulation war?

Strategically oil bearing states will be last to fall because nuclear war would destroy oil wells. This was well demonstrated by the American attack on Iraqi tanks and jets placed between oil wells. The oil fires in Kuwait have created a greater crisis than the war itself. The positive underground pressures, present in over eighty per cent of the limestone formation oil wells in the Middle East, can generate pressures of eight thousand pounds per square inch and left unchecked some wells could burn for two to three hundred years darkening the sky and lowering the world-wide temperature and causing massive famines.

In reference to Question 75, it is obvious that the oil producing states will therefore be the last to be attacked because of the world-wide environmental danger imposed by a wider, oil-driven firestorm created by a nuclear attack on Iraq.

84. When will the sealing of the 144,000 Christian evangelists occur?

This is the last great commission to spread the eternal gospel to those who live on earth and includes the hundred and forty-four thousand of Revelation 14:1-5. Each of the names of the tribes in ancient Hebrew signifies the spiritual attribute or gift and must therefore be all Christians, Gentile or Jew, i.e. the two witnesses of Revelation 11. Modern national Israel includes the half tribe of Benjamin and the tribe of Judah and some Levites. The sealing of the 144,000 occurs just before the great persecution of believing Messianic Jews and Gentile Christians.

The twelve tribes that are sealed are the spiritual not genetic tribes of Israel. Many of Jewish blood may not be able to trace their ancestry except those with Jewish names. In Russia alone it is estimated that there are fourteen million Jews of at least 25 percent of Jewish genetic heritage. This is parallel with the two witnesses which have prophesied previously for 1,260 days and then are put to death and martyred for another 1,260 days until the end of the seven-year period.

The two sticks which are put together in Ezekiel 37:15-17 are Christians Gentiles and saved Jews which are joined into one congregation as Jesus prophesied in John 17. The great multitude which followed after in Revelation 7:9-17 are those which are saved out of the tribulation by the refining fires of the tribulation under the saving grace of God given through these 144,000 Christian and Messianic Jewish evangelists.

The seal of God is completed on all of the Christians and Jews who have turned to Christ by the 1,260 day or half-way point through the seven-year period.

Matthew 24: 14

14 And this gospel of the kingdom shall be preached in all the world for a witness unto all nations; and then shall the end come.

[**The last great commission was to spread the eternal gospel to all those who live on earth and in the end meaning the tribulation would come. There would also be tribulation saints that would accept the gospel from those who are sealed before the destruction which occurs upon the earth. This sealing process, as shown in Revelation 7:1-4 occurs before any damage is done to the environment.**]

As in Revelation 7:1-4 this sealing occurs before any damage is done to the environment. The four angels signifying the first four trumpets and vials are held back until the sealing of the 144,000 which must occur prior to the first seal being opened, because the Tribulation and persecution and martyrdom Christians and Jews is 1,260 days. From the second to the fifth seals must, therefore, start on day 1,260 followed by a five-month period as identified in Revelation 9: 1-12, time for the battle of Armageddon.

The time for collecting of the three opposing armies released from Revelation 9: 13-19 and Revelation 16: 12-16 can be calculated.

The total time period is 2,520 days plus 45 days with time intervals identified Daniel 8: 13-14, Daniel 8: 26, Daniel 9: 27, Daniel 12: 7, and 11-12. There are also quotes in Revelation giving time period including Revelation 11:1-3, and 9, 13, Revelation 12: 6, 13-14, Revelation 13: 5. Counting back 1,150 days from day 2,565, which is 2,300 evening and morning sacrifices from Daniel 8: 13-14 and 26, this indicates 1,150 days prior to the 2,565 day. This places the Battle of Armageddon as starting at day 1,415, immediately after the five-month United Nations occupying force in the Arab countries and East Jerusalem.

The one leading this force, according to Revelation 9:11 is the Angel of the Abyss or Abbadon, the name given to the seventeenth level of the Scottish Right Masons to call upon his death to enter the heavenly Masonic Lodge. It is obvious that we are again speaking the same political, economic beasts of the Euro-Russian Empire in Revelation 17:16 and the ten Kingdoms which will hate the prostitute nation of Mystery Babylon the Great, America is the whore Mystery Babylon whose flesh will be eaten and burned with fire.

85. What is included in the second woe?

The second woe consists of the sixth trumpet and the sixth vial and is the Chinese and the Kings of the East counter attack. This again, according to Figure 77-1 is day 1,415 in which the Euphrates River has dried up and the three armies converge for the final battle of Armageddon.

Rev. 9:13-21

13 And the sixth angel sounded, and I heard a voice from the four horns of the golden altar which is before God,

14 Saying to the sixth angel which had the trumpet, Loose the four angels which are bound in the great river Euphrates.

15 And the four angels were loosed, which were prepared for an hour, and a day, and a month, and a year, for to slay the third part of men.

16 And the number of the army of the horsemen [were] two hundred thousand thousand: and I heard the number of them.

17 And thus I saw the horses in the vision, and them that sat on them, having breastplates of fire, and of jacinth, and brimstone: and the heads of the horses [were] as the heads of lions; and out of their mouths issued fire and smoke and brimstone.

18 By these three was the third part of men killed, by the fire, and by the smoke, and by the brimstone, which issued out of their mouths.

19 For their power is in their mouth, and in their tails: for their tails [were] like unto serpents, and had heads, and with them they do hurt.

20 And the rest of the men which were not killed by these plagues yet repented not of the works of their hands, that they should not worship devils, and idols of gold, and silver, and brass, and stone, and of wood: which neither can see, nor hear, nor walk:

21 Neither repented they of their murders, nor of their sorceries, nor of their fornication, nor of their thefts.

The army of 200,000,000 brings to mind the quote by Mao Tse Tung that in his communist Chinese 'Red' book he could raise an army of 200,000,000. The ecodisaster nuclear war in the Middle East will force these Kings of the East to raise such an army to protect their national survival.

According to Revelation 9:18 a further one-third of all mankind is killed by this stage of Armageddon. This must be added to the fourth of world population, primarily downwind, that would be killed by Russian supplied Iraqi nuclear attack on the Arab and Egyptian Desert Storm I allies., and the subsequent fallout.

86. What events occurred in the third woe and how is it timed in the tribulation period?

Jeremiah 4:5-6

5 Declare ye in Judah, and publish in Jerusalem; and say, Blow ye the trumpet in the land **[The Feast of Trumpets!]***: cry, gather together, and say, Assemble yourselves, and let us go into the defenced cities.*

6 Set up the standard toward Zion: retire, stay not: for I will bring evil from the north **[Russian and allied attack!]***, and a great destruction.*

Joel 1:14-15

14 Sanctify ye a fast, call a solemn assembly, gather the elders [and] all the inhabitants of the land [into] the house of the LORD your God, and cry unto the LORD,

> *15 Alas for the day! for the day of the LORD [is] at hand, and as a destruction from the Almighty shall it come.* **[Nuclear Holocaust!]**

Joel 2:1-2

> *1 Blow ye the trumpet in Zion* **[The Feast of Trumpets!]**, *and sound an alarm in my holy mountain: let all the inhabitants of the land tremble: for the day of the LORD cometh, for [it is] nigh at hand;*
>
> *2 A day of darkness and of gloominess, a day of clouds and of thick darkness, as the morning spread upon the mountains: a great people and a strong; there hath not been ever the like, neither shall be any more after it, [even] to the years of many generations.*

The third woe is the seventh trumpet and vial at the last day of the seven years. The saints which came out of the great tribulation are in the new Jerusalem in heaven in Revelation 4. The seventh vial and trumpet coincide with this third woe or the judgement of the return of Jesus Christ from Jeremiah 15, verse 46, at the sound of Babylon's capture, the earth will tremble, its cry will resound among the nations. Revelation chapter 8 creates an image that the great earthquake noted in the sixth seal, Revelation 6: 12-17 is the same as the great earthquake that occurs in Revelation 8: 5.

The end of the wrath of Satan which is 666 is contained within 777, meaning the seventh seal, the seventh trumpet, and the seventh vial. '777' is **the wrath of God which are explained in Revelation 11: 18 as: 1) a time for judging the dead, 2) for rewarding the prophets and saints, and 3) for destroying those who destroy the earth.** The righteous are rewarded in a New Earth and Heaven, and the wicked cast into the second death, with one Second Coming with one judgment of the righteous and the unrighteous.

Revelation 11:19 culminates in the one great earthquake and hail storm which again at the same time that the wrath of God is all inclusive of the wrath of Satan but culminates in the spiritual wrath of God '777' to reward those faithful to be resurrected into righteousness and to judge the evil dead and those who destroyed the earth both individuals and nations. **[The Wrath of God (Jesus) is only the eternal separation from the creator!]**

This is the last event of the Tribulation period and according to our quote and time periods given above must happen by the 2,520 day followed by a 45-day period of massive earth upheaval. Then the physical resurrection and reconsecration of the temple will occur in Jerusalem according to Daniel 8: 13-14 and 26. A New Earth will then be eternally united with heaven.

The seventh seal which comprises the seven trumpets and vials starts from day 1,250 and occurs concurrent with the second to the seventh seals on day 1,260. The judgment of the seventh seal is specifically stated in Revelation 11:18 as the judging of the dead, the rewarding of the prophets and saints, and the destruction of those that destroy the earth. The wrath of God which is contained within the seventh seal, trumpet and vial, on a spiritual level, encompasses also the wrath of Satan which includes the six first seals, vials and trumpets.

The blowing of the Shofar with the trumpets is the calling together of the elect that would be saved out of the tribulation. At the time that the vials of judgment are poured against all the enemies of God and the nations that would stand beside and protect both Gentile Christians and Messianic Jews.

87. What is the significance of the understanding that there is one great earth upheaval or megaquake in interpretation of the scriptures?

This great earthquake is the same as the earthquake of Ezekiel 39 and Jeremiah 50:29-30 and 41. The Lord impressed upon me that he is a God of order and simplicity. The Introduction gives an overview of the writing principles God had given for this book's writing. There is but one Tribulation that the church will be saved through The Second Coming of Jesus will occur once at the end of the Times of Tribulation. Only one judgment occurs at this single world-wide megaquake. Heaven and the New Earth is the destination of the righteous. Hell and the Second Death is the destination of the unrighteous in Christ. There is only one chance for the remaining unsaved on earth. That door will be open 'a little while' but Jesus will forever shut that door at his coming in judgment.

Revelation 3:7

> 7 And to the angel of the church in Philadelphia write; These things saith he that is holy, he that is true, he that hath the key of David, he that openeth, and no man shutteth; and shutteth, and no man openeth;

88. What will be the fate of the Modern Babylon - Iraq and the Oil Producing Islamic Alliance and, the Daughter of Babylon the Great, America?

God has given prophecies regarding the ancient nation of Babylon , modern day Iraq, that there will be utter destruction. America, also is the modern day Daughter of Babylon and is the Babylon of Revelation 17 and 18. Although it has been given the anointing of Israel to be the chief Christian Nation to bring the gospel to the world, its duality of character brings blessings and cursings with judgments against America. Follow along with me as we explore the two Babylons and their fate. America is also referred to as Mystery Babylon, for it was a mystery to John the Revelator and the ancient prophets, but this day is revealed. This is indeed the END TIMES, and Jesus is Coming Soon! Praise the Lord!

Revelation 9:13-19

> 13 And the sixth angel sounded, and I heard a voice from the four horns of the golden altar which is before God,

14 Saying to the sixth angel which had the trumpet, Loose the four angels which are bound in the great river Euphrates. **[Iraqi attack unleashes Armageddon]**

15 And the four angels were loosed, which were prepared for an hour, and a day, and a month, and a year, for to slay the third part of men.

16 And the number of the army of the horsemen [were] two hundred thousand thousand: and I heard the number of them.

17 And thus I saw the horses in the vision, and them that sat on them, having breastplates of fire, and of jacinth, and brimstone: and the heads of the horses [were] as the heads of lions; and out of their mouths issued fire and smoke and brimstone.

18 By these three was the third part of men killed, by the fire, and by the smoke, and by the brimstone, which issued out of their mouths.

19 For their power is in their mouth, and in their tails: for their tails [were] like unto serpents, and had heads, and with them they do hurt.

We know from Jeremiah 51:37, that there will be a total destruction in one day of Babylon and that all nations will attack Babylon. (Isaiah 17:12, Jeremiah 51:41-43, Jeremiah 51:63-64)

Isaiah 17:12

12 Woe to the multitude of many people, [which] make a noise like the noise of the seas; and to the rushing of nations, [that] make a rushing like the rushing of mighty waters!

Jeremiah 51: 41-43

41 How is Sheshach taken! **[Sheshach-Babylon]** *and how is the praise of the whole earth surprised! how is Babylon become an astonishment among the nations!*

42 The sea is come up upon Babylon **[see Isaiah 17:12]**: *she is covered with the multitude of the waves thereof.* **[numerous armies]**

43 Her cities are a desolation, a dry land, and a wilderness, a land wherein no man dwelleth, neither doth [any] son of man pass thereby. **[radiation]**

Jeremiah 51: 63-64

63 And it shall be, when thou hast made an end of reading this book, [that] thou shalt bind a stone to it, and cast it into the midst of Euphrates:

64 And thou shalt say, Thus shall Babylon sink, and shall not rise from the evil that I will bring upon her: and they shall be weary. Thus far [are] the words of Jeremiah.

There is a shout from heaven for joy in heaven and earth over the fall of Babylon the Great in Revelation 18.

Jeremiah 51:29

29 And the land shall tremble and sorrow: for every purpose of the LORD shall be performed against Babylon, to make the land of Babylon a desolation without an inhabitant. **[Iraqi Empire]**

Jeremiah 51:35

35 The violence done to me and to my flesh [be] upon Babylon **[Missile attack by Iraq against Israel]**, *shall the inhabitant of Zion say; and my blood upon the inhabitants of Chaldea, shall Jerusalem say.* **[Israel]**

Jeremiah 51:37

37 And Babylon shall become heaps, a dwellingplace for dragons, an astonishment, and an hissing, without an inhabitant. **[total destruction]**

Isaiah 13:20-22

20 It shall never be inhabited, neither shall it be dwelt in from generation to generation: neither shall the Arabian pitch tent there; neither shall the shepherds make their fold there.

21 But wild beasts of the desert shall lie there; and their houses shall be full of doleful creatures; and owls shall dwell there, and satyrs shall dance there.

22 And the wild beasts of the islands shall cry in their desolate houses, and dragons in [their] pleasant palaces: and her time [is] near to come, and her days shall not be prolonged.

Isaiah 17:12

12 Woe to the multitude of many people, [which] make a noise like the noise of the seas; and to the rushing of nations, [that] make a rushing like the rushing of mighty waters!

Jeremiah 51:41-43

41 How is Sheshach taken! **[Sheshach = Babylon]** and how is the praise of the whole earth surprised! how is Babylon become an astonishment among the nations!

42 The sea is come up upon Babylon: **[many invading armies]** she is covered with the multitude of the waves thereof.

43 Her cities are a desolation, a dry land, and a wilderness, a land wherein no man dwelleth, neither doth [any] son of man pass thereby.

Jeremiah 51:63-64

63 And it shall be, when thou hast made an end of reading this book, [that] thou shalt bind a stone to it, and cast it into the midst of Euphrates:

64 And thou shalt say, Thus shall Babylon sink, and shall not rise from the evil that I will bring upon her: **[Total annihilation]** and they shall be weary. Thus far [are] the words of Jeremiah.

Jeremiah 51:48, "Then heaven and earth and all that is in them will shout for joy over Babylon for out of the north destroyers will attack her declares the Lord." This is the same as ***Revelation 18:2-3***

2 And he cried mightily with a strong voice, saying, Babylon the great is fallen, is fallen, and is become the habitation of devils, and the hold of every foul spirit, and a cage of every unclean and hateful bird. **[God has a double portion for America under judgment, for it called itself by His Name and fornicated with**

other gods and became rich on the filth of mammon gained through the Masonic NWOrder!]

3 For all nations have drunk of the wine of the wrath of her fornication, and the kings of the earth have committed fornication with her, and the merchants of the earth are waxed rich through the abundance of her delicacies. [This is clearly the fate of America, the Daughter of Babylon!]

89. What is the summary of the events which will occur during the last three and one-half years of the Tribulation period?

On the Feast of Tabernacles at day one, an Islamic/Palestinian-Israeli peace treaty will be signed in which the Jewish tabernacle of Moses is erected on the Temple Mount beside the Dome of the Rock and the El Aksa Mosque. This will be a symbol of New Age tolerance of religion. The New Age Messiah will enter the tabernacle on a wing of the tabernacle on day 1,230, Feast of Purim at the Dome of the Rock. Thirty days later, during the Passover, Iraq will attack its surrounding Arab nations, Egypt and Israel. The Arab nations and Egypt which it will attack are those included in Desert Storm 1.

At the end of the Feast of Unleavened Bread, on day 1,265 and for a period of five months, the United Nations will have an occupying force in the Arab nations that were attacked by Iraq and East Jerusalem. These forces will be withdrawn as Iraq takes over control of the entire Middle East, except for the remnant of Israel and the Battle of Armageddon merges the three armies starting on day 1,415. This occurs as the riverbed of the Euphrates dries up and the Kings of the East, including Moslem and Communist countries, bring in armies large enough that the total number of men involved in the conflict will equal 200 million.

The conventional battle will wage war to the north of Israel, with further consolidation of the power of Iraq until its final day of destruction. On the 2,520th day, the Feast of Trumpets, in which a nuclear exchange will destroy all the other nations first which came against Israel, with the last to be destroyed being Iraq. Ten days later, on the Feast of Atonement, the 2,530th day, Israel will mourn for the Messiah prophesied.

Isaiah 53:4-12

4 Surely he hath borne our griefs, and carried our sorrows: yet we did esteem him stricken, smitten of God, and afflicted.

5 But he [was] wounded for our transgressions, [he was] bruised for our iniquities: the chastisement of our peace [was] upon him; and with his stripes we are healed. **[Jesus bore all the sins of the whole world.]**

6 All we like sheep have gone astray; we have turned every one to his own way; and the LORD hath laid on him the iniquity of us all.

7 He was oppressed, and he was afflicted, yet he opened not his mouth: he is brought as a lamb to the slaughter, and as a sheep before her shearers is dumb, so he openeth not his mouth.

8 He was taken from prison and from judgment: and who shall declare his generation? for he was cut off out of the land of the living **[Jesus crucified]**: *for the transgression of my people was he stricken.*

9 And he made his grave with the wicked, and with the rich in his death; because he had done no violence, neither [was any] deceit in his mouth.

10 Yet it pleased the LORD to bruise him; he hath put [him] to grief: when thou shalt make his soul an offering for sin, he shall see [his] seed **[Jesus was resurrected. He lives!]**, *he shall prolong [his] days, and the pleasure of the LORD shall prosper in his hand.*

11 He shall see of the travail of his soul, [and] shall be satisfied: by his knowledge shall my righteous servant justify many; for he shall bear their iniquities.

12 Therefore will I divide him [a portion] with the great, and he shall divide the spoil with the strong **[Gentile Christians and Jewish Christians]**; *because he hath poured out his soul unto death: and he was numbered with the transgressors; and he bare the sin of many, and made intercession for the transgressors.*

In Psalm 22:1-31, the same picture of a suffering Messiah is shown plainly to the Jews of the Old Testament.

After one month of dedication in the New Eternal Temple, the Eternal Reign of Jesus from his throne in Jerusalem will continue forever from the 17th Day of Heshvan, on day 2,565. This is the same day as the first day of the forty days of reign that began during the flood in the days of Noah. This is the fulfillment of the prophesied 'latter rain'. All those who did not obey God and follow Noah were destroyed from the earth. As Grant Jeffrey shows in his book, "Armageddon - Appointment with Destiny", it is also the date in which the Balfour Declaration, November 2nd, 1917 declared that Palestine would become a Jewish national homeland for the first time in 2,000 years.

90. What is the level of destruction that results from this last three and one-half year period of this age of history?

As we return to the events of the end of the tribulation, we see further evidence of the level of destruction.

Isaiah 24:17-20

17 Fear, and the pit, and the snare, [are] upon thee, O inhabitant of the earth.

18 And it shall come to pass, [that] he who fleeth from the noise of the fear shall fall into the pit; and he that cometh up out of the midst of the pit shall be taken in the snare: for the windows from on high are open, and the foundations of the earth do shake.

19 The earth is utterly broken down, the earth is clean dissolved, the earth is moved exceedingly. **[The one great earth upheaval.]**

20 The earth shall reel to and fro like a drunkard, and shall be removed like a cottage; and the transgression thereof shall be heavy upon it; and it shall fall, and not rise again. **[Utter destruction of the present earth.]**

This is a great day of the Lord Almighty.

Isaiah 24:21-23

21 And it shall come to pass in that day, [that] the LORD shall punish the host of the high ones [that are] on high, and the kings of the earth upon the earth. **[Satan, demons, unsaved men and women.]**

22 And they shall be gathered together, [as] prisoners are gathered in the pit, and shall be shut up in the prison, and after many days shall they be visited.

23 Then the moon shall be confounded, and the sun ashamed **[nuclear destruction and obliteration of the light of the sun, moon and stars, will herald the White Throne judgment.]** when the LORD of hosts shall reign in mount Zion, and in Jerusalem, and before his ancients gloriously.

II Peter 3:10-13

10 But the day of the Lord will come as a thief in the night **[It will come to those of the world, both unsaved and those "virgins" of Christians that do not seek the truth and pursue it like precious gold!]**; *in the which the heavens shall pass away with a great noise, and the elements shall melt with fervent heat, the earth also and the works that are therein shall be burned up.*

11 [Seeing] then [that] all these things shall be dissolved, what manner [of persons] ought ye to be in [all] holy conversation and godliness,

12 Looking for and hasting unto the coming of the day of God, wherein the heavens being on fire shall be dissolved, and the elements shall melt with fervent heat? **[The earth will be formless and empty as in Genesis 1:1-2.]**

13 Nevertheless we, according to his promise, look for new heavens and a new earth, wherein dwelleth righteousness.

Zephaniah 1:2-3

2 I will utterly consume all [things] from off the land, saith the LORD. **[The Lord pledges to totally consume all things from off the land!]**

3 I will consume man and beast; I will consume the fowls of the heaven, and the fishes of the sea, and the stumblingblocks with the wicked **[The wicked will be judged at the Lord's Coming, not 1,000 years later.]**; and I will cut off man from off the land, saith the LORD. **[All will die in a world-wide holocaust, except for a very few as at the time of Noah's ark.]**

Zephaniah 1:14-18

14 The great day of the LORD [is] near, [it is] near, and hasteth greatly, [even] the voice of the day of the LORD: the mighty man shall cry there bitterly.

15 That day [is] a day of wrath **[day 2,520]**, a day of trouble and distress, a day of wasteness and desolation, a day of darkness and gloominess, a day of clouds and thick darkness,

16 A day of the trumpet and alarm against the fenced cities, and against the high towers. **[Shofar - the last Trumpet!]**

17 And I will bring distress upon men, that they shall walk like blind men **[darkness and radiation eye burns]**, because they have sinned against the LORD: and their blood shall be poured out as dust, and their flesh as the dung. **[nuclear incineration]**

18 Neither their silver nor their gold shall be able to deliver them in the day of the LORD'S wrath; but the whole land shall be devoured by the fire of his jealousy: for he shall make even a speedy riddance. **[all who do not have the Seal of God]**

Zephaniah 3:8

8 Therefore wait ye upon me, saith the LORD, until the day that I rise up to the prey: for my determination [is] to gather the nation

[**Armageddon = Judgment ... of armies**], *that I may assemble the kingdoms, to pour upon them mine indignation, [even] all my fierce anger: for all the earth shall be devoured with the fire of my jealousy.* **[Nuclear annihilation of the whole world at the instant of taking out the righteous. For the earth to continue, the Lord will have to resurrect it to become the New Heavens and Earth!]**

Revelation 6:8

8 And I looked, and behold a pale horse: and his name that sat on him was Death, and Hell followed with him. And power was given unto them over the fourth part of the earth, to kill with sword, and with hunger, and with death, and with the beasts of the earth.

In Revelation 6:8, one-quarter of the earth's population is decimated by the initial nuclear attack by Iraq and Russia. This includes the second to the fifth seals and the first five trumpets and vials. In the sixth trumpet and vial, Revelation 9:18 indicates that one-third of the remaining population of mankind will be killed. **The total population of the earth, therefore, will be cut in half by the tribulation by the nuclear holocaust, on day 2,520, the end of the sixth trumpet and vial.**

This agrees very closely with the half of the population which the New Age Movement believes that their Shambhalah or destructive force must eject all those who do not have the capacity to evolve into a new form of human called Homo Universalis. They rationalize that this is not murder but merely the removing of those elements, like spiritual recycling, which will prevent the evolution of the world into a stable new species called Homo Universalis that will respect the environment, live in peace and have a stable population, under New Age socialism worshipping Mother Earth, achieving their true supernatural deity as this more highly involved man. The strong delusion is that man can create a sustainable Paradise on earth without the change in man's nature by the indwelling Spirit of the living God.

91. When Christians die where do they go?

All Christians will live in the New Jerusalem.

John 14:1-6

> 1 Let not your heart be troubled: ye believe in God, believe also in me.
>
> 2 In my Father's house are many mansions: if [it were] not [so], I would have told you. I go to prepare a place for you.
>
> 3 And if I go and prepare a place for you, I will come again, and receive you unto myself; that where I am, [there] ye may be also.
>
> 4 And whither I go ye know, and the way ye know.
>
> 5 Thomas saith unto him, Lord, we know not whither thou goest; and how can we know the way?
>
> 6 Jesus saith unto him, I am the way, the truth, and the life: no man cometh unto the Father, but by me.

Revelation Chapter 21 and 22 describes the new Jerusalem where all of the Christians cohabit with the Lord forever. We see from Revelation 21:9 that the new Jerusalem is pictured as coming down to earth during a description by one of these seven angels who had the seven vials full of the seven last plagues. The bride of the Lamb is the Church Gentile Christians and believing Messianic Jews. The great high wall of Twelve Gates is the twelve spiritual attributes and the walls of city were composed of the believers. The various colors of stone signifying the various spiritual gifts. They were given to the ancient Israelite people and is explained by the high priest's garment was the twelve stones.

When Jesus comes to this new Jerusalem we see references going back to

Daniel 7:13-14

> 13 I saw in the night visions, and, behold, [one] like the Son of man came with the clouds of heaven, and came to the Ancient of days, and they brought him near before him.

14 And there was given him dominion, and glory, and a kingdom, that all people, nations, and languages, should serve him: his dominion [is] an everlasting dominion, which shall not pass away, and his kingdom [that] which shall not be destroyed.

It is at the time of this last kingdom of Clay and Iron of the unification of the economic power and military power of the resurrected Roman Empire that Jesus Christ will come and return and set up his reign on earth from …

Daniel 2:44

44 And in the days of these kings shall the God of heaven set up a kingdom, which shall never be destroyed **[It will endure forever, not 1,000 years.]**: *and the kingdom shall not be left to other people, [but] it shall break in pieces and consume all these kingdoms, and it shall stand for ever.* **[Rock = Jesus Christ]**.

For this interpretation, Daniel was given a position of high authority within the Babylonian empire and made him rule over the entire province of Babylon and in charge of all of King Nebuchadnezzar's wise men. This is a great sign to Christians to comfort them and a great prophetic sign for evangelization of those who would believe about Jesus Christ.

The appearance of the empire of Clay and Iron signifies that Jesus will soon come and remove all evil people and nations from earth and create an eternal empire on the new earth united with a new heaven.

Daniel's vision he saw the complete outline of history up to the time of Jesus' empire being set up on earth which we now know follows a great nuclear war as a result of the wrath of Satan and man's following his own judgment to choose good and evil. God will have proved man totally helpless in creating Utopia on earth without God. Jesus will prove it by setting up an eternal kingdom. God's ultimate judgment may fall on those who will not submit their wills to the peace and security of God's infinite love and holiness.

Isaiah 65:17-25

17 For, behold, I create new heavens and a new earth: and the former shall not be remembered, nor come into mind. **[Earth will be new after destruction makes it formless and empty.]**

18 But be ye glad and rejoice for ever [in that] which I create: for, behold, I create Jerusalem a rejoicing, and her people a joy. **[God's house, the New Jerusalem will come down to earth and be eternally united.]**

19 And I will rejoice in Jerusalem, and joy in my people: and the voice of weeping shall be no more heard in her, nor the voice of crying.

20 There shall be no more thence an infant of days, nor an old man that hath not filled his days: for the child shall die an hundred years old but the sinner [being] an hundred years old shall be accursed. **[All the wicked are removed at Jesus' coming and death will be no more.]**

21 And they shall build houses, and inhabit [them]; and they shall plant vineyards, and eat the fruit of them.

22 They shall not build, and another inhabit; they shall not plant, and another eat **[Man will live in an Eden-like Earth without the wicked or Satan and his demons.]**: *for as the days of a tree [are] the days of my people, and mine elect shall long enjoy the work of their hands.* **[Eternal life.]**

23 They shall not labour in vain, nor bring forth for trouble; for they [are] the seed of the blessed of the LORD, and their offspring with them. **[Man will have eternal generations on the New Earth.]**

24 And it shall come to pass, that before they call, I will answer **[Man and God will communicate as Adam did before the fall.]**; *and while they are yet speaking, I will hear.*

25 The wolf and the lamb shall feed together **[wolf and lamb nations]**:, *and the lion shall eat straw like the bullock* **[lion and ox nations]** *and dust [shall be] the serpent's meat* **[Satan will be**

destroyed by the Second Death]. *They shall not hurt nor destroy in all my holy mountain, saith the LORD.*

Those who are resurrected in the New Earth and Heaven will have a world as described in Isaiah 65:17-25. Jerusalem will be a delight to all the nations of the world instead a point of controversy that brings the world to the brink of nuclear annihilation. The New Jerusalem will be the habitation place for God's people for eternity. This is the New Earth eternally bound to the New Heaven.

Rev. 21:1-8

1 And I saw a new heaven and a new earth: for the first heaven and the first earth were passed away; and there was no more sea.

2 And I John saw the holy city, new Jerusalem, coming down from God out of heaven, prepared as a bride adorned for her husband.

3 And I heard a great voice out of heaven saying, Behold, the tabernacle of God [is] with men, and he will dwell with them, and they shall be his people, and God himself shall be with them, [and be] their God.

4 And God shall wipe away all tears from their eyes; and there shall be no more death, neither sorrow, nor crying, neither shall there be any more pain: for the former things are passed away.

5 And he that sat upon the throne said, Behold, I make all things new. And he said unto me, Write: for these words are true and faithful.

6 And he said unto me, It is done. I am Alpha and Omega, the beginning and the end. I will give unto him that is athirst of the fountain of the water of life freely.

7 He that overcometh shall inherit all things; and I will be his God, and he shall be my son.

8 But the fearful, and unbelieving, and the abominable, and murderers, and whoremongers, and sorcerers, and idolaters, and all liars, shall have their part in the lake which burneth with fire and brimstone: which is the second death.

God will now dwell with righteous men and he will eternally live with them, for Jesus will make all things new.

Daniel 2:44-45

> 44 And in the days of these kings shall the God of heaven set up a kingdom, which shall never be destroyed **[There will not be a millenium and it will endure forever, not 1,000 years.]** : and the kingdom shall not be left to other people, [but] it shall break in pieces and consume all these kingdoms, and it shall stand for ever.
>
> 45 Forasmuch as thou sawest that the stone was cut out of the mountain without hands **[Rock = Jesus Christ]** , and that it brake in pieces the iron, the brass, the clay, the silver, and the gold; the great God hath made known to the king what shall come to pass hereafter: and the dream [is] certain, and the interpretation thereof sure.

Dreams and Visions:

We, as Gentile and Jewish Believers, already rule and reign with Jesus for Two Millenia as Kings and Priests. After Satan is released for a "little season," the kingdom of Jesus Christ will NEVER BE SET ASIDE AT THE END OF THE NEXT MILLENIUM. Jesus, the "stone cut out of the mountain" will break the Kingdom of Clay & Iron, the last secular empire, and it will never rise or be succeeded by another Godless government. Thus saith the Lord! Amen, Come Lord Jesus!

Chapter 4

NEW WORLD ECONOMY: ONE WORLD ECONOMY

92. How has the unification of Germany been engineered by Russia?

Jacque Monet is the father of the common market. In Hal Lindsey's "Late Great Planet Earth," we see Monet quoted "As long as Europe remains divided it is no match for the Soviet Union. Europe must unite." The last two years has been a blur of political miracles from October '89, the fall of the Berlin Wall to the currency union, July 1, 1990 of East and West Germany to the G7 Houston Summit in July of '90. A plea was made to provide massive aid to the ailing Russian economy.

This was the pay off for the Russians to allow the East Germans to unite with West Germany or should I say West Germany was absorbed into East Germany. Even Russian Soldiers now receive their Russian pay in Deutchmarks financed by the West German Government. Germany committed over 15 billion dollars to USSR to assist it into a market economy and as recent as the last week in June of '91, President Gorbachev has requested a hundred plus billion dollars in financial aid over a five year period.

As a West German summitteer stated, "If we don't give aid to the USSR we may lose the chance and then a conservative coup is quite probable with a hard line communist." Such a coup did occur, at least for an apparent three-day period between August 3 and 6, 1991, in which Mikhail Gorbachev and his government were temporarily removed from power.

Communications were not cut off or transportation by airline. Mr. Yeltsin, then President of Russia, was not removed from power or detained by house arrest, Mr. Gorbachev was not executed along with his family, there was a show of force but no helicopters to spot snipers and no obvious use of force other than very minimal confrontation with picketers.

The small numbers out of the huge population of Moscow of 8-1/2 million with tremendous coverage shows that the coup was a media event. Staging it was necessary to threaten the West with revolution in fifteen republics with potential strategic nuclear weapons about to have a very bloody and destructive revolution that would affect the entire world. This rationale was certainly contrived by Gorbachev and his government to not only remove any opposition in the K.G.B. and the military, but to loosen the purse strings of western nations, with most success being European countries and especially Germany.

This gives considerable ammunition to western politicians, such as Mr. Bush, during a recession to assure massive loan guarantees to the Soviet Union in the range of many billions of dollars. This is while refusing to give tiny loan guarantees in the range of ten billion dollars to returning Soviet Jews trying to emigrate to Israel for resettlement.

As mentioned in Question 61, both the United States and Russia have considerable invested in a reunification of Germany which was directly engineered and orchestrated by Mr. Mikhail Gorbachev. His plan was stated clearly in his book, "PERESTROIKA: A New Thinking for Our Country and the World".

As of April, 1991 Russia has obtained $24 billion in loan guarantees from the International Monetary Fund and a guarantee of three per cent of the total I.M.F. assets on joining membership, a plan for the near future. At the end of 1992, the European Currency Unit will become the electronic currency exchange standard for the European community in a move toward total economic and political unification of the European super state.

The vast military machine of the Soviet Union has been built on approximately 30-45 per cent of Gross National Product being diverted into production of weapon systems far in excess of that produced by the United States. This has been only developed for one purpose which is primarily world conquest, through the threat of a first strike offensive. Production of these systems has increased dramatically during the years of Gorbachev and his plan of Perestroika.

Following the demise of Gorbachev's government in August 3, 1991, Mr. Yeltsin with his Confederation of Independent States has not resolved the problem of unification of the Soviet military machine. This is part of the tactics to push western nations, particularly European and Germany, to support the Soviet Union's current economic problems with huge amounts of cash.

With the integration of a free market economy in the former Soviet Union, the radicalization of the Moslem fundamentalists in alignment with the major powers of Russia and its co-nuclear Eastern bloc states, a window of opportunity is opened from now until half-way through the seven-year period. This last seven years is opened by the Arab-Israeli peace treaty and the start of the Jewish sacrifice within the tabernacle on the Temple Mount of Jerusalem. The window of opportunity will close exactly 1,260 days later.

93. What is the economic and military tightrope the Soviet Union must walk as it enters into the New World Order?

Paul Kennedy, historian, states in "The Rise and Fall of the Great Powers" that an empire supports its military to secure that territory and interest based on its economy.

Russia is the leading producer of oil in the world. It has the largest amount of arable land in the world of any nation. Russia must become a member of the global economy to retain its empire. Mikhail Gorbachev has attempted to turn communism into a market communism. Gorbachev can complete the revolution charted by Validimir Lenin. The tightrope Mr. Gorbachev must balance upon has economic doom, if there is no reform, and political doom with rising nationalism and a break up of the empire, if there is economic reform.

Economic policy set forth by Gorbachev has been carried further by Mr. Yeltsin in developing a free market economy with spiraling inflation and a direct attempt by the I.M.F. to regulate the total number of rubles in circulation. Russians have saved 40 per cent of their total income for seventy years. In spite of very rocky economic times, there appear no alternatives to Mr. Yeltsin's reforms. Each day news brings further reports from the former Soviet Union of economic chaos, the further spread and proliferation of nuclear technology and the fire sale of nuclear scientist brain power to Moslem states, vieing to join the nuclear club.

This is a period of time of regrouping of the Soviet Union, retrenching its position, but at no point denies its underlying Marxist-Leninist philosophy. Gorbachev has merely propounded New Age Marxist-Leninist economic reform to develop a form of market Communism integrated with the world economy to support its military machine and ultimate goals of world conquest. The Russian bear is now asleep. When it stirs and wakes destruction will suddenly be upon a New Age Socialist Environmentalist World.

94. **What kind of evidence is there that there is a world economic conspiracy moving toward a one world government, a one world bank and a one world currency?**

Pastor William Getts and the book "The Economy to Come" stated however,

> "...as I have read and researched material like Mars New World Order, Hal Lindsey in 1980's Count Down to Armageddon, Mystery 666 by Don Stanton and The Naked Capitalist by Clion Skousen, Tragedy and Hope by Carol

Quigley and others, I've become convinced that there is indeed an international non-governmental group of financiers, intellectuals, industrialist and politicians whose goal is the development of a one world government, a one world bank and a one world currency."

Many elements of this conspiracy of the common goals from different origins is reflected in the terms, "spins" of Constance Cumbey's eye opening book on a New Age, **"The Hidden Dangers of Rainbow."** The lie is always the same, **"Man can determine good from evil."** The goal is the same, world economic and political unity in peace as it says in the *1 Thessalonians 5:3, "For when they shall say, Peace and safety; then sudden destruction cometh upon them, as travail upon a woman with child; and they shall not escape."* This, of course, refers to the peace which will be brought by the Imam Mahdi False Messiah and the New Age Movement, the World Economic Masonic Order and Perestroika as a front for the advancement of the **New World Order. Each tries to attempt to forward its own form of Utopia without God.** In all cases the gods are the same with ultimately the worship of Satan by false gods or worship of fallen man, in the image of Satan.

95. How have we arrived at this point in world economic unification?

There are many well known facts that when we take a two here and a two there, they make a very convincing four. The Tri-lateral Commission is in Hal Lindsey's words "an international non-elected group of the western world's most powerful bankers, media consultants, scholars, and government officials bent on radically changing the world."

Since July 1990, capital moved freely between all European countries and by December 31st, 1992, the European Currency Unit will be the first world electronic currency standard that will replace the American dollar as a world currency standard upon which other currencies are measured against. Direct attempts by the I.M.F. and the World Bank to shore up the Russian ruble and control the number of rubles in circulation and to support the ruble by April, 1992 with $24 billion shows that the ruble will be directly tied as well to the European Currency Unit which will come into being by December 31st, 1992.

The July '92, G7 Summit invited Boris Yeltsin and promised $1 billion in immediate aid and the $24 billion in loan guarantees. This is still tied to Russia raising the price it charges former Soviet client states for oil to rise to world oil prices. At that rate, according to a Fall '90 Time magazine report, this would require 90 per cent of Czechoslovakia's GNP to pay for its oil needs only. The second condition the G7 insist on is speeded reforms to a market economy. As Russia runs out of easily recoverable oil, this will put the hooks in the jaw God refers to in Ezekiel 38 and 39, that will bring Russia and its allies down on the Middle East to take over world oil reserves. (See Question #111).

Pastor William R. Goetz documents will see the development of this conspiracy and the development of its goals. Following World War II, the world control of trade could not survive the post-war period. Prior to that posting of tariffs by Britain, France, Holland, Portugal and the United States controlled this imperial system.

Maynard Keynes and Harry Dexter White developed the Bretton-Woods system. It was a solution to the manipulation of national currencies by their governments to protect their currencies and weaken that of other nations which, of course, would produce international financial instability. Secondly, the problem of protective tariffs raised indiscriminately by nations would result in closing markets to underdeveloped nations in the outing international free trade. In this system it fixed currency exchange rates and developed the International Monetary Fund and the World Bank. These two institutions not only set exchange rates, but have given authority to supply credit to the world's 'have-not' countries and to lend money to nations destroyed by war. The

"Most Favoured" Nation Status System of trade was proposed, underdeveloped nations were given this Most Favoured Status and thus were free from paying tariffs. This stimulated international trade.

The agreement which controlled this tariff system was the General Agreement on Tariffs and Trade or G.A.T.T. The Bretton-Woods plan relied on the United States being the logical enforcer of control, with the U.S. dollar being the basic world currency. It was backed by the 'Gold Standard' and a healthy United States economy in 1944 when the Bretton-Woods was put together, because the U.S. consumed the vast majority of the total world's exported goods and thus the greatest economic power in the world. Dealing with violators of the system was easy by utilization of tariff restrictions and credit control.

With the gradual stumbling of the U.S. economy and the start of the Vietnam War, there was an increase in the U.S. balance of trade deficit combined with the removal of the Gold Standard in 1971 by President Nixon which removed the stability from the American dollar. This started the demise of the Bretton-Woods plan which was met by the head of the Illuminati World of Royal Arch Masons, David Rockefeller, in July 1973, to recruit 200 leading international bankers, businessmen, politicians and labour leaders to develop a new world stabilized economic base. This was led by Zbigniew Brzezinski (Special Presidential Advisor for National Security under the Carter administration) specifically selected by Rockefeller for policy formulation and selecting these world class experts.

Rockefeller envisioned a Tri-lateral Commission with its transformation into reality by Zbigniew Brzezinski to reshape the world economy based on a Tri-lateral or three-sided economic base of the United States, a united Europe and Japan. A new United States of Europe with American and Japanese industrial alliances would control this New World Order. These three entities comprised more than seventy per cent of world trade at that time who would then be able to enforce the New World Economic Order.

David Rockefeller is the current world head of the Illuminati. This organization started from five Austrian Banking families in 1726, on May Day, a pagan high holy day and the only Communist holiday.

Rockefeller envisioned the Tri-Lateral Commission, the U.S.A., Europe and Japan. They now have the power to enforce Bretton-Wood's replacement, thus a **One World Economic System** is taking over with the new European power base two and a half times the manufacturing power of the United States and more population than the USSR, in the European economic community. The coronation has started with <u>German economic re-unification</u> in July 1, 1990 and German unification completed in October of 1990, with the final crown of all the nations joining with total economic union by December 31, 1992. The Club of Rome and other Masonic Organizations is co-ordinating all these efforts with the World Constituent Parliament Association (W.C.P.A.). Their goal is a New World Order Built on the Economic New Order of electronic world funds control through the Mark of the Beast.

96. **What biblical indications show that the creation of a United Europe is the start of the creation of the Empire of Clay and Iron?**

Revelation 17:8-11

> *8 The beast that thou sawest was, and is not; and shall ascend out of the bottomless pit, and go into perdition: and they that dwell on the earth shall wonder, whose names were not written in the book of life from the foundation of the world, when they behold the beast that was, and is not, and yet is.* **[The Kingdom of Babel or Babylon will be resurrected at the Time of the End in the N.W.O.!]**

9 And here [is] the mind which hath wisdom. The seven heads are seven mountains, on which the woman sitteth. **[Seven successive secular kindgoms!]**

10 And there are seven kings: five are fallen **[Kingdoms prior to Rome!]** *and one is* **[Rome at the time of John]**, *[and] the other is not yet come; and when he cometh, he must continue a short space* **[N.W.Order!]**.

11 And the beast that was, and is not, even he is the eighth, and is of the seven, and goeth into perdition. **[Russian Beast Dictator of East and Western Europe and the Middle East!]**

The city of seven hills at the time of Jesus was referred to as the city built on seven hills. This final world order will be built on the seven world post-flood secular world empires. Also, it will rely on the economic power of the G7 economic nations to enforce its economic and military control over sectarian violence and any threats to the economic well being of the New World Order.

It will start from Rome, from the Treaty of Rome and the resurrected Roman Empire would stand a short time before being swallowed up and destroyed by communist take-over. The seventh empire of a United States of Europe is taken over by the eighth, a Beast Empire formed from the ashes of a militarily revitalized Russia and allies and conquered United European Community coming down to take over the Middle Eastern Nations controlling the worlds oil reserves and driving the world economic engine forward.

97. Who will ultimately control this economic order?

The economic order will have been originally set up by world Royal Arch Masonism, enforced by the American NSA controlled Mark of the Beast, with the increasing exchange of oil for wealth, this power will shift during the first three and one-half years of the seven-year period, to the Babylon empire, further strengthened by the religious unification of the false Moslem Messiah. This will precipitate the Russian beast and the nations of the European United States of Europe to attack Iraq and its Babylonian empire and to destroy America in opposition to communist secular atheist goals.

98. What are the organizations in the United States and Britain which are the guiding power reorganizing economic unification of the United States and Europe and what is their goal beyond economic unification?

The U.S. cousin of the Tri-Lateral Commission is a Council on Foreign Relations or the C.F.R. founded by David Rockefeller's grandfather in 1921. C.F.R. President, Winston Lord, was quoted by Pastor Getts, "The Tri-Lateral Commission doesn't secretly run the world, the Council on Foreign Relations does that." Every American Secretary of State except James Burns has been a member of the C.F.R.

One of the C.F.R.'s own members, Carol Quigley, is summarized by W. Clion Skousen, from Quigley's massive 1,300-page book Tragedy and Hope as one of the elite insiders. He knew the scope of the power complex, and he knew that its leaders hoped to eventually attain total global control. The British branch of the C.F.R. is the Royal Institute of International Affairs.

The purpose is to reunite Britain and the United States, U.S.A. and E.E.C. under a world government. It is felt by a Royal Arch Mason as laid out in nine lectures on Anglo-Israel, by Reverend W. H. Poole in the 1860's, that the United States and Britain are the lost tribes of Israel. They will use their Masonic justification to attempt to place a Davidic king over all the tribes in which this new system will rule the world. (Ref. Goetz, Wm. "The Economy to Come", p. 62-67)

99. How is the existence of a unified Europe in the New World Order completely dependent on an Islamic/Palestinian-Israeli peace treaty?

Europe runs on Middle East crude and desperately needs an Arab/Israeli treaty. The only power which can make the Arab bow to form a treaty is of course the Russians who arm them. The only one which can make the Israelis sign is the United States, who supplies them with their protection and supplied them with nuclear weapons until Israel develop their own capabilities.

With eighty per cent United States spending, the Israelis have developed the Arrow Theater Air Defense (THAD) Anti-ICBM rocket system capable of disintegrating incoming nuclear missiles at up to 7,000 to 8,000 miles. This is far superior to the Patriot system which was just coming off the drawing board on August 2, 1990 when the Gulf War opened. It probably required the time to January 19th to produce enough Scuds to neutralize the expected number of Scuds available with missile launchers for Saddam Hussein, i.e. 1,000 Scuds.

100. Why has Canada and other nations accepted a new (V.A.T.) Value Added Tax at transaction as the G.ST.?

The stage is set, Canada is the fifty-seventh country to adopt a sliding value added tax (V.A.T.) or taxation at transaction. This is called a government service tax or G.S.T. and was the only trade protectionist barrier allowed by the General Agreement on Trade and Tariffs, sponsored by the Trilateral Commission. This is a first stage in abolishing cash. One must do away with income tax tied to cash to achieve a cashless society, where all transactions may be controlled by a world debit card.

In a personal conversation in August of 1991 with the Minister of Finance, Mr. Mazankowsky, at a Conservative Annual Dinner in Halifax, Nova Scotia, a number of important questions were placed. As Minister of Finance for Canada he responded very candidly to my questions. He stated that it was the intention of the

Conservative government to abolish income tax in six to eight years and to replace it with a G.S.T. of 25 to 27 per cent, thereby eliminating the need for cash, which would coincide with a move to the debit card by the end of the decade at the latest.

Obviously, the only way to eliminate income is to eliminate income tax. Once the cashless society is present, the elements of a system such as referred to in Revelation 13, become imminently possible.

Revelation 13:16-18

> *16 And he causeth all, both small and great, rich and poor, free and bond, to receive a mark in their right hand, or in their foreheads:* **[invisible bar code-identicode]**
>
> *17 And that no man might buy or sell, save he that had the mark, or the name of the beast, or the number of his name.*
>
> *18 Here is wisdom. Let him that hath understanding count the number of the beast: for it is the number of a man; and his number [is] Six hundred threescore [and] six.*

The cashless society which precedes the Mark of the Beast will be for an increasing convenience and prosperity, and crime and drug use elimination, but in the middle of the seven years the system will demand that all who are involved with the economy of this new world system must take the mark, probably an invisible bar code on the forehead or right hand. The bar code itself may be an identification or it may be further verified by a retinal scan or fingerprint scan to confirm the identity of the transactor. All of our economic experts know that the debit card is even more transparent to fraud than the credit card which suffers from an epidemic of fraud that keeps interest rates of credit cards much higher than banks or other lending institutions. But because this system is the only one which will give absolute control, our institutions and governments are going to sacrifice the truth.

We know that the computer is based on the hexadecimal or 666 modulus numbering system. The number 666 not only refers to the number for man but also the Trinitarian Masonic system and the world computer system. It also refers to the three sixes as arrows in a triangle, the symbol of recycling. This is a recycling of the ancient symbol of the three snakes in a triangle head eating tail, the symbol of reincarnation.

Each of these new high tech debit cards is but a prelude to the placement of a number which cannot be lost on the forehead or hand. New systems are currently available which allow a retina scan of the eye with a laser to identify an individual and show proof that the number found on the forehead is indeed the property of the person who is confirmed by the retina scan. There is a very accurate scanner currently being used by the U.S. military and other companies. It analyzes fingerprints at the same time that a scan of an invisible infra red bar code can be identified by laser scanner.

Whether the mark is visible or invisible, technology now exist for the first time in history which will allow a total computerized economy allowing central control of the world so that no one may buy or sell if they do not have this identification.

The Mark of the Beast will be based on the German mark and the European economic currency unit or E.C.U. as the world's standard. It is now called EURO. Currently for every dollar in circulation world-wide, there are seven computer dollars which have no basis in reality and are not backed up by cash and there are seventeen dollars in real circulation for every dollar value in precious metals world-wide. As a result, the creation of the New World Order and limitless cash under the control of World Masonism are completely dependant on removing income tax and making the society a cashless society.

101. How have the Russians and Americans played high stakes economic and military chess over the past twenty years?

A number of stages have occurred in the opposing models to produce a Utopia without God. The Russians encouraged their Arab allies to raise the price of oil in the '70's and created an oil crisis in North America. The American response to this was to continue to arm Israel further with more nuclear weapons. Chess on the world stage has high stakes.

Glasnost and Perestroika are simply a response to the Reaganomics policy of interlocking world debt by taking the United States from a net creditor nation to a net debtor. This was undertaken so that other countries will not adversely discriminate against the U.S. dollar and cause significant devaluation of the U.S. currency world-wide. Most of this money, over one trillion dollars, was not spent on health care or social services, but almost entirely on the development of expensive high technology weapons of death under Reagan and Bush.

These weapons are used like video game toys to destroy two to three hundred thousand Iraqi citizens without any need. It has caused untold damage to the area that will be felt for hundreds to thousands of miles downwind. The Kuwait oil fires may have magnified or initiated the intensity of the greatest tropical storm in history to strike Bangladesh and kill a hundred and forty thousand people.

The combination of the Mount Pinotubo volcanic eruption in the Philippines in the fall of 1991, and the Gulf War has created a dramatic increase in world pollution and has markedly increased **the destruction of the ozone layer**, particularly over the southern pole and the southern regions of South Americans and a new more ominous hole has appeared in the ozone during the winter of 1991-92 over eastern Canada, Canada of the Arctic, Greenland, Sweden, Norway and the northeastern regions of the Baltics and Russia.

The damage is extensive enough in South America, from the annual summer surge in growth of the Antartic Ozone Hole that during this winter animals developed cataracts, and little of the fruit or grains grew. They were burnt white by the ozone destruction resulting in shortwave U.V.B. light burning the plants to the point that there was no harvest. This is but a warning to the world about what will happen even from a localized nuclear war. Particles generated by such a type of conflict would reduce world temperatures and preserve gases, such as nitric oxide gases, through this cooling effect. The effect would accelerate the ozone destruction to occur over a matter of days, weeks, or months.

102. What are Glastnost and Perestroika in relationship to current Soviet military and economic policy?

Glastnost and Perestroika, which are not really 'openness' and 'restructuring', but can simply be paraphrased, "I'm really a cuddly Russian bear that just wants to play market economy like other big boys and may even make you rich if you protect me from my hardline communist opponents." and, "We have no intentions on global control of oil or shipping and wouldn't think of strangling the carotid arteries of Japan and Europe at the oil choke point of the outlet of the Strait of Hormuz in the Persian Gulf or the choke point on the Red Sea."

The Russian threatened to have a civil war like a tantrum if they do not receive sufficient cash. This money will, of course, be used to modernize the arm forces. There has been more active Russian spying during Gorbachev's Glasnost and Perestroika than prior to the so-called thawing of the cold war.

Russian communism has been able to infiltrate many Masonic political organizations including MI-5 and MI-6 in Britain, as well as P-2 in Italy which caused the collapse of the Italian Government in the 1980's. Surely Masonism is the harlot religion which has prostituted itself for a financial gain. Is it not fitting that prostitute religion should be destroyed by godless Atheism prior to the judgment of God on all those who remain on earth and have not repented.

According to Revelation 17: 16, the beast which takes over the European Empire of Clay and Iron will hate this New Age religion and Neo-Babylonian America and destroy them with fire and eat their flesh. Surely our holy God is merciful and just, but this great blasphemy would be destroyed by godless man worshipping secular atheism. The conquest of secular atheism will be answered by the return of Jesus himself, Almighty God.

Chapter 5

THE U.S.S.R. AND WORLD MILITARY DOMINANCE

103. How has the Soviet Union achieved conventional and military superiority to the United States of America?

Hal Lindsey's "1980's Count Down to Armageddon," documents the slow at first and rapidly recent growth in Russian military superiority. Until the end of the sixties the U.S.A. was far ahead of the nuclear arms race. This turn of events started with President Kennedy and the Cuban Missile crisis aftermath July 17, 1979, Admiral Elmo R. Zumwalt, Jr. gave testimony to the U.S. Senate Committee on Foreign Relations. He was on the Joint Chiefs of Staff and Director of Arms Control for the Secretary of Defense in 1962 and in 1963. Admiral Zumwalt quoted by Hal Lindsey,

> "The U.S. recognizes that its strategic nuclear superiority is unacceptable to the Soviet Union. We understand that your attempt to install missiles in Cuba was an effort to redress that imbalance. We propose now to let you catch up to us, we shall then have a situation of mutual assured destruction or M.A.D., or mutual deterrence. We propose to stop at the 1,054 ICBMs and 656 SLBMs we are now building, you should do the same. We propose to keep our missiles with a combination of size and accuracy that you will know from your own calculation that we cannot destroy yours in a first strike so that you could always retaliate if we strike first. You should do the same with regards to size and accuracy."

Both sides decided they should reduce the continuing radiation produced by warheads to minimize the kill of innocents if military targets should be struck. Each side accordingly should forego a civil defense so that cities of each would be hostages against their own government first strike. With the signing of SALT, the Russians had to now be granted a 55 per cent advantage in ICBMs and a 300 per cent advantage in mega tonnage and throw weight. We have reduced fallout but the Russians have not. Russian civil defense is fine tuned with concrete bunkers in all major housing complexes in all cities and towns. Population evacuation plans and industrial survival procedures are in place.

President Clinton's has reduced the military preparedness of the United States and has cancelled the full deployment of the US space shield against incoming ICBMs. He has given military hardware technologies to Russia, China, and the Islamic world at an unprecedented rate. We are incapable of staging the kind of response with our former allies in Desert Storm, and cannot fight a two front war. We are now vulnerable to a devastating strike from Russia at the timing of the N.W.O. European Globalists, newly armed with the EURO and the MARK generously supplied via American telecommunications and military technologies. This insane Illuminated scheme of the current government will lead to the loss of American sovereignty, and result in a militia lead counter-revolution fought on American soil.

The Marxist-Leninist, Gorbachevist, Community trinity would hurl the world into an Atheism and communist nightmare bend on destroying Jews and Christians. Gorbachev condemns Stalin and the Katyn forest massacre of five thousand Polish officers, by KGB Russians, when for years they blamed it on German Nazis during World War II.

104. What is the basic ideology set forth by Peter the Great and repeated by Lenin?

The communist ideological lies that communism will change man's nature is not dying as news media pretend. As often stated by Lenin referring to the advance of the Russian Empire at the time of Peter the Great, **"Communism moves like a hammer two** steps back and one step forward to drive the nail into the coffin of the capitalist world." It was often stated by Lenin that, "the capitalists will sell the rope that we will hang them with".

Hitler himself was disturbed by communism and used it to try to balkenize the Germans against spreading communism into Germany, "I will not tolerate the triumph of Jews through Bolshevization of the world." Clearly he knew another little known fact that Nelson Rockefeller, the grandfather to David of the CFR and Tri-Lateral Commission, sent ten million dollars in arms out of New York harbour at no cost to support Vladimir Lenin, for the Bolshevic Revolution. It is no strange coincidence that Mikhail S. Gorbachev was head of the KGB after his predecessor Andropov.

105. How do the Russians propose to balance political and military goals to seize world control?

As Paul Kennedy's thesis proposes, the Russians must move quickly and decisively to balance between political and military suicide. They will lunge for their goals of world control by stealing technology through spying from the West, obtaining free capital to modernize industry and the military industrial complex, while sitting on the largest production of oil in the world, outside the Middle East.

106. How will world energy consumption and distribution of reserves affect history in the Middle East and around the world? Will oil be found in Israel?

According to Rob Linstead, Ph.D., Christian Author and Engineer, in the book, **The Next Move Current Events in Bible Prophecy**, the world's energy requirements increase by seven per cent per year and double the world consumption every ten years. World oil reserves are thought to be in the range of two trillion barrels with three-quarters in the Middle East and North Africa. About half of all that oil is in the countries bordering the Persian Gulf.

It is felt, for example, that only one-quarter of the territory of Iraq has been explored and that it is the second largest oil reserve in the world with its best fields geologically unexplored as yet.

Doctor Linstead also relates the story of a Christian Geological Engineer, Andy SoRelle, who in the early 1980s explored for oil while in the Meggido Valley near Haifa at 21,000 feet. After reading and believing that Deuteronomy, Chapter 33, verse 24 talks about Asher dipping his foot in oil. This, of course, would be the tribe of Asher having a territory that would look like it was a foot dipping in oil on a map.

Dr. Linstead reviews scripts that prophesied the finding of oil in the Middle East, in Israel, and in Arab countries. In Genesis 49:1 and Jacob called unto his sons, and said, "Gather yourselves together, that I may tell you that which shall befall you in the last days," and in Genesis 49:20, "Out of Asher his bread shall be fat, and he shall yield royal dainties." Verse 22, "Joseph is a fruitful bough, even a fruitful bough by a well; whose branches run over the wall:"

Genesis 49: 25-26

25 [Even] by the God of thy father, who shall help thee; and by the Almighty, who shall bless thee with blessings of heaven above, blessings of the deep that lieth under, blessings of the breasts, and of the womb: **[oil]**

26 The blessings of thy father have prevailed above the blessings of my progenitors unto the utmost bound of the everlasting hills: they shall be on the head of Joseph, and on the crown of the head of him that was separate from his brethren.

We can see again the reference to oil exploration.

Deuteronomy 32:13

13 He made him ride on the high places of the earth, that he might eat the increase of the fields; and he made him to suck honey out of the rock, and oil out of the flinty rock; **[geological formation for oil deposits]**

Flinty rock is a description of the kind of rock formation where geologists find oil.

Deuteronomy 33:13

13 And of Joseph he said, Blessed of the LORD [be] his land, for the precious things of heaven, for the dew, and for the deep that coucheth beneath, **[deep oil reserves in the boot of Asher in the Meggido Valley]**

Deuteronomy 33:19

19 They shall call the people unto the mountain; there they shall offer sacrifices of righteousness: for they shall suck [of] the abundance of the seas **[sandseas yield oil]**, *and [of] treasures hid in the sand.* **[Oil is explored from deserts of Middle East]**

Oil is the treasure hid in the sand of Israel and Arab countries.

Deuteronomy 33: 24-26

24 And of Asher he said, [Let] Asher [be] blessed with children; let him be acceptable to his brethren, and let him dip his foot in oil.

25 Thy shoes [shall be] iron and brass; and as thy days, [so shall] thy strength [be].

26 [There is] none like unto the God of Jeshurun, [who] rideth upon the heaven in thy help, and in his excellency on the sky.

The references to the map of Asher's territory dipping his foot in oil of the deep and his feet will be made of iron and brass shining metal structure of oil refinery as seen through the eyes of the prophet, envisioned foretell of large supplies of oil in the territory of Israel.

107. How will the finding of oil in Israel directly influence Russia and all its allies to invade northern Israel?

The finding of oil will not only be the strength of Israel, but also the reason for the Arab/Israeli, to Russian/Arab conflict, coming to take loot. These nations of Ezekiel 38: 1-6 will eventually converge on Israel where the majority of oil appears to be. Looking at the territory of Asher, the toes are at Haifa, the largest oil refinery in Israel and one of the largest in the world and at the mouth of the valley of Meggido, between the Mediterranean and Galilean Seas.

Ezekiel 38: 4, 10-13

> *4 And I will turn thee back, and put hooks into thy jaws,* **[Russia captive to oil just as Assyria put hooks in the jaws of captives]** *and I will bring thee forth, and all thine army, horses and horsemen, all of them clothed with all sorts [of armour, even] a great company [with] bucklers and shields, all of them handling swords:*
>
> *10 Thus saith the Lord GOD; It shall also come to pass, [that] at the same time shall things come into thy mind, and thou shalt think an evil thought:*
>
> *11 And thou shalt say, I will go up to the land of unwalled villages; I will go to them that are at rest, that dwell safely, all of them dwelling without walls, and having neither bars nor gates,*
>
> *12 To take a spoil, and to take a prey; to turn thine hand upon the desolate places [that are now] inhabited, and upon the people [that are] gathered out of the nations, which have gotten cattle and goods, that dwell in the midst of the land.*
>
> *13 Sheba, and Dedan, and the merchants of Tarshish, with all the young lions thereof, shall say unto thee, Art thou come to take a spoil? hast thou gathered thy company to take a prey? to carry away silver and gold, to take away cattle and goods, to take a great spoil?*

It is therefore a primary political trigger for Russian to invade the Middle East. It will arm many allies and be the chief commander of a final invasion to culminate in the Valley of Decision, the Valley of Meggido. This will occur at the 1,260th day, thirty days after the sacrifice has been stopped in the Tabernacle of Moses on the Temple Mount.

Desperate need for oil world-wide will focus the world on the country of Israel. Dr. Linstead quotes from Oil and Gas Journal, published December 24, 1984 by L. F. Ivonhoe state that,

> "There is no longer any scientific question of whether but only when and how our global petroleum age will end during the first half of the twenty-first century. The end will be in sight for most nations by the year 1999."

(ibid. p. 60).

As Dr. Linstead refers to the above article,

> "...the region, Middle East, is a wild card of the energy deck. Production in this area is controlled by world demand and local politics rather than any capacity. Any world oil gluts or crisis will henceforth be due to Iraq petroleum deliveries from the super oily region of which online production facilities and active reserves can make or break the international price of any fuel."

(ibid. p. 60)

108. What types of oil production problems do the Soviets have and how will this affect future oil supplies to the new market economies of Eastern bloc countries following the apparent demise of the Soviet Empire?

The Soviets have serious oil problems as Dr. Linstead shows. An article in the Chicago Tribune, April 4, 1984 entitled "Soviets admit serious oil field problems" says, "The Soviet Union, the world biggest oil producer admitted for the first time Tuesday it has serious problems with oil production in Western Siberia and said the main reason was that wells were more difficult to tap." The communist party daily Pravda said, "The Tyumen region which provides more than half the country's oil, has been below target for six months, and the prospects for improvement were not good." Since the writing of that article, there have been numerous explosions in gas pipe lines in Western Siberia and the Russians have been unable to maintain proper technology to get deep reserves which are the majority of oil and they are very difficult tundra oil fields.

As of April, 1992, most oil and gas exploration has been stopped in all western countries, and in Canada exploration and development of the Hibernia oil fields has been stopped by Gulf Canada. They are in the process of selling six ships at a price of between $600 and $800 million Canadian and moving all their oil recovery technology to the Soviet Union to cash in on oil recovery in proven sources. This adds further strength to the Soviet economic base with oil production from Russia being number one in the world.

109. What are current U.S. oil and gas reserves?

Another article Dr. Linstead reviews in the Wichita Eagle-Beacon, May 1985 entitled "Off shore oil and gas reserves far overstated U.S. says," discusses the facts. "The U.S. interior department was quoted as saying that there is a fifty-five per cent less oil and forty-four per cent less natural gas world-wide than was estimated in 1981. They also said that it has lowered its sights off Alaska by seventy-three per cent for oil and seventy-eight per cent for natural gas."

110. Which nation in particular would benefit from increasing Arab tensions over Israeli occupation in the Middle East?

Dr. Linstead reviews a few comments in the Readers Digest, February 1982 article, in **"Count Down in the Middle East"**, and states:

"Only the Soviet Union stands to benefit from a growing Arab tension over the Israeli occupation. The Soviet have entrenched all around the rim of the east, Middle East

heartland in Afghanistan, Yemen, Ethiopia, Libya. Experts say the Russians and their allies would need substantial supplies of foreign oil by the end of this decade if not before. There's only one place to obtained it in quantity: the Persian Gulf."

111. What are expected consumption requirements of Eastern bloc countries such as Czechoslovakia expected to be following modernization?

It was reported in Time Magazine, fall 1990, that Czechoslovakia is an example of an Eastern Bloc country that will use ninety per cent this year and a hundred and ten per cent next year, of its gross natural production, at world oil prices, to pay for energy needs only in oil. Russia currently has subsidized oil to Eastern Bloc countries at below world prices for a number of years which will end with the termination of the Warsaw Pact and the restructuring world market economy of the former USSR.

These consumption requirements of the expanding market economy of Eastern Bloc countries will make essential the tying together, not only of the economic power of Europe through the European Currency Unit, but the oil power of the oil producing states of the Mid-East to supply European and former Warsaw Pact nations with energies to develop their market economy.

112. Has there been geological exploration in the 'boot of Asher' territory and what have the results been?

A very important article was also reviewed by Dr. Linstead, first written in the Jerusalem's Post Magazine, September 11, 1981, entitled **"A Matter of Belief"**. Mr. Andy SoRelle is a Christian geologist who offered to look for oil for the Israel government in the Sinai after the Israeli take over of the territory and discovered five very prosperous oil fields which were later turned over to Egypt with the Sinai after the Camp David 1978 meeting and Israeli-Egyptian treaty.

Several years later still bent on living in Israel and looking for oil, he read and believed ***Deuteronomy 33:24.***

24 And of Asher he said, [Let] Asher [be] blessed with children; let him be acceptable to his brethren, and let him dip his foot in oil.

He found a vast quantity of oil at 21,000 feet but lost the drill fish or front of the drill bit after spending twenty million dollars on the exploration. The site is only hundreds of feet from the largest oil refinery in Israel at Haifa, one of the largest oil refineries in the world.

The author of the article of the Jewish geologist, Jackie Sherman, as a result of that article began to read the Bible and accept Jesus Christ because of what the Bible said in a concrete way to him as a scientist. Dr. Linstead spoke with Andy SoRelle again after his visit in Israel, his response to the question, twenty million dollars and several years later, aren't you discouraged? He said, "Why should I be discouraged by God's timing? If Noah could wait a hundred and twenty years for it to rain, I can wait two years for oil." He related that with three million dollars and he might be able to retrieve the fish or drill bit and bring the well back into function. He claimed that he foresaw immense potential. He said, "I think it may be the biggest well in the Middle East." **He continues to drill in other well sites in the 'boot of Asher' area of Israel and in the Valley of Meggido**. This location is the very site prophesied as the place where the world conflict to end the Age will start.

113. Does God bless both Arabs and Jews regarding the great blessing of 'plentiful oil'?

The decedents of Esau are the Saudi Arabians, Iraqis, and areas of the United Air Emirates and Kuwait. Isaac give Esau the blessing told in Genesis 27:39, "Behold, thy dwellings shall be the fatness **[the oil]** of the earth, and of the dew of heaven from above." Jacob, forefather of all Israel and the head of Israel being Judah and half tribe of Benjamin received the blessing of Genesis

27:28. "Therefore God give thee of the dew of heaven, and the fatness **[oil]** of the earth, and plenty of corn and wine:" Isn't it awesome the power of the Bible to give us some sense of the true greatness of our God and its complete foreign knowledge of all events.

We wonder at the timeless blessings of God to Ishmael for the Arabs to live where most of the oil in the world is located and to Isaac for Israel to find oil deep in the ground at the territory of the boot of Asher. This would occur when they returned to Israel in unbelief. As Dr. Linstead says, **"...what a sure word of prophecy God has given us."**

114. What role have the Russians had in the Iraqi invasion of Kuwait?

As James McKeever newsletter "End Times News Digest", December 1990, quotes from the McIlvany Intelligence Advisor, August 1990, quoting Senator Bill Richardson,

> *"The chances of a full scale military operation against the Iraqi forces is really unthinkable to the U.S. State Department. Since it would cause unfriendly vibes with the Soviets, the Iraqi Government has had a friendship treaty with the Soviets since 1972 and all very friendly."* In essence, the USSR's military committed to help Iraq. The Soviets have eight military facilities or bases in Iraq according to Robert Morris. His 1987 book **Our Globe Under Seige, Part 3.** Morris quoted columnist Paul Scott who listed these facilities several years ago, eight military bases including naval and air installation. *"The primary enemy is not Iraq, it's the Soviet Union. If you look closely, you will see the Machaevelli communist fingerprints all over the dead body of Kuwait."*

Grant R. Jeffrey in his book, **"Messiah: War in the Middle East and the Road to Armageddon"**, analyzes very clearly the role of the Soviet Union and its secret agenda in the Middle East.

President Gorbachev asked for a forty-eighty-hour advanced notice before U.N. forces launched operation Desert Storm ground war against Iraq. However, Iraq was notified very quickly by President Gorbachev and, therefore, when the Arab campaign started President Bush waited until thirty minutes before the attack and kept Gorbachev on the phone for twenty-eight minutes.

Several other bits of information were reviewed by Grant Jeffrey including the presence of Russian military advisors daily conducting intelligence assistance to Iraq and the movement of 200,000 Russian troops and tactical battlefield nuclear weapons from the Soviet southern command theatre to move up to the Russian-Turkey border after Turkey moved 180,000 NATO troops to the the Turkish-Iraqi border to protect bases which the Americans and the U.N. forces were utilizing during the air campaign.

It is impossible that Russia, and Mikhail Gorbachev in particular, was totally unaware of Iraq's plans to invade her neighbour, and was the mastermind of a plan that reviewed in the January 21, 1991 Newsweek, where Hosne Mubarak, President of Egypt, was presented with a plan by Saddam Hussein approximately 2-1/2 years earlier for South Yemen, Syria, Iraq and Egypt to attack and divide the spoils of Saudi Arabia, Kuwait, Bahrain, Qatar, and the Arab Emirates and redistribute the territory and wealth to recreate the new Babylonian Moslem oil empire. This, indeed, was the most significant story of the Gulf War and certainly the most significant for setting the stage for the coming Russian-Arab invasion of the Middle East.

The ultimate destruction of the Neo-Babylonian Oil Empire, and the destruction of the New Age religious system Mystery Babylon, will occur during this Time of Jacob's trouble.

Chapter 6

ISRAEL IN THE END TIMES

115. How is the recreation of the nation of Israel important prophetically?

Israel returned to the land in unbelief in 1948 and in 1967 and 1973 it expanded its territories. Since the time of the prophecy going forward, this is the first time that Israel has been resurrected, in fulfillment of the absolute Word of God.

In the Words of Jesus:

Matthew 24: 32-33

> *32 Now learn a parable of the fig tree; When his branch is yet tender, and putteth forth leaves, ye know that summer [is] nigh:*
>
> *33 So likewise ye, when ye shall see all these things, know that it is near, [even] at the doors.*

The ultimate victory is the nation of Israel. The return of Jesus is very near when the nation of Israel returns to the land. Grant Jeffrey shows the exact interpretation of Ezekiel's prophecy on the precise day of May 14th, 1948, exactly 2,520 biblical years after the partial return in unbelief at 536 B.C.

The countries surrounding them attacked and were defeated during the 1967 and 1973 wars. Israel has become a very formidable military power with at least 25 per cent of its total G.N.P. used by its military, plus U.S. military aid and the extreme dedication of its people into developing a counter-offensive and defensive military posture foremost in the world.

116. Have new archeological discovery aided in discovery of the ashes of the red heifer necessary for temple sacrifice?

The discovery of the Dead Sea Scrolls and what is known as the Copper Scroll gave direction to the tomb of Zadoc the priest and various digging sites at an ancient Jewish settlement at Qumran on the Dead Sea. Excavations by Vendell Jones has found a cave in which the ashes of the red heifer are very likely buried. These ashes are an important but not essential element in reinitiating sacrifice in the rebuilt Jewish temple.

Using genetic cloning techniques Israelis are now growing red heifers from Switzerland on ranches in Israel. The Temple Priests must use the burnt ashes of the heifer to be ceremonially clean before the Temple Mount can be sanctified and the Tabernacle built and start the daily sacrifice.

117. What other elements have been prepared for the reinitiation of the priesthood and temple sacrifice?

All the elements are now built historically accurate including the process. Completion of the instruments of the priesthood and the numerous priesthood Yeshiva schools established to train the Cohens and Levites to be the priests in the New Temple brings us one step closer. It has only been the last several years when both major groups of Jews within Israel have agreed that the rebuilding of the temple in reinitiation of sacrifice has been called for and they agreed on at all level.

The Jewish people believe that they cannot purify a Sanhedrin until they have the ashes, they cannot purify the priesthood without the ashes and without the priesthood they cannot sacrifice again. In June of 1991, the Sanhedrin was voted in by Rabbis world-wide in preparation for sanctification by use of the ashes of the red heifer to purify a Levitical priesthood for proper temple sacrifice. This is according to purification procedures from the Bible.

See Question 40 - Dreams & Visions

118. Is there recent evidence for the return of the Ark of the Covenant and the reinitiation of Temple sacrifice?

There are numerous theories about the location of the Ark. Neverless, there is excellent evidence the Ark of the Covenant is located in the old city of Jerusalem.

119. How will the fate of Christians and Jews be bound together during these end times?

From Revelation 11: 3 we see that the two witnesses in 11: 3 are considered in 11: 4, olive trees and lamp stands and are, therefore, Christian Gentiles and Believing Jews, which worship Jesus as the son of God.

Two Witnesses = Saved Jews + Gentiles!

Revelation 11:3-8

3 And I will give [power] unto my two witnesses, and they shall prophesy a thousand two hundred [and] threescore days, clothed in sackcloth.

4 These are the two olive trees, and the two candlesticks standing before the God of the earth.

5 And if any man will hurt them, fire proceedeth out of their mouth, and devoureth their enemies: and if any man will hurt them, he must in this manner be killed.

6 These have power to shut heaven, that it rain not in the days of their prophecy: and have power over waters to turn them to blood, and to smite the earth with all plagues, as often as they will.

7 And when they shall have finished their testimony, the beast that ascendeth out of the bottomless pit shall make war against them, and shall overcome them, and kill them.

8 And their dead bodies [shall lie] in the street of the great city, which spiritually is called Sodom and Egypt, where also our Lord was crucified.

Malachi 4: 4-6

4 Remember ye the law of Moses my servant, which I commanded unto him in Horeb for all Israel, [with] the statutes and judgments.

5 Behold, I will send you Elijah the prophet before the coming of the great and dreadful day of the LORD:

6 And he shall turn the heart of the fathers to the children, and the heart of the children to their fathers, lest I come and smite the earth with a curse.

[Christian Gentiles and Believing Jews will be one at the Time of the End.]

Ezekiel 37:15-28

15 The word of the LORD came again unto me, saying,

16 Moreover, thou son of man, take thee one stick, and write upon it, For Judah, and for the children of Israel his companions: then take another stick, and write upon it, For Joseph, the stick of Ephraim, and [for] all the house of Israel his companions:

17 And join them one to another into one stick; and they shall become one in thine hand.

18 And when the children of thy people shall speak unto thee, saying, Wilt thou not shew us what thou [meanest] by these?

19 Say unto them, Thus saith the Lord GOD; Behold, I will take the stick of Joseph, which [is] in the hand of Ephraim, and the tribes of Israel his fellows, and will put them with him, [even] with the stick of Judah, and make them one stick, and they shall be one in mine hand. **[Jewish Christians + Gentile Christians]**

20 And the sticks whereon thou writest shall be in thine hand before their eyes.

21 And say unto them, Thus saith the Lord GOD; Behold, I will take the children of Israel from among the heathen, whither they be gone, and will gather them on every side, and bring them into their own land:

22 And I will make them one nation in the land upon the mountains of Israel; and one king shall be king to them all: and they shall be no more two nations, neither shall they be divided into two kingdoms any more at all:

23 Neither shall they defile themselves any more with their idols, nor with their detestable things, nor with any of their transgressions: but I will save them out of all their dwellingplaces, wherein they have sinned, and will cleanse them: so shall they be my people, and I will be their God.

24 And David my servant [shall be] king over them; and they all shall have one shepherd: they shall also walk in my judgments, and observe my statutes, and do them.

25 And they shall dwell in the land that I have given unto Jacob my servant, wherein your fathers have dwelt; and they shall dwell therein, [even] they, and their children, and their children's children for ever: and my servant David [shall be] their prince for ever.

26 Moreover I will make a covenant of peace with them; it shall be an everlasting covenant with them: and I will place them, and multiply them, and will set my sanctuary in the midst of them for evermore.

27 My tabernacle also shall be with them: yea, I will be their God, and they shall be my people.

28 And the heathen shall know that I the LORD do sanctify Israel, when my sanctuary shall be in the midst of them for evermore. **[New Jerusalem.]**

The stick of Judah and the stick of Ephraim mean the Jews that turn to their Messiah, Jesus, and the spiritual remnant of Ephraim or Gentile Christians shall be joined together into one nation. Hence the creation of a Jewish and Christian Zionist nation under one God and one king, Jesus Christ.

This shows that it was never Jesus's intention to have Jews and Christians as separate, and in the Old Testament it shows very clearly that at the times of the end the witness of Moses and the witness of Elijah would bind Christian and Believing Messianic Jews together. God says that without these witnesses being bound together he will strike the earth with a curse and, as we know, in the times of Noah, only the ark could save the survivors from imminent destruction.

The End Times 'Noah's Ark' from this new world-wide holocaust of fire will result from the binding together of Gentile Christians and Believing Jews into Christian and Jewish world-wide unity resulting in the eventual conversion of many surviving Jews and then Gentiles to accept Jesus as Lord.

In the book, **"Israel, the Church, and the Last Days"** by Daniel Juster and Keith Intrater, both Messianic Jewish pastors, they confirmed that the key to evangelizing the world is to have Gentile Christians reach out to evangelize Jews first and save the nation of Israel, as well as Jews, during the time of Jacob's trouble. It is in this act that the key to converting the world. This will "Unify" the body of Christ, and to Gentile Christians and Messianic Jewish believers unity will confirm that all prophecy points to Jesus as the only true Messiah to save a dying world.

120. What is the witness of Moses?
Exodus 2: 10

10 And the child grew, and she brought him unto Pharaoh's daughter, and he became her son. And she called his name Moses: and she said, Because I drew him out of the water.

Moses was drawn out of the sea of the chaos of nations, just as Jews will be drawn out of the sea of the chaos of nations and returned to Israel at the times of the end, during the great Exodus – termed Exodus 2. They will come from the land of the north, the

Soviet Union and Russia in particular, and all of the nations of the earth.

Isaiah 29: 18

18 And in that day shall the deaf hear the words of the book, and the eyes of the blind shall see out of obscurity, and out of darkness.

This is the same scroll mentioned by Isaiah, Ezekiel, Daniel, and Revelation that went unsealed at the times of the end which will not only win Jews to accept Jesus as Lord, but all the surviving nations on earth will be turned to accept Jesus as Lord during eternity.

Isaiah 40: 4-7

4 Every valley shall be exalted, and every mountain and hill shall be made low: and the crooked shall be made straight, and the rough places plain:

5 And the glory of the LORD shall be revealed, and all flesh shall see [it] together: for the mouth of the LORD hath spoken [it].

6 The voice said, Cry. And he said, What shall I cry? All flesh [is] grass, and all the goodliness thereof [is] as the flower of the field:

7 The grass withereth, the flower fadeth: because the spirit of the LORD bloweth upon it: surely the people [is] grass.

Isaiah 49: 22-23

22 Thus saith the Lord GOD, Behold, I will lift up mine hand to the Gentiles, and set up my standard to the people: **[cross of Jesus]** *and they shall bring thy sons in [their] arms, and thy daughters shall be carried upon [their] shoulders.* **[Christians returning saved Jews to Israel]**

23 And kings shall be thy nursing fathers, and their queens thy nursing mothers: they shall bow down to thee with [their] face toward the earth, and lick up the dust of thy feet; and thou shalt

> know that I [am] the LORD: for they shall not be ashamed that wait for me.

Gentiles will lift up the banner of Tabernacle of Moses to all the peoples of the earth and will bring, "on their shoulders" with, financial aid, and prayer, the sons and daughters of Israel back to the land, after the Times of Jacobs Trouble or "The Tribulation."

Isaiah 56: 8

> 8 The Lord GOD which gathereth the outcasts of Israel saith, Yet will I gather [others] to him, beside those that are gathered unto him.

The others who will be gathered besides the exiles of Israel are Christians that will be returned to the land as spiritual Israel in representation of the lost tribes.

Isaiah 60: 10-13

> 10 And the sons of strangers shall build up thy walls, and their kings shall minister unto thee: for in my wrath I smote thee, but in my favour have I had mercy on thee.
>
> 11 Therefore thy gates shall be open continually; they shall not be shut day nor night; that [men] may bring unto thee the forces of the Gentiles, and [that] their kings [may be] brought.
>
> 12 For the nation and kingdom that will not serve thee shall perish; yea, [those] nations shall be utterly wasted.
>
> 13 The glory of Lebanon shall come unto thee, the fir tree, the pine tree, and the box together, to beautify the place of my sanctuary; and I will make the place of my feet glorious.

Isaiah 60:16

> 16 Thou shalt also suck the milk of the Gentiles, and shalt suck the breast of kings: and thou shalt know that I the LORD [am] thy Saviour and thy Redeemer, the mighty One of Jacob.

Isaiah 60: 18-22

18 Violence shall no more be heard in thy land, wasting nor destruction within thy borders; but thou shalt call thy walls Salvation, and thy gates Praise.

19 The sun shall be no more thy light by day **[you will not worship the sun god]**; *neither for brightness shall the moon give light unto thee* **[you will not worship the moon god]**: *but the LORD shall be unto thee an everlasting light* **[Jesus, the Son's reign will never set]**, *and thy God thy glory.*

20 Thy sun shall no more go down; neither shall thy moon withdraw itself: for the LORD shall be thine everlasting light, and the days of thy mourning shall be ended.

21 Thy people also [shall be] all righteous: they shall inherit the land for ever **[process New Earth plus Heaven = New Jerusalem.]**, *the branch of my planting, the work of my hands, that I may be glorified.*

22 A little one shall become a thousand, and a small one a strong nation: I the LORD will hasten it in his time.

In Isaiah 61: 1-6, when Jesus quoted in the synagogue, verse 1 and 2, he stopped mid-sentence, at the portion to proclaim the year of the Lord's favor at his first coming.

Then he proclaimed the events of his second coming.

Isaiah 61: 2-11

2 To proclaim the acceptable year of the LORD, and the day of vengeance of our God; to comfort all that mourn;

3 To appoint unto them that mourn in Zion, to give unto them beauty for ashes, the oil of joy for mourning, the garment of praise for the spirit of heaviness; that they might be called trees of righteousness, the planting of the LORD, that he might be glorified.

4 And they shall build the old wastes, they shall raise up the former desolations, and they shall repair the waste cities, the desolations of many generations.

5 And strangers shall stand and feed your flocks, and the sons of the alien [shall be] your plowmen and your vinedressers.

6 But ye shall be named the Priests of the LORD: [men] shall call you the Ministers of our God: ye shall eat the riches of the Gentiles, and in their glory shall ye boast yourselves.

7 For your shame [ye shall have] double; and [for] confusion they shall rejoice in their portion: therefore in their land they shall possess the double: everlasting joy shall be unto them.

8 For I the LORD love judgment, I hate robbery for burnt offering; and I will direct their work in truth, and I will make an everlasting covenant with them.

9 And their seed shall be known among the Gentiles, and their offspring among the people: all that see them shall acknowledge them, that they [are] the seed [which] the LORD hath blessed.

10 I will greatly rejoice in the LORD, my soul shall be joyful in my God; for he hath clothed me with the garments of salvation, he hath covered me with the robe of righteousness, as a bridegroom decketh [himself] with ornaments, and as a bride adorneth [herself] with her jewels.

11 For as the earth bringeth forth her bud, and as the garden causeth the things that are sown in it to spring forth; so the Lord GOD will cause righteousness and praise to spring forth before all the nations.

At his second coming and during the eternity which will follow it, aliens which will be Christians, will also receive great blessing by living safely in the land. All the ancient ruins will be restored and the nation of Israel will feed on the wealth of nations. In Isaiah 65: 9, it shows that both descendents of Jacob, which are all the spiritual tribes of Israel and, in particular, the saved Jews or Judah, will possess the nation of Israel. This indicates the joining of Christians and Messianic Jews in national unity.

The nation of Israel was born in one day, May 14, 1948, as shown in verse 7 and 8, Jeremiah 3: 16-18 also showed that the Ark of the Covenant will no longer come into their mind, nor be remembered, nor another one be built and that all the nations will gather in Israel to give honor to the Lord, and that at that time, the house of Judah or Jews, and the house of Israel or Christians, will join together in return for the northern land, or Russia, and all the other countries of the earth.

New Jerusalem = Heaven on Earth!

Dreams & Visions:

"And Lo, I open the gates to the Garden of Eden and all those that are My People will come in and I will wipe the tears from their eyes and their will be no more remembrances of the world that has passed away. In My Holy Kingdom, the New Jerusalem that has come down out of heaven, My Bride will be dressed for the wedding supper for her Groom!"

Isaiah 65:17-25

17 For, behold, I create new heavens and a new earth: and the former shall not be remembered, nor come into mind.

18 But be ye glad and rejoice for ever [in that] which I create: for, behold, I create Jerusalem a rejoicing, and her people a joy.

19 And I will rejoice in Jerusalem, and joy in my people: and the voice of weeping shall be no more heard in her, nor the voice of crying.

20 There shall be no more thence an infant of days, nor an old man that hath not filled his days: for the child shall die an hundred years old; but the sinner [being] an hundred years old shall be accursed.

21 And they shall build houses, and inhabit [them]; and they shall plant vineyards, and eat the fruit of them.

22 They shall not build, and another inhabit; they shall not plant, and another eat: for as the days of a tree [are] the days of my people, and mine elect shall long enjoy the work of their hands.

23 They shall not labour in vain, nor bring forth for trouble; for they [are] the seed of the blessed of the LORD, and their offspring with them.

24 And it shall come to pass, that before they call, I will answer; and while they are yet speaking, I will hear.

25 The wolf and the lamb shall feed together, and the lion shall eat straw like the bullock: and dust [shall be] the serpent's meat. They shall not hurt nor destroy in all my holy mountain, saith the LORD.

Revelation 3:12

...the name of the city of my God, [which is] new Jerusalem, which cometh down out of heaven from my God: and [I will write upon him] my new name.

Revelation 22:2-3

2 In the midst of the street of it, and on either side of the river, [was there] the tree of life, which bare twelve [manner of] fruits, [and] yielded her fruit every month: and the leaves of the tree **[Cell Groups]** *[were] for the healing of the nations.* **[Preservation of a Remnant of the Nations]**

3 And there shall be no more curse: but the throne of God and of the Lamb shall be in it; and his servants shall serve him:

121. What is the spiritual state of Israel and America at present?

Ezekiel 32: 17-27

17 It came to pass also in the twelfth year, in the fifteenth [day] of the month, [that] the word of the LORD came unto me, saying,

18 Son of man, wail for the multitude of Egypt, and cast them down, [even] her, and the daughters of the famous nations, unto the nether parts of the earth, with them that go down into the pit.

19 Whom dost thou pass in beauty? go down, and be thou laid with the uncircumcised.

20 They shall fall in the midst of [them that are] slain by the sword: she is delivered to the sword: draw her and all her multitudes.

21 The strong among the mighty shall speak to him out of the midst of hell with them that help him: they are gone down, they lie uncircumcised, slain by the sword.

22 Asshur [is] there and all her company: his graves [are] about him: all of them slain, fallen by the sword:

23 Whose graves are set in the sides of the pit, and her company is round about her grave: all of them slain, fallen by the sword, which caused terror in the land of the living.

24 There [is] Elam and all her multitude round about her grave, all of them slain, fallen by the sword, which are gone down uncircumcised into the nether parts of the earth, which caused their terror in the land of the living; yet have they borne their shame with them that go down to the pit.

25 They have set her a bed in the midst of the slain with all her multitude: her graves [are] round about him: all of them uncircumcised, slain by the sword: though their terror was caused in the land of the living, yet have they borne their shame with them that go down to the pit: he is put in the midst of [them that be] slain.

26 There [is] Meshech, Tubal, and all her multitude: her graves [are] round about him: all of them uncircumcised, slain by the sword, though they caused their terror in the land of the living.

27 And they shall not lie with the mighty [that are] fallen of the uncircumcised, which are gone down to hell with their weapons of war: and they have laid their swords under their heads, but their iniquities shall be upon their bones, though [they were] the terror of the mighty in the land of the living.

We see that Moses returned with the Ten Commandments and found that Aaron and the people had sinned greatly and worshipped a golden calf idol. This is as the state of Israel is now returned to the land in unbelief. There is only a small remnant of Jews looking forward to the return of the Messiah and turning to God which will allow the Lord to show that he is their Messiah and came 2,000 years ago as Jesus of Nazareth.

The following verses demonstrate clearly that the Holy Spirit can be denied and that one's name can be blotted out of the Book of Life. Only those hearing from God in prayer daily and with their lamps filled with the anointing and direction of the Holy Spirit will enter into the Kingdom of Heaven. I, who stood at the gates of heaven at eight, knew that I did indeed deserve to go to hell for doing abortions, however justified by personal crises. Those who do not hear and heed these words, will regret the destruction that is coming upon the earth and risk the loss of eternal life with Jesus.

Matthew 25:1-13

1 Then shall the kingdom of heaven be likened unto ten virgins, which took their lamps, and went forth to meet the bridegroom.

2 And five of them were wise, and five [were] foolish.

3 They that [were] foolish took their lamps, and took no oil with them:

4 But the wise took oil in their vessels with their lamps.

5 While the bridegroom tarried, they all slumbered and slept.

6 And at midnight there was a cry made, Behold, the bridegroom cometh; go ye out to meet him.

7 Then all those virgins arose, and trimmed their lamps.

8 And the foolish said unto the wise, Give us of your oil; for our lamps are gone out.

9 But the wise answered, saying, [Not so]; lest there be not enough for us and you: but go ye rather to them that sell, and buy for yourselves.

10 And while they went to buy, the bridegroom came; and they that were ready went in with him to the marriage: and the door was shut.

11 Afterward came also the other virgins, saying, Lord, Lord, open to us.

12 But he answered and said, Verily I say unto you, I know you not.

13 Watch therefore, for ye know neither the day nor the hour wherein the Son of man cometh.

Revelation 3:10-13

10 Because thou hast kept the word of my patience, I also will keep thee from the hour of temptation, which shall come upon all the world, to try them that dwell upon the earth.

[God will save his people through the tribulations as He did his people in Egypt!]

11 Behold, I come quickly: hold that fast which thou hast, that no man take thy crown. **[Loose Your Salvation!?!]**

12 Him that overcometh will I make a pillar in the temple of my God, and he shall go no more out: and I will write upon him the name of my God, and the name of the city of my God, [which is] new Jerusalem, which cometh down out of heaven from my God: and [I will write upon him] my new name.

13 He that hath an ear, let him hear what the Spirit saith unto the churches.

Exodus 34: 15-24

15 Lest thou make a covenant with the inhabitants of the land, and they go a whoring after their gods, and do sacrifice unto their gods, and [one] call thee, and thou eat of his sacrifice;

16 And thou take of their daughters unto thy sons, and their daughters go a whoring after their gods, and make thy sons go a whoring after their gods.

17 Thou shalt make thee no molten gods.

18 The feast of unleavened bread shalt thou keep. Seven days thou shalt eat unleavened bread, as I commanded thee, in the time of the month Abib: for in the month Abib thou camest out from Egypt.

19 All that openeth the matrix [is] mine; and every firstling among thy cattle, [whether] ox or sheep, [that is male].

20 But the firstling of an ass thou shalt redeem with a lamb: and if thou redeem [him] not, then shalt thou break his neck. All the firstborn of thy sons thou shalt redeem. And none shall appear before me empty.

21 Six days thou shalt work, but on the seventh day thou shalt rest: in earing time and in harvest thou shalt rest.

22 And thou shalt observe the feast of weeks, of the firstfruits of wheat harvest, and the feast of ingathering at the year's end.

23 Thrice in the year shall all your men children appear before the Lord GOD, the God of Israel.

24 For I will cast out the nations before thee, and enlarge thy borders: neither shall any man desire thy land, when thou shalt go up to appear before the LORD thy God thrice in the year.

This is a significant warning to Israel not to give land to any other nation for peace for this will be committing national suicide and violate the direct orders of God. Created as a state in verse 24, the nations will be driven before the nation of Israel if it celebrates all the feasts and follows all the commandments of God in preparation for temple worship. Israel is also warned in Exodus 32: 17-35 to not worship false gods such as Mammon or money for this will cause a great plague.

At the Time of the End they will be offered entry into the New World Order. Israel will be offered the Mark of the Beast to enter this computerized electronic world economic system. Israel is applying for E.C. membership or special trade status. This will cause great destruction on the land of Israel if they accept taking the Mark of the Beast. Israel will have made a 'covenant with death' in signing its initial peace treaty with the Beast.

The mark is offered at the half-way mark in the seven-year period. It is only this in the end that will save a remnant from Israel from ultimate and total destruction when they turn and mourn as Psalm 22 says, and Isaiah 53, for the Son of God that they have pierced who was their expected Messiah. During this time of Jacob's trouble then they will recognize their Messiah.

2 Samuel 8: 12-13

12 Of Syria, and of Moab, and of the children of Ammon, and of the Philistines, and of Amalek, and of the spoil of Hadadezer, son of Rehob, king of Zobah.

13 And David gat [him] a name when he returned from smiting of the Syrians in the valley of salt, [being] eighteen thousand [men].

As when David was rebuked by Nathan and told that he would build a temple to his own God, but that his son would. This is a foreshadowing that the Jews as they return now will build the tabernacle but that the temple building itself will be built by Jesus when he returns to establish his throne of his kingdom forever. Chapters 40 to 48 of Ezekiel describe the Messiah himself building the Temple of the New Heavens and New Earth and this is further confirmed by Amos, chapter 9, verses 11-12, and 14-15.

Amos 9: 11-12

11 In that day will I raise up the tabernacle of David that is fallen, and close up the breaches thereof; and I will raise up his ruins, and I will build it as in the days of old:

> 12 That they may possess the remnant of Edom, and of all the heathen, which are called by my name **[Christian nations]**, saith the LORD that doeth this.

Amos 9: 14-15

> 14 And I will bring again the captivity of my people of Israel, and they shall build the waste cities, and inhabit [them]; and they shall plant vineyards, and drink the wine thereof; they shall also make gardens, and eat the fruit of them.

> 15 And I will plant them upon their land, and they shall no more be pulled up out of their land which I have given them, saith the LORD thy God.

We see that David's fallen tent which is a tabernacle of Moses will be erected again, so that they may possess a remnant of Edom and all the nations. That is the Jews and Christians will be returned to the land of Israel in safety from the holocaust of the New Age Movement and the resulting world-wide conventional and nuclear war. The exiled people will be returned, and their ruined cities will be rebuilt, and Israel will live in their own land, on the New Earth, never to be uprooted again. As God says in Deuteronomy 4: 39-40, if we keep God's decrees and commands, all his feast days and all his commandments as are written on our heart, then Jews and Christians will live long in the land of Israel. His blessing comes from:

Genesis 12:3

> 3 And I will bless them that bless thee, and curse him that curseth thee: and in thee shall all families of the earth be blessed.

Christians will be blessed because they bless the Jews returning to Israel and assist them.

Passover = Israel + America Attacked!

Dreams and Visions:

While praying and reading the scriptures, I received the following vision of the times spoken of by Dimitru Duduman, when the revolution would start and the America would have the places like Sodom and Gomorrah attacked.

In the spirit, the angel Gabriel took me to the West Coast and I saw foreign and oriental looking troops with blue hats carrying machine guns, I saw helicopters with the signs of the United Nations, and many thousands of Americans in lines waiting to receive the Mark of the Beast. He told me to watch as the Chinese navy on the West Coast base we gave them became a secondary staging ground for the invasion. The primary invasion was our own military bases–the angel showed me our New World Order US government officials gave these invaders.

I was horrified as I watched. Deep below many airports and military bases, I saw those with Red badges, who were to be executed for the word of their testimony, and they did not shrink from the faith in Jesus. Others, marked by blue, worked in factories and were periodically brought to reprogramming camps and rooms were unspeakable inhumane acts were performed on them to have them repent of their belief in the Truth and the Word. Elsewhere, those with the Green Emblem, smiled and went about life with peace on their well fed faces, and they feared not, for they had felt righteous in that they were saving the planet, or they knew falsely in their hearts that surely the Lord would not cast them out to outer darkness! Surely, once saved, they thought, I have eternal security, and the Lord Jesus I once received will not reject those he has taken into his arms. Then Gabriel cringed as if in pain seeing this most, for he said that their believes would bring them to destruction for they knew Him not!

I asked what is the end of these things. He said, those that will hear the words of the witnesses of Jesus and the prophets of the END, would be stirred and be saved throughout the kingdom of the Beast. These would be high level masons, murderers, bankers, military men, teachers, doctors, labourers, and all the corporations of the Beast would turn over those who would receive the Mark of the Sovereign Lord on their right hand or forehead. Even those who had taken the Oath to the Evil One and those most detestable, were among their numbers! As I watched, He said, "Behold, see those who feel secure in their righteousness, are lost while these most terrible before men are now washed righteous in the Blood of the Lamb!" In the spirit I fell on my face weeping for those that call themselves by the name of the Lord, and the fate that they will face in outer darkness.

Suddenly, I was back beside the angel Gabriel, and he said, "America is Babylon and the Nation of the Anointing of Israel to bring the gospel to the world. All these things must come to pass, so that all Mercy and Justice of a Righteous God will be served." I again asked what will happen to America? He said, "Revolution will start when the Evil One is revealed in the Tabernacle, and the Holy People are trampled underfoot with the attack on America and the nations that call themselves after the name of Jesus."

Revelation 17:15-18

> *15 And he saith unto me, The waters which thou sawest, where the whore sitteth, are peoples, and multitudes, and nations, and tongues.* **[America]**
>
> *16 And the ten horns which thou sawest upon the beast* **[The Ten World Regional Masonic Leaders!]**, *these shall hate the whore* **[America]**, *and shall make her desolate and naked, and shall eat her flesh, and burn her with fire.* **[First Strike Thermonuclear Attack!]**

17 For God hath put in their hearts to fulfil his will, and to agree **[European and Middle Eastern/Islamic Leaders]**, *and give their kingdom unto the beast, until the words of God shall be fulfilled.*
18 And the woman which thou sawest is that great city **[New York]**, *which reigneth over the kings of the earth.*

Dreams and Visions:

In October 1998, after a busy office, I was praying and reading in Jeremiah. Suddenly, I was taken in the spirit by the angel Gabriel to the Parliament of Europe in Strasbourg, France. There he told me to observe the meeting that was happening with eighteen representatives of the European Union around a large board table. In the center, there was a silver challis and they passed a short, approximately 18 inch, silver sword with a golden handle to all the members at the table and swore a blood oath by cutting their right thumb and marking the blood on the right ear after bleeding into the challis with blood mixed with wine. They come together in worship of Satan and setup his kingdom on earth. They also swore to destroy America.

"By the blood of Hiram and the enlightenment of Osiris, I do pledge to the most excellent and illuminated One, to carry forth my pledge and duty to the New Order of the Ages. By my blood and with this sign, I seal my honor to do all that we have purposed here today, on pain of death by disembowelment and having my heart wrenched from my bosom. So say the Noble Knights of the Order."

I was completely overwhelmed that countries that we consider our allies would scheme to destroy our nation in order to set up the New World Order. I asked the angel when and he again had me turn my attention to the debate as to when America would be attacked. They all came to one accord to destroy America when the EURO Dollar was completely in control of the European Economy and the all of the Illuminated Sons had removed their wealth from

America and the US Stock Market into the European Banking System. Thus the signs were set and the plot hatched to destroy America. This evil plot would be brought to the fullness, and not a day earlier.

122. During the time of Jacob's trouble what destruction, and where will Israel be damaged?
Zechariah 14:1-15

1 Behold, the day of the LORD cometh, and thy spoil shall be divided in the midst of thee.

2 For I will gather all nations against Jerusalem to battle; and the city **[West Jerusalem]** *shall be taken, and the houses rifled, and the women ravished; and half of the city shall go forth into captivity, and the residue of the people shall not be cut off from the city.* **[Day 1,415]**

3 Then shall the LORD go forth, and fight against those nations, as when he fought in the day of battle. **[Day 2,520]**

4 And his feet shall stand in that day upon the mount of Olives, which [is] before Jerusalem on the east, and the mount of Olives shall cleave in the midst thereof toward the east and toward the west, [and there shall be] a very great valley; and half of the mountain shall remove toward the north, and half of it toward the south. **[with the Great Earthquake]**

5 And ye shall flee [to] the valley of the mountains; for the valley of the mountains shall reach unto Azal: yea, ye shall flee, like as ye fled from before the earthquake in the days of Uzziah king of Judah: and the LORD my God shall come, [and] all the saints with thee.

6 And it shall come to pass in that day, [that] the light shall not be clear, [nor] dark:

7 But it shall be one day which shall be known to the LORD, not day, nor night: but it shall come to pass, [that] at evening time it shall be light. **[The Messiah will appear]**

8 And it shall be in that day, [that] living waters shall go out from Jerusalem; half of them toward the former sea, and half of them toward the hinder sea: in summer and in winter shall it be.

9 And the LORD shall be king over all the earth: in that day shall there be one LORD, and his name one.

10 And the land shall be turned as a plain from Geba to Rimmon south of Jerusalem: and it shall be lifted up, and inhabited in her place, from Benjamin's gate unto the place of the first gate, unto the corner gate, and [from] the tower of Hananeel unto the king's winepresses. **[Jerusalem resurrected in New Earth]**

11 And [men] shall dwell in it, and there shall be no more utter destruction; but Jerusalem shall be safely inhabited.

12 And this shall be the plague wherewith the LORD will smite all the people that have fought against Jerusalem; Their flesh shall consume away while they stand upon their feet, and their eyes shall consume away in their holes, and their tongue shall consume away in their mouth. **[Nuclear Holocaust]**

13 And it shall come to pass in that day, [that] a great tumult from the LORD shall be among them; and they shall lay hold every one on the hand of his neighbour, and his hand shall rise up against the hand of his neighbour.

14 And Judah also shall fight at Jerusalem; and the wealth of all the heathen round about shall be gathered together, gold, and silver, and apparel, in great abundance.

15 And so shall be the plague of the horse, of the mule, of the camel, and of the ass, and of all the beasts that shall be in these tents, as this plague. **[Animals destroyed by nuclear weapons.]**

The Lord says that the city of Jerusalem will be attacked by all the nations. The United Nations will act as representative and the eastern half of the city. previously under Arab control, will be handed back to the Arabs to become their capitol of a new Palestinian state including the occupied territories. At this time the Lord will fight against the nations and the great earthquake which will result from the war will allow Jews to flee to safety in central and southern areas of the country, away from the attack on the north and occupied territories, as well as the area of West Jerusalem. In verse 12 it shows that the type of plague that God will strike against the nations which attacked Jerusalem will be one of a nuclear war. In verse 14 it shows that all the wealth of the surrounding nations, which are oil producing, will be collected and be under the control of Israel, forever.

123. What promise does God give regarding the joining of Christians and Jews into one kingdom, and his promises of divine protection?

Ezekiel 37: 15-28

15 The word of the LORD came again unto me, saying,

16 Moreover, thou son of man, take thee one stick, and write upon it, For Judah, and for the children of Israel his companions: then take another stick, and write upon it, For Joseph, the stick of Ephraim, and [for] all the house of Israel his companions:

17 And join them one to another into one stick; and they shall become one in thine hand.

18 And when the children of thy people shall speak unto thee, saying, Wilt thou not shew us what thou [meanest] by these?

19 Say unto them, Thus saith the Lord GOD; Behold, I will take the stick of Joseph, which [is] in the hand of Ephraim, and the tribes of Israel his fellows, and will put them with him, [even] with the stick of Judah, and make them one stick, and they shall be one in mine hand.

20 And the sticks whereon thou writest shall be in thine hand before their eyes.

21 And say unto them, Thus saith the Lord GOD; Behold, I will take the children of Israel from among the heathen, whither they be gone, and will gather them on every side, and bring them into their own land:

22 And I will make them one nation in the land upon the mountains of Israel; and one king shall be king to them all: and they shall be no more two nations, neither shall they be divided into two kingdoms any more at all:

23 Neither shall they defile themselves any more with their idols, nor with their detestable things, nor with any of their transgressions: but I will save them out of all their dwellingplaces, wherein they have sinned, and will cleanse them: so shall they be my people, and I will be their God.

24 And David my servant [shall be] king over them; and they all shall have one shepherd: they shall also walk in my judgments, and observe my statutes, and do them.

25 And they shall dwell in the land that I have given unto Jacob my servant, wherein your fathers have dwelt; and they shall dwell therein, [even] they, and their children, and their children's children for ever: and my servant David [shall be] their prince for ever.

26 Moreover I will make a covenant of peace with them; it shall be an everlasting covenant with them: and I will place them, and multiply them, and will set my sanctuary in the midst of them for evermore.

27 My tabernacle also shall be with them: yea, I will be their God, and they shall be my people.

28 And the heathen shall know that I the LORD do sanctify Israel, when my sanctuary shall be in the midst of them for evermore.

Ephraim represents the northern ten lost tribes, now Gentile Christianity, and Judah represents saved Messianic Jews and modern Israel as it now stands. God promises to join these two together to make one congregation. He promises that the nations will never be divided into two kingdoms and that the covenant of peace will be an everlasting covenant. This will be a sign to the nations to glorify the Lord's name that God has made Israel holy when his sanctuary is among them forever.

Jeremiah 3: 18

> *18 In those days the house of Judah shall walk with the house of Israel, and they shall come together out of the land of the north to the land that I have given for an inheritance unto your fathers.*

[after the tribulation period]

This is the land given to Abraham by God, which will include the Christians and Jews who reside in the land of Israel.

As God said to Peter, that upon this confession that Jesus was Lord, that he would rebuild his congregation which included believing Jews and Gentile Christians, and that this was the rock cut out without human hands that would be the cornerstone of his kingdom on a new earth. The law of Moses and the way to righteousness was shown to Moses by God utilizing the tabernacle, the tent of meeting, the holy of holies, and all of the holy objects representing way to grow daily in righteousness that each Christian must walk in with the Lord, in a personal relationship. [See Q. 124]

124. What is the plan of salvation presented through the representations of the Tabernacle of Moses, and made possible through the sacrifice of Jesus pointed to by all the prophecy and fulfillment in the Old and New Testament?

Pastor Clyde Williamson of Kereth Connection Ministries, Toronto, Canada presents a simple but profound representation of all of the stages of obtaining a continuing state of salvation through yieldedness, forgiveness, wisdom, understanding, and worship. The witness of Moses was the plan of salvation presented to the Jews and the fulfillment proven by Christians. Returning Jews to Israel during the great, final exodus out of the land of the north and all other countries on earth, and presenting the gospel to the whole of Jewry world-wide as well as the Gentile world, is the last event before the End will come.

Jesus came, not to annul the covenant, but to fulfill it and show that he was the physical representation of the way of salvation represented by the Tabernacle of Moses and the Temple. Jesus became the sin offering and took all the sins of the world upon himself so that we may obtain his righteousness by accepting his free gift. By this we may never fear God and, therefore, be made perfect in God's love and accept him as our Heavenly Father without fear of judgment.

The "Abomination of Desolation" is the Aaronic Priesthood sacrificing an unacceptable blood sacrifice of bulls and sheep on the Temple Mount. The blood of Jesus which still rests on the Mercy Seat of the Ark, is a witness against them and will unleash the judgement on the scholars and those who reject their messiah, Jesus. The final treaty will allow this abomination in exchange for East Jerusalem and the splitting of the Holy City of God, in Isaiah the Lord says "I will annul your covenant with death!" Jesus sets his judgements upon his apostate Jewish people to purify them in the fires of His Mercy and Judgement to keep a faithful remnant for Himself!

In the Syd Roth's book, **"Time is Running Short"**, as a Messianic Jew he confirms, again, the central key to the salvation of the world is the salvation of Jews and Israel. This book shows how understanding the Jewish holy days and learning to bring Jews to Christ is key to bringing salvation to the rest of the world during the times of tribulation which are quickly coming upon our world.

Genesis 37: 5-10

5 And Joseph dreamed a dream, and he told [it] his brethren: and they hated him yet the more.

6 And he said unto them, Hear, I pray you, this dream which I have dreamed:

7 For, behold, we [were] binding sheaves in the field, and, lo, my sheaf arose, and also stood upright; and, behold, your sheaves stood round about, and made obeisance to my sheaf.

8 And his brethren said to him, Shalt thou indeed reign over us? or shalt thou indeed have dominion over us? And they hated him yet the more for his dreams, and for his words.

9 And he dreamed yet another dream, and told it his brethren, and said, Behold, I have dreamed a dream more; and, behold, the sun and the moon and the eleven stars made obeisance to me.

10 And he told [it] to his father, and to his brethren: and his father rebuked him, and said unto him, What [is] this dream that thou hast dreamed? Shall I and thy mother and thy brethren indeed come to bow down ourselves to thee to the earth?

Joseph is a type of Judah, with all the lost tribes represented by his brothers that will serve Israel. The lost tribes represent Ephraim or spiritual Israel - the Christians. The great famine is the famine of the Word of God during the rise of the great heresy of the New Age Movement, and the false Messiah. This will force all Christians and Jews to return to places of refuge for safety, to buy 'the grain of the Word'.

The witness of Elijah will be the turning of Christian to Jews and Jews to Christians, that in their desperation at the end of Jacob's trouble, they will accept the Lord and His divine protection. These are the elect of the earth that the Lord will save and protect for eternal life on a New Earth and New Heaven.

BIBLIOGRAPHY

1. **Ankerberg, John & Weldon, John**
   One World — Biblical Prophecy and the New World Order. 1991. Moody Press, Chicago.

2. **Brown, Lester R.**
   State of the World — A Worldwatch Institute Report on Progress Toward a Sustainable Society. W. W. Norton & Inc., 500-5th Ave., New York, N.Y. 10110.

3. **Dyer, Charles H.**
   The Rise of Babylon Sign of the End Times. 1991. Tyndale House Publishers, Inc., Wheaton, Illinois. [70A p. 147-179]

4. **Goetz, William R.**
   The Economy to Come and Other Signs of Earth's Impending Climax. Horizon House Publishers, Beaverlodge, Alberta, Canada. [65A - p. 45-72; 94A - p; 95A - p; 98A - p.]

5. **Gorbachev, Mikhail**
   Perestroika — New Thinking for our Country and the World. 1987. Harper & Row Publishers, New York. [92A - p. 190-209]

6. **Hunt, Dave**
   Global Peace and the Rise of Antichrist. Harvest House Publishers, Eugene, Oregon 97402. [30A - p. 143 etc.]

7. **Intrater, Keith**
   From Iraq to Armageddon. 1991. Destiny Image Publishers, P. O. Box 351, Shippensburg, PA 17257. [75A - p. 151-171]

8. **James, Edgar C.**
   Arabs, Oil & Armageddon. 1991. Moody Press, Chicago.

9. Armageddon and the New World Order. 1991. Moody Press, Chicago.

10. **Jeffrey, Grant R.**

Armageddon — Appointment with Destiny. 1988. Frontier Research Publications, P.O. Box 129, Station "U", Toronto, Ontario M8Z 5M4.

[55A - p. 106; 76B - p. 145; Figure 2, p. 143-147; 114A - p. 105-106; 15A - p. 40-42; 117B - p. 160-161; 118B - p. 108-128]

11. Heaven — The Last Frontier. 1990. Frontier Research Publications, P. O. Box 129, Station "U", Toronto, Ontario M8Z 5M4.

12. War in the Middle East & the Road to Armageddon. Frontier Research Publication, P.O. Box 129, Station "U", Toronto, Ontario M8Z 5M4.

[35A - p. 57, Table Weapon Type; Russia Outspends the U.S., 51A - p. 77, 105; Gorbachev Gambit; 99A - p.; Scud Missile — Patriot # Required, 114A - p.; 117B - p.160-161]

13. **Kennedy, Paul**

The Rise and Fall of the Great Powers. 1988. Fontana Paperbacks, 8 Gravton St., London W1X 3LA. [93A - p.; 105A - p. The former Soviet military must be supported by a market socialist capitalism.]

14. **Knight, Steven**

The Brotherhood. Grafton Books, Collins Publishing Group, 8 Grafton Street, London W1X 3LA.

15. **Lawrence, Troy**

New Age Messiah Identified. 1991. Huntington House Publishers, p. O. Box 53788, Lafayette, Louisiana 70505. [72A - p. 113-45; 73A - p. 133-158]

16. **Lewis, David Allen**

Prophecy 2000 — Unprecedented Events — The 1990s. 1991. New Leaf Press, Inc., P.O. Box 311, Green Forest, AR 72638. [50A - p. 26-27; 56B - p.; 116A - p. 142-144; 117A - p. 152-55; 118A - p. 165-178]

17. **Lindsay, Hal**

The 1980's: Countdown to Armageddon. 1982. Bantam Books. [103A - p. Russian military superiority.]

18. The Late Great Planet Earth. 1981. Bantam Books. [92A - p.]

19. The Road to Holocaust. 1990. Bantam Books.

20. There's a New World Coming. 1984. Bantam Books, Toronto.

21. **Linsted, Rob**

The Next Move — Current Events in Bible Prophecy. Bible Truth, P. O. Box 8550, Wichita, Kansas 67208. [106A - p. 50-56; 106B - p. 62-65; 106C - p. 56-65; 107A - p. 60; 108A - p. 61; 109A - p. 61; 110A - p. 61; 112A - p. 56-65; 116A - p. 93-97]

22. **Mann, Ralph**

Glastnost — Gateway to World Revival. Ralph Mann, Mission Possible Foundation, P.O. Box 2014, Denton, Texas 76202. [52A - p. 62-76]

23. **Matrisciana, Caryl & Oakland, Roger**

The Evolution Conspiracy. Harvest House Publishers, Eugene, Oregon 97402.

24. **MacDonald, Ken & Agnes**

The Second Coming — Tough Questions Answered. Berean Publications, '91, P. O. Box 12, Newcomerstown, Ohio, U.S.A. 43832.

25. **McAlvany, Donald S.**

Toward a New World Order — The Countdown to Armageddon. 1990. Hearthstone Publishing Ltd., P. O. Box 815, Oklahoma City, Oklahoma 73101. [29A - p. 38-40; 48B - p. 160-164; 102A - p. Increased Russian spying.]

26. McKeever, James

Christians Will Go Through The Tribulation — And How To Prepare For It. 78 Omega Publications, P.O. Box 4130, Medford, Oregon 97501. [126A - p. - 2nd half of the book]

27. The Future Revealed. 1982. Omega Publications, P.O. Box 4130, Medford, Oregon 97501.

28. The Rapture Book — Victory in the End Times. Omega Publications, P. O. Box 4130, Medford, Oregon 97501.

29. Revelation for Laymen. 1980. Omega Publications, P. O. Box 4130, Medford, Oregon 97501. [76A - p. 213. Table comparing Bowls and Trumpets]

30. McMahon, T. A. & Oakland, Roger

Understand the Times. 1990. T.W.F.T. Publishers, P. O. Box 8000, Costa Mesa, California 92628.

31. Miller, P. A.

Forbidden Knowledge — Or Is It. 1991. Joy Publishing, P.O. Box 827, San Juan Capistrano, CA 92675. [75A - p. 107-113]

32. Relfe, Mary Stewart

The New Money System. 1982. Ministries, Inc., P.O. Box 4038, Montgomery, Alabama, U.S.A. 36104.

33. Rosen, Moishe

Beyond the Gulf War Overture to Armageddon. Here's Life Publishers, Inc., P. O. Box 1576, San Bernardino, CA 92402.

34. Rosenthal, Marvin

The Pre-wrath Rapture of the Church. 1990. Thomas Nelson Publishers, via Lawson Faue, Ltd., Cambridge, Ontario.

35. Roth, Sid

Time is Running Short. 1990. Destiny Image Publishers, P.O. Box 351, Shippensburg, PA 17257. [124A - p.]

36. **Rumble, Dale**

And Then The End Shall Come. 1991. Destiny Image Publishers, P.O. Box 310, Shippensburg, PA 17257.

37. **Short, Martin**

Inside the Brotherhood — Further Secrets of the Freemasons. Grafton Books, Collins Publishing Group, 8 Grafton St., London W1X 3LA.

38. **Walvoord, John F.**

Armageddon, Oil and the Middle East Crisis. 1990. Zondervan Publishing House, 1415 Lake Drive, S.E., Grand Rapids, MI 49506. [75A - p. 53-63]

39. **Webber, David**

The Image of the Ages. 1991. Huntington House Publishers, P.O. Box 53788, Lafayette, LA 70505.

40. **Williamson, Clyde**

The Esther Fast Mandate. 1987. Almond Publications, Box 336, Etobicoke, Ontario, Canada M9C 4V3.

41. **Zodhiates, Spiros**

The Hebrew-Greek Key Study Bible. 1984. Baker Book House, Grand Rapids,